SHAKESPEARE: TIME AND CONSCIENCE

SHAKESPEARE:

TIME AND CONSCIENCE

Grigorii Mikhailovich

By Grigori Kozintsev

TRANSLATED FROM THE RUSSIAN

BY Joyce Vining

 HILL AND WANG ❖ NEW YORK

Originally published in Russian under the title
Our Contemporary: William Shakespeare

English translation copyright © 1966 by Hill and Wang, Inc.
All rights reserved

Library of Congress catalog card number: 66–18167

First edition May 1966

Manufactured in the United States of America
by American Book–Stratford Press, Inc.

Contents

Introductory Note

The meaning of the concept "classic art" does not seem to require lengthy meditation. The words are not hard to understand. Nevertheless, aside from the accepted properties, classic works are further characterized by an ability to present to each epoch its own vital interests.

Hamlet told the actors that theatre must "hold as 'twere the mirror up to Nature—to show Virtue her own feature, scorn her own image, and the very age and body of the time his form and pressure." The mirror of classic art has its own secret, one not easily penetrated; its works seem to accompany the advance of the centuries.

Shortly before his death, the futurist poet Mayakovsky penned a few lines on the force of poetry and its victory over time:

> But the word gallops headlong, with tightened girth,
> ringing for centuries, and trains creep up
> to lick the calloused hands of poetry.

Shakespeare's words still ring, resonant and full. His verse is still blistering its hands today. People are improved and cleansed by the poetry, their hearts penetrated by its warmth, their consciences stirred by its noble anger. In Shakespeare's tragedies, they discover the unmasked face of Virtue and of Scorn. His plays seem to be written by someone close to us, by a man of our time.

G.K.

Landscapes

Landscapes

DURING A RECENT TRIP TO ENGLAND, I was able to see many places connected with Shakespeare and his art. Besides old houses and castles, I remember other scenes—imaginary landscapes whose outlines had been suggested long before my trip by the very poetry of Shakespeare. Sometimes reality coincided with my preconceptions. Frequently, however, I had envisioned something other than what I was shown. My attempts to understand the reasons for the coincidences and differences prompted ideas about some of the characteristic traits of Shakespearean poetics. But the title of this chapter is not an absolute definition of the matter to be discussed; I shall include portraits, objects, and statues as well as landscapes.

I shall begin with objects.

You have to go pretty far. We roam long streets, lined with bookshelves instead of houses. We cross bridges over halls replete with cabinets. Passing tiers of books, we descend a spiral staircase into cellars filled with complete runs of periodicals and piles of brochures. In front of us is a door; my companion invites me in. The room is small, with several chairs and a table with a reading stand. He asks me to take a seat, and wait. I am in one of the studies of the British Museum.

As a director of Shakespearean tragedy, I naturally wanted to see a first edition of the plays while I was in England. Mr. Childs, the library's assistant director, asked me a few questions about my profession and the reasons for my interest in this particular edition. Having given all this a thought, he asked me to follow him.

3

So here I sit, beside a table, waiting. The door opens. Mr. Childs holds a large volume in red morocco. This, however, is not the binding, but only a case. Mr. Childs opens the leather box and takes out a book.

"We had to go through this," he says, "because I didn't think it would be enough to see this edition in a showcase, under glass." He carefully lowers the book onto the stand. "You must not only look at it, but handle it as well. I shall leave you alone with it."

Before me is one of the greatest bibliographical rarities—a first edition of Shakespeare, or "Folio" as they call it.

. . . The man died in 1616. His will was detailed. It even mentioned some sort of second-best bed. But there was no reference to his writings. A playwright's manuscripts were then rarely of interest in themselves. Plays were the property of a company of actors, and so Shakespeare's plays belonged to a theatre troupe.

Three years later, the head of this troupe, and its leading actor, died—Richard Burbage would no longer play Othello, Lear, or Hamlet.

In 1613, during a performance of *Henry VIII* at the Globe, one of the theatre's cannon was badly shot off. Fire smoldered in the thatch over the stage. The theatre burned to the ground.

Shakespeare's last direct descendant died in 1670. His house and land passed to others. Aside from a rotted coffin and a decomposed body, there might have been nothing left of the poet save the two poems published during his lifetime and eighteen plays which were probably published without his consent. More than half of his dramatic work could have been lost. But his work was preserved—not by patrons or scholars, but by his friends, his co-workers in the rugged world of the theatre.

John Heminges and Henry Condell collected the texts of thirty-six plays. On the title page, the two actors claimed that the book was published according to original manuscripts. This claim, however, has not met with scholarly acceptance. Some manuscripts were probably incomplete, and others dappled with the cuts and insertions usual in stage copies. Several plays had to be restored from individual scripts. Someone remembered; someone had prompted; ad libs were taken for the author's own words. Thus, the first collection came to be. It was published in 1623, in folio.

Heminges and Condell found adequate words to set forth their aims in publishing the collection. They stated in the foreword that it was not profit that attracted them; no, they merely wished "to keep the memory of so worthy a friend and fellow alive as was our Shakespeare." So worthy a friend and fellow—this is a good, clear definition of the man, even when taken as referring to an intimate not only of two actors but of all humanity.

Heminges and Condell grew old and died. They were buried side by side. The theatres of England were closed by the Roundheads. But the Folio had just begun to live.

I am alone with this book. I open its leather cover to expose age-darkened paper, carefully smoothed by experts, with the heavy black-letter type of early printing.

Mr. William
SHAKESPEARES
Comedies,
Histories, &
Tragedies.

An engraving by the Dutch artist Droeshout is centered under the title. Against a dark background is etched the face of a man with large calm eyes and a receding hairline, but with hair hanging over his ears. Who is he? The author of immortal plays, or a mere figment of the artist's imagination? In lines written in memory of Shakespeare, Ben Jonson advised against scrutinizing the features here portrayed; he counselled the reader, rather, to seek understanding of the subject's mind and soul.

It took time before this advice could be followed. When the old royal library was given to the British Museum in 1757, its holdings did not include Shakespeare. Two years later, the library was opened to the public, but Shakespeare's works were not standing on its shelves. A collection of old English plays, the gift of David Garrick, served as the foundation for a Shakespeare collection. Actors, at least, still preserved the memory of their worthy friend and fellow. The museum received this collection in 1779. One year later, the Folio was missing.

Today Shakespeare is published and republished in all languages. The British Museum, however, has only five copies of the Folio, of which only three preserve the portrait. Each copy is carefully studied, measured, and described in detail. One page is

12⅞ by 8½ inches, another 12⅞ by 8⅜. It is good to see history interest itself even in the measurements of books.

The pages of the Folio vary by eighths of an inch, but there is no tangible measure for a line of poetry. Heine once wrote bitterly that perhaps the time would come when a shopkeeper would weigh cheese and verse on the same scales. Criticism is another scale, used to measure the artistic, and indeed it is hard not to ponder the early obsolescence of much of Shakespeare criticism. Yet the works themselves retain all their vital powers. That which is weighed on scales cannot rival creation in dimensions beyond perception.

The man who worked not far from this room, in a large circular hall, on his *Das Kapital,* well understood the multiplicity, sensitivity, and near intangibility of the measures of art. Delighted with Timon's monologue on the effect of gold on man, Marx, even remembering Crab, remarked that "Launce alone, with his dog Crab, is worth more than all the German comedies put together." "In the first act alone of *The Merry Wives of Windsor,*" he noted elsewhere, "there is more life and movement than in all German literature."

Life and movement can come to art only in terms of the invisible dimensions of the artistic. Life and movement are breathed forth from the very book I hold.

Carefully, I turn the pages of the Folio. There is a peculiar charm in first editions; the old print and the grade of paper retain something of the time that produced them. Rough, durable paper —and rough, strong words. Not everyone valued them. "Your touch will always meet sleekness," Radishchev wrote at the end of the eighteenth century about admirers of the effete and flattering phrase. "Nothing rough and wholesome will ever pain your tactile sense." But the centuries have not been able to erode the healthy ruggedness of Shakespeare's poetry.

How good it was to make the acquaintance of the Folio as I did—in an empty library study, holding it in my own hands. But how much harder to get hold of the life reflected in this book.

To define a color as brick-red is to say little about the color. The buildings of Birmingham, Amsterdam, and Hamburg are made of brick, but their colors are quite disparate in tone. In

Stratford, the houses along the road are built of a special toylike brick. Past the car window flit white plaster walls ruled in black timber, with tiled roofs and red shutters. An occasional door is brightly painted in yellow. The color of the brick changes from its former reds to grays and whites. Small hotels and pubs, their names swinging from brackets affixed to a corner of the building, will appear around a bend. And somehow all this—the oak beams, the cast-iron railings, the signs with "The Red Lion," "The Unicorn," "The Saint George," or "The Swan" on them—returns the passer-by to the time of Shakespeare.

The automobiles trundle along. In the one ahead, the driver thrusts his head out the window and motions with his fingers: you can pass. Two-storied green buses and fashionable, expensive cars, which resemble halved aerial bombs, go by. A little old Ford moves unhurriedly along, with an elderly bespectacled woman at the wheel. Multicolored motorrollers gather speed. On easy asphalt, the twentieth century passes the sixteenth.

The sixteenth century is restored to polished perfection. It is laundered and ironed out to starched whiteness. Appetizing, like the wrapper on a chocolate bar.

A peaceful river, trees bending over the water, a boat. Two girls sit at the oars—one in a bright red sweater, the other in green.

This is the Avon. We are in Stratford-upon-Avon. Here Shakespeare was born; this is not to be forgotten. You cannot eat an omelette without the eggs being supervised by his portrait, which sits, of course, at the top of the menu. When you stub out a butt, you risk rubbing it into the face of the author of *Romeo and Juliet;* it's on the ash tray. Looking over the magazines in a newsstand, you discover that the famous Stratfordian even wrote comic books.

"Don't fray your nerves into lace edges," pleads an advertisement in a souvenir booklet of the Memorial Theatre. "Shakespeare takes heavy toll of the human battery, and aftercare for his crumpled audiences is a neglected therapy. . . ."

Where is salvation?

"At Stratford, however, you can be lacerated by Othello or pulverized by Lear and only ten minutes later respond to expert treatment at the Welcombe Hotel. . . ." Its solaces include "an à la carte menu as varied as the soliloquies."

"Would you like to take the short tour?" asks the custodian of the birthplace. They have apparently worked out a speedy scientific short cut for seeing a museum. Familiarization at a trot. You walk quickly, stopping momentarily at a few sights noteworthy by reason of their fame or their curiosity. Then you buy post cards with historically oriented pictures.

But we are taking the long tour through the house where Shakespeare was born. The curator of the museum is an educated man who enjoys his work; it is a pleasure to speak with him. He shows us his small collection as though its few exhibits were made up of simple, ordinary things. His casual approach to all these objects makes them all the more real.

You can get the same feeling in Leningrad, at the corner of Liteiny Avenue and Basseinaya Street. Having mounted to the second floor, you pause on an ordinary stair landing in front of a quite unremarkable door. The brass plate on the door reads "Nikolai Alekseevich Nekrasov." You ring. The door opens. A vestibule. Rooms. This is not a museum housing a few artifacts that once belonged to a nineteenth-century poet; it is simply an apartment. People live here. But the master and his family are not at home.

The owner of an unpretentious *dacha* in Yalta has gone for a stroll along the embankment or, perhaps, has recently gone to Moscow. He left his medicine on the night table. Yet for some reason his overcoat lies under the glass of a showcase, along with a pince-nez on lace. Here they rarely call the absentee by his surname; it is, "Anton Pavlovich[1] planted these bushes. . . ."

The people in the little Stratford house had left it to go about their business, for, as Hamlet said, "every man hath business and desire." So the inhabitants have gone, having generously left permission for us to enter the premises in their absence. We walk, look, disturbing no one. You catch yourself thinking that these people had left their rooms just before our arrival, not three and a half centuries ago.

We go through the smallish and clean whitewashed rooms, with their oak beams and brick fireplaces. We open the low doors, descend the wooden staircase. We are not only passing through an apartment, but through a life. In one room is a bed and a cradle. Here Shakespeare was born. A few more steps, a few more years.

[1] Chekhov [trans.].

In the kitchen, near the hearth, is a pole that is attached to the ceiling. A small stick with a hoop is nailed to it fairly close to the floor. This hoop held the waist of a child; a boy moved his short legs and learned to walk. Going through a few more years, you enter another room. It holds a school desk scarred by the knives of sixteenth-century children. The desk was brought here from the Stratford Grammar School, where Shakespeare studied Greek and Latin.

Are those his things? Probably not. They are things of his day, but it is doubtful that he himself lay in this particular cradle, or once sat behind this desk. Not only is there little to differentiate one sixteenth-century school desk from another, but most everyday articles of necessity to people throughout the centuries prove alike in some way. If this one bed has smallish carved posts and a canopy, what of it? The beds of all women in childbirth remember similar pain and similar happiness. And the first steps of all children, be they guarded by a wooden enclosure or by this pole and hoop, are alike.

Life in the Stratford house was simple, human. The father worked here as a glover, the mother cooked, and they ate around a heavy oak table; they bore children. And when the time came, they died. Their life is tangible, insofar as it bespeaks a familiar humanity.

Passing through the light, clean rooms, you think of his art. Here, as a child, he learned to walk, later to travel the roads of every nation as an intimate of its people, as their Shakespeare. His hyperbole is sometimes unusual, his tales fabulous, but the essence of human life, as he portrayed it, has something in common with all lives, and with your own life—just as the sixteenth-century cradle resembles all cradles, and your own cradle. In his art people recognize the injustice that fell to his lot, and the apparent happiness. It is not by chance that the conditions in which great artists lived rarely represent anything exotic or even curious to the modern observer. The style of palace halls and fashionable villas changes far more markedly than that of houses where men of genius worked.

One wants to memorize this small house, its low-pitched white-washed rooms, its plain everyday contents. In producing Shakespeare, we directors frequently present his characters as though they had been created by a man who grew up amidst parquet floors and columns. Externals—a "short cut" to Shakespeare's art.

However, this house was not only the great man's place of birth, but his property as well. And here begins the second story, interesting in its own right. There are thus two tales, each developing parallel to the other: the fate of Shakespeare and that of his property.

John Shakespeare, citizen of Stratford-upon-Avon and owner of the house, left the property to his son William. Later it passed to the poet's eldest daughter, then to other relatives. Eventually, there were no more direct descendants; the line had ended. Strangers took possession of the property. The new owners turned part of the building into a small hotel. On a bracket by the door was hung a sign on which a country house painter had drawn the portrait of a girl. Here, where the poet had spent his youth, guests lolled about, and the master of the house dealt in bed and board.

Medals were struck in honor of Shakespeare premières. Innumerable volumes about his works began to appear in print. But in the house where the poet's life had begun now rings the sound of an axe. There is the stench of blood and raw meat. No need to anticipate dramatics: a butcher had set up shop on the ground floor. Dressed carcasses hung about, and housewives came to buy their sausage and sirloin.

Shakespeare's characters were celebrated by Garrick, Edmund Kean, Mochalov.[2] Goethe, Stendhal, Pushkin, and Belinski[3] called the poet great. His fame grew, and his property changed hands. In 1847, a poster appeared on fences; its bold script proclaimed that "the truly heart-stirring relic," "the most honoured monument of the greatest genius that ever lived," would be sold at auction on the sixteenth of September. The print shouted "immortal bard," and "a most glorious period" of English history. The elevated style was calculated to inflate prices, to reinforce any increase of the value as announced. A historical and descriptive guide to Shakespeare's birthplace calls it "a masterpiece of publicity." Certainly society was stirred by it.

The *Times* found "something grating to the ear" in the announcement, and feared that the house might fall into "the dese-

[2] Pavel Stepanovich Mochalov (1800–1848), Russian tragedian [trans.].

[3] Vissarion Grigorievich Belinski (1811–1848), Russian literary critic [trans.].

crating grasp of those speculators who are said to be desirous of taking it from its foundations and trundling it about on wheels like a caravan of wild beasts, giants, or dwarfs, through the United States of America." But the government still saw no necessity for buying the house and preserving it. Nevertheless, there were men of that mind who organized a committee to raise funds to purchase the historic building. Contributions were collected in a variety of ways, one of them being the staging of special dramatic performances in London and in the provinces. A playbill from *The Merry Wives of Windsor* is displayed on one of the walls in the Stratford museum. One of the roles was played by an amateur; the bill lists his name as Charles Dickens.

For three thousand pounds the committee bought both this house and the house once belonging to Shakespeare's daughter. Restoration of the buildings was undertaken between 1857 and 1864. At first, about one thousand people visited the museum; in 1956 there were 230,000 visitors. The floors have been polished to a high sheen by the feet of people from every continent. Wandering through the house with me now are an Indian with a black beard and white turban, some students from France, and a Swedish family.

Of course, the visitors include all sorts. I am indignant at the sight of the traces left behind by flippant tourists who want *their* names immortalized, too. The glass in ancient windows is scratched with signatures. What barbarity! I read the names: Walter Scott, Henry Irving, Ellen Terry. . . . Perhaps I was a bit hasty!

In front of the house is a garden where they raise the trees and flowers found in Shakespeare's poetry. This is a momument after my own heart. The garden keeps the verses warm; it changes from day to day; it is one with the entire earth. Every summer, it breaks out in a festival of color. Its fragrance rises. Ophelia's garland is plaited once more. Here's "rosemary, that's for remembrance. . . . And there is pansies, that's for thoughts," and daisies, for flightiness. A bed of violets—the emblems of love; remember, they all withered when Ophelia's father died. A light breeze sways the branches of a willow, Desdemona's melancholy friend.

Yet, earlier, when not all these flowers grew in the garden, and when the trees were fewer and not so tall, a young provincial set out from the house, off on the road to seek his fortune, as the old expression goes. Many legends have cropped up about this youth. According to tradition, he worked as a tutor for a Catholic family, and as an assistant schoolmaster in the school where he once studied. Some lord or other accused him of poaching, and the young man was drawn to the road by wandering players. There are not a few such notions, but they are largely unfounded and have proved dubious.

But the times through which he wandered are known from the words of contemporaries and, most important, from the poet himself. He travelled the savage world of his day. Hordes of vagabonds made their way along the heavily trafficked high road. Ploughmen, for example, were turned out of their fields so that arable land could be converted into pasture: wool was commanding a high price then. Here King Lear met his subjects, poor naked wretches. Stone towers stood sullen in heavy fog, while the witches prophesied the crown to Macbeth and blood to the people. From village to village, the death knell marked the carousals of the Black Death. Tired horses pulled heavy loads; people squabbled. Rumors of rebellion were rampant. A bloody comet shot past the earth. Conspirators surrounded the throne. The executioner's axe ticked off the reigns.

A fat idler left the tavern at dawn. Coachmen's lanterns blinked yellow in the inns. Foul places! Ulcers on the horses' backs; rotten peas and lentils. The fleas are oppressive. No chamber pots even; you have to urinate in the fireplace. Falstaff is surrounded by careerists and gallows birds, and his sherry has lime added to it by the innkeeper to take away its extremely sour taste.

The kingdom of the glorious Queen Bess, restored for the tourist trade, is pleasant to view from a car. A tidy sixteenth century gladdens the eye, stimulates the appetite—it would be a crime to complain of Stratford restaurants. These clean little storybook pictures, however, vanish from memory when you but recall Shakespeare's rough words. Instead of the peace of a road smoothed by steam rollers, you see an arduous one, dirty and pockmarked. You see beams swollen by dampness, ramshackle houses, crooked destinies.

The 1690's. A German traveller, upon crossing London Bridge, finds its tall pikes interesting; the heads of the executed rot on their points. The German stopped, counted: thirty-four heads. Boats sailed on the Thames and moored at the distant shore. There, outside the city limits, stood high tapering towers. Inscriptions are furnished by an old engraving, "Long View of London." "Beere-bayting" is over one of the of the buildings. "The Globe" over the other. In the one, bears were harassed by dogs, and in the other, Shakespeare performed and was performed. Inside the tower there was an open platform for acting. The audience surrounded the stage, sitting in galleries or standing on the ground. There was no roof. Over the theatre hung the sky, and a banner with *Totus mundi agit histrionem* blowing in the wind.

However, acting became a more complicated matter when just one troupe, and not the whole world, was involved. The players had to have a patron to be granted the right to act. Burbage's company was under the patronage of the Earl of Leicester, and later under that of the Lord Chamberlain. Otherwise, according to the law, they would be treated to the branding iron and lash as vagabonds.

William Shakespeare, one of Leicester's men and then one of the Lord Chamberlain's, worked with Burbage's troupe for over twenty years. There were few permanent actors, only eight to fourteen of them. With these, Shakespeare spent almost half of his life. With them he acted, wrote new plays and revised old ones, shared in the general profits, and invested in the construction of a new building. They worked together year round. Performances began after noon, so writing and rehearsing often had to take place at night, in the haste demanded by the theatre. The troupe played before the court and in the dining halls of the great. Summer sent them wandering about other cities, to perform in castles and inns. When things didn't go well, the company lived in poverty. They struggled against competitors, who planted spies and stole plays. Children's troupes came into fashion, and the take was threatened. Actors were frequently condemned in the churches. The Puritans got theatres closed as breeding places of dirt and disease.

Scholarship has uncovered a number of facts concerning Shake-speare's work. In recent years, scholars have even reconstructed an Elizabethan theatre in detail. They have restored texts and have come to understand the acting technique of the period. The results of these studies are important. Enough has already been written on the universality of the genius and the immortality of his work. It is high time that we turn our eyes from the elect of God and look at the laborer, his co-workers, and the audience for whom he wrote. The acquisition of all this knowledge will do nothing to harm respect for his genius or a conviction of his immortality.

Perhaps, among other things, the price of a ticket was significant in itself. While the building constructed by Burbage was not particularly comfortable, he strove for moderately priced performances. Shakespeare wrote for various audiences, of course, but the ones who paid only a penny at the door were those who decided the fate of the play. Shakespeare stood right with them, face to face, on the stage where his fellows, the actors, were speaking the lines he wrote. These audiences surrounded Burbage's troupe on three sides; the players spoke directly to them. The strange conditions under which the performances took place have often been described: the whirls of tobacco smoke, the hawkers of both food and drink, the card games. It was quite possibly like this. But it is more probable that when Iago spoke to Othello of Desdemona's infidelity, the card playing and nibbling stopped. Shakespeare's plays were not written for a sluggish, disinterested audience.

Calling these audiences coarse and unreceptive seems a waste of breath. Christopher Marlowe emerged from the world of London apprentices, and the century before that the violence of the French student milieu prompted more than throat cutting, as attested by the poetry written by François Villon. It was an era of great and decisive change. One contemporary tells us that gentlemen began to trade in sheep, knights became mining barons, and the sons of peasants went on to the university. People of position held in great respect became cattle breeders, butchers, and tanners.

The rifts in society were medieval by nature. The feudal village was no more, but others were organized and took its place. Into them were driven those who had formerly considered themselves free men. The lash whistled even louder in the hands of the new masters; the locks were even stronger on the new fences. Belief in the greatness of man became anger at a human race incapable of attaining that greatness. Hamlet could appear on the stage because he had already walked in the midst of life. It was not only the Danish prince who suffered the loss of his illusions, but also many of those who paid their penny for admission.

Shakespeare frequently gave voice to the thoughts of his audiences. He sensed the transformations in sixteenth-century life, as did many of his contemporaries, but it was only he who could shape the general anxiety and rage into words. He was the poet of the penny-ticket holder, and his creative work was born not of social strife, but of the unremitting and unwearying work of a popular playwright and actor. He wrote quickly, without revision. Two thousand spectators filled the theatre; they were waiting for him. There is no reason to insinuate that the playwright did not value their applause. Gentlemen of learning were unable to persuade him to write in an elevated classic style. As a youth, he wrote two poems that agreed with a Renaissance aesthetic and that opened the door to patrons of the arts. This kind of work was not continued. All the fury of the age could rage inside a clumsy tower without a roof, but it was impossible to express these tempests in imitation of Seneca. If words ran out, he made new ones; when grammar got in the way, he ignored it. His art, too, had no roof.

Shows, tours, plague epidemics, parliamentary bans, competition, youthful hopes, and reality viewed with the eyes of maturity. And again by the old road—past peaceful fields, smallish trees, and graveyards with unstable stones—the poet returned to his modest home town, to the place where his people were buried. Tired after many hard years of work, he would soon die here himself. He had filled his stage with a horde of heroes, the young, the old, the gay, the sad; they all left the stage to take their thoughts and passions into life itself. He had changed the language of poetry and drama, giving names to objects and feelings which had gone nameless till then. He later fell sick. When it came time to write his will, things had gotten worse for him: his hand trembled; the signature came out crooked; the letters were uneven.

April of 1616 was drawing to a close. From the side of the road, the steeple bell summoned the people of Stratford to bid farewell to a fellow townsman. The coffin was borne from the Church of the Holy Trinity. (They should have had it repaired long ago. The roof needed new tiles: rain leaked into the chancel and dampness marred the walls. There were panes missing in the windows.) The lid was nailed down, and the casket lowered into the ground. Then the coffin was covered with earth. Shakespeare was no more. In his place, people began to be shown someone totally unlike him.

There was the doll that stood on the north wall of the old church. A London artisan had made the bust to order; it was of a fat man with bulging eyes and a carved moustache, twirled, and dashing. He varnished it, painted it white, smeared the cheeks with pink and the doublet with red. The artisan tucked a pen into the fat fingers, since his client had said that the departed was a writer. And for greater solemnity, he put a tasseled pillow under the paper on which this cut-rate Shakespeare was writing.

In the naïveté of old country sculpture, one finds a poetic purity, a spontaneous expression of feeling. There is nothing of this in the Stratford idol, but rather something sinister in the self-satisfied vacuity of its painted face. I look at this doll, and it comes to me: this is the one who rewrote Shakespeare's tragedies for the comics.

And this is how death robbed life of Shakespeare. At first, it made a blockhead of him with an inane piece of provincial trash. Then it began to be a whole career. No expense was spared— marble got into the act.

A bell grandly marks the hours from Westminster Abbey. They have built a literary pantheon here, in the midst of the history and glory of a nation. An illustrious company has assembled at Poets' Corner: Johnson, Keats, Shelley, Burns. Everyone's hair is dressed and curled. Here a forehead is wreathed in laurel; there a brow is raised to heaven in dawning inspiration. And in the middle of one wall stands a full-length marble gentleman leaning his elbow on a pile of elegantly bound tomes. With remarkable accuracy, the sculptor has molded buttons on the doublet, lacings on the collar, and beautifully pressed lace cuffs. The stockings are slightly puckered, but this happens in reality. As in the best-known sculpture, the statue's eyes are vacant.

They say this is Shakespeare.

Why the de luxe editions under his elbow? Evidently, his plays were this well bound in the versions pirated by a rival company. But could so elegant a gentleman really be interested in receipts from a performance and the income from renting a theatre? I anticipate your question: Yes, these ignoble interests were essential to Shakespeare's creative work. Otherwise, you get a tasseled pillow under the author's scratch paper.

When the gentle, patient Chekhov was presented with a silver

pen on an anniversary, he quite seriously got angry. The gift struck
Anton Pavlovich as an insult.

It is hard to see William Shakespeare in this man with his
stockings wrinkled *au naturel.* It is probably some other Shakespeare. If the surname was shared by another littérateur, then,
judging by the statue, this one really could have done his writing
with a silver pen.

In the Tate Gallery, where the best collection of English painting is housed, there are quite a few paintings of Shakespearean
figures.

In 1852, John Everett Millais painted a beautiful girl, half-
submerged in a beautiful stream. I had long known "Ophelia"
from reproductions, but only the original bears witness to the
industry of the painter. Trees, flowers, water, dress, grass are all
depicted with the same scrupulous care. A tiny yellow-breasted
bird seems to be chirping away from a branch. The painting could
not be reproached with naturalism, however; such a bird would
only twitter musically, tastefully. It is a well-known fact that
Elizabeth Siddal posed for Ophelia in her bath. Millais later
replaced the walls of the bath with the shores of the Ewell River.
All this strikes me as visible in the picture: bath water, a her-
barium, and a gracefully posed drowning woman.

Ford Madox Brown, another painter of the same period, chose a
different scene. An old man sleeps, his fingers holding a little
flower. A lady in a cloak of unpleasant pink stretches her hand to
the sleeper. Here, too, are musicians, their director raising his
baton, unconcerned spectators. According to the catalogue, this is
"Lear and Cordelia."

It is easy to identify the external situations of the tragedies, but
it is impossible to feel the tragedy. The poetry and tragic intensity
of the figures were not within the artists' range of interests. The
sculptor who paid such attention to Shakespeare's stockings should
shake the hand of the painter who busied himself copying the bird
chirping over the corpse of Polonius's daughter.

"Hamlet and Ophelia" by Dante Gabriel Rossetti. A pale
maiden proffers letters to a cassocked man who wears a sword at
his side. The girl's face is devoid of life; the man looks like a
sleepwalker. The objects that surround the figures look as if they

are made of embossed pigskin; there are curtains, furniture, and a strange staircase with two impassable flights. A dead lackluster world. Really, is this young lady capable of going mad from love or despair? Could this gentleman stab a man to death, and pour poison down his throat as well?

Seeing Rossetti's painting, it is hard not to consider the many conventions that have been adopted by art. The group of young artists now under discussion was organized in 1848. Millais, Holman-Hunt, Rossetti, and their adherents called themselves the Pre-Raphaelite Brotherhood. They despised middle-class civilization and its soullessness. Academicians canonized the high Renaissance; the brotherhood called for the traditions of pre-Raphaelite art and for "truth to nature." Although the words of their artistic manifestoes were provocative, painting did not rise from its knees. It prayed to the Blessed Virgin and occupied itself with allegories and parables. The revolt itself, born in the salon, was limited to the salon. Art did not change the world, but only the look of middle-class living rooms. Mannered society neither resembled the heroism of medieval legends nor the gay clarity of early Renaissance fabliaux and novellas. This outlook on life was especially removed from the Shakespearean.

Suddenly a silly thought arises, and the fantastic notion takes hold of me. What if . . . I picture these figures coming to life, affectation in their movements and a singsong tone to their declamations. They leave their gilded frames and step onto the stage of the Globe. And I can distinctly hear a beautifully deafening whistle replete with the energy of life, and a concert of catcalls, the shouts of London apprentices, impatient foot-stamping, and extravagant sixteenth-century abuse. And the whole house of cards crumbles, dashed by the guffaws of the Elizabethan audience.

I am wandering through the halls of the museum. There are many excellent pictures, but they are extraneous to the matter under discussion here. It's already late; time to go. Beside the staircase leading down hangs a mid-sixteenth-century portrait, hardly in a place of honor. It is of a man with an elegant beard, dressed in a shirt embroidered with flowers, leaves, and branches. The fingers of his left hand rest on the hilt of his sword; his elbow clasps a steel helmet to his side; the other hand holds a lance. The strangeness of the picture lies in that his toilette is limited to a luxurious shirt and military arms. The man has forgotten to put on shoes, stockings, or trousers. And thus he stands, dressed to the nines, and barefoot—one of the tribe of discoverers of new worlds, merchant adventurers. The artist dressed him, it seems, for a court masque, but perhaps he just pictured ancient heroes in this sort of garb.

There are many such figures in Elizabethan miniatures, and even though in most of them the miniaturist drew only the face, the rest of the model's figure can be guessed. However the hair be crimped, and however expensive the lace on the collars, one can sense the bare feet of these people, the strong rough feet of travellers and soldiers, feet which stand on the warm, dusty ground. At that time, nothing on this earth had yet come into order.

Somehow, the following phrase appeared in one of our translations of *Hamlet:* "The time is out of joint."[4] Before this, Russian tragedians had been exclaiming for years: "The continuity of times has been destroyed." The new treatment delighted the critics. The Kroneberg translation was recognized as faulty, as distorting the essential idealism of the Shakespearean figure of speech. "Dislocated time," on the other hand, was accepted by scholarly opinion as almost literally reproducing the English line. It forcibly reminded the reader of physical dislocation and removed him from the world of abstract ideas. The phrase came into common usage —not in conversational Russian, it's true—but in the language of critical reviews.

I was reminded of this passage in *Hamlet* while in an aged church of one of the Oxford University colleges. A knight's sepulcher was in front of me; the stern and courageous warrior lay on a stone couch, with his hands strictly placed, palms together, on his chest. A dog stood guard over him at the head of the bed; a lamb was placed at his feet. A sword lay ready by his right hand. This was a worthy representation of the death of a knight: the peaceful clarity of the plastic forms breathed eternal immobility. Time had come to the sculptor's aid; it had yellowed the stone, giving it a stately nuance of antique ivory.

---

[4] The Russian word used here literally denotes physical dislocation. Its application to a time or an age was unheard of, so that the expression was remarkably striking in Russian [trans.].

But it was worth turning to the right and looking upwards, to see an indecent spectacle of Elizabethan times jar the peace of the Romanesque sepulcher. An unbelievable performance was taking place on the wall. What hadn't been sculptured there! There were columns, cupids, and cockle shells, a globe, and skulls sprouting curlicues. In the middle of all this cinnabar and aquamarine profusion was portrayed a merry rubicund gentleman. Two ladies with golden hair sounded golden trumpets over his head; these figures were evidently borrowed from some erotic tale, for the sculptor paid particular attention to their breasts and hips.

Under the whole construction was inscribed, "He died of melancholy."

Freethinkers and blasphemers, they wanted to set out for the other world with their theatrical trumpeters, gay mesdemoiselles, a globe, and a volume of Ovid. Returning from a maritime expedition, completing an experiment, or finishing a line for a sonnet, they found themselves in an iron world of profit. It but remained to pronounce a last speech at the scaffold, bragging of one's knowledge of the classics, or to construct similarly funereal buffoonery on the stage.

The two sepulchers, unnatural neighbors, led me to meditate once more on the story of *Hamlet*. Knightly virtues and humanistic dreams were poisoned by the King of Denmark, by his government, and by the reality of Elsinore. Concepts of life and death, created by different epochs. . . . Everything proved to be unstable; things found continuation in nothings; no affirmations proceeded from the negations. There was a disunification of the past, of the present, and of the future. . . . It seemed to me that the phrase "the continuity of times has been destroyed" was the more successful and that "dislocation of the time" was but a mannered metaphor with little real association.

Of course, government power had many ways of supporting the bond of times. One of England's most popular edifices served this purpose relatively well. Its thick walls, bolted doors, and bars seemed a symbol of succession: They served the past; the present could not manage without them; and they would not prove quickly outmoded in the future. I am speaking of the Tower. The drama of vicissitude was a popular genre in that era, and it was performed more than once in this set. Elizabeth Tudor was sent here by her sister Mary. Here Thomas More and Anne Boleyn sat behind bars. Here they put crowns on heads, and then chopped the heads off. There were few Elizabethans of note who had not lodged here. Ben Jonson was an habitué. Some were brought by politics, some by an unrestricted mind as far as religious dogma was concerned, and some by wildness and debt.

A stone wall is hung with the portrait of a bearded man with large pearl earrings. It is in a high spacious dungeon, with a canopied bed and a tapestry. One of the heroes of the times spent a number of years in this chamber—Sir Walter Ralegh, vice-admiral of the British fleet, poet, historian. He had brought tobacco and the potato to Europe, hoisted Elizabeth's flag over the New World, and had organized the colony of Virginia, England's first in the Americas. Ralegh had been fond of carousing in The Mermaid, and the inn became part of literary history. Shakespeare, too, frequented it. Ralegh sat at the head of the table. Amid clouds of tobacco smoke, they discussed the fate of the world and matters of aesthetics. They came here after distant travels to talk about Italian architecture, French fashion, and ancient ruins. Geography was frequently intertwined with fairy tales, and history with legend. The travellers enjoyed describing their encounters with herds of horses that had human faces, and with beautiful women who gazed at passers-by not with eyes, but with precious stones.

A new reign, and Ralegh found himself under lock and key. His imprisonment was not harsh: his family came for stays, and he could wander around the courtyard. James I even freed him for a time, for a last expedition. Still, Sir Walter's head was chopped off later. This is why he was waiting here in the Tower for twenty years. Meanwhile he occupied himself with the composition of his *History of the World,* which spanned the story of man from the creation of the world to the death of Alexander of Macedon.

The chronicle of King Richard III is indivisible from the Tower. Reading it, one can distinctly visualize the terrible grandeur of the notched towers and the silent horror of the casemates. Shakespeare called its stones gray, and memory calls the Tower ancient; Shakespeare placed Richard, Duke of Gloucester, by its walls, and the stones are remembered as bloody. And so they seem, even now.

The epithet is still valid. Along the street, they have placed a number of signs reading, "Bloody Tower." From the snack bar, where coffee and hot dogs are sold, you go to the left, through the gate. Over your head are embrasures with window frames set into them, and middle-class lace curtains behind the glass. Just beyond the gate stands a large plaster dog of commercial manufacture; there is a slot in its head—for contributions to the R.S.P.C.A. Rains have washed the stone walls, but have not been able to remove the London soot which has eaten into their surface. Crowds of tourists visit the place where once the scaffold was erected. A small tablet lists whose heads had been chopped off: Lord Hasting's, Anne Boleyn's, Essex', and other famous ones. The attendants are dressed in ancient uniforms and hats.

An elderly raven strolls unhurriedly over the flagstones. The sulky-looking gentleman is unwell, and somber in his shabby black morning coat. The years do not cheer him. The surrounding crowds are boring. This bird summons forth sinister associations. More living details: an axe and a wooden block are displayed in one of the halls. There are dents on the block—the traces of blows. There are several of them, each demanding closer scrutiny, and meditation. Here is the original prop of tragedy, and it merits some time spent in just standing here quietly.

As for the halls and fortifications, they have long since been civilized and adapted to modern needs throughout.

Ancient cannon stand on the grounds of a castle in Edinburgh. This time the weather is bad; it is foggy and raining lightly. Everything seems unreal. Perhaps it is here that the ghost of Hamlet's father walked? . . . One of the weapons is made ready for battle. Soldiers arrive wearing plaid Scottish trousers and white gaiters. An officer gives the command. A flash of fire, and smoke rises over the fortifications. No need to fear disquieting events; Scotland is a peaceful place. This is merely the signal for the opening of the film festival.

The procession goes through the streets: an orchestra of the noted bagpipes, men in kilts, and, finally, the movie stars. They wear the same smiles as on the Promenade de la Croisette in Cannes or under Hollywood palms.

There are hillocks lying beneath the castle embrasures. A graveyard. But why are the knolls so small and the markers so strangely uniform? Dogs are buried here. The canine necropolis is kept in perfect order. Attitudes toward the living animal are somewhat worse: everywhere there are signs saying, "No dogs allowed." Nonetheless, they have brought animals into these churches. It was on this very spot that, by orders of Cromwell, they made a stable out of an ancient cathedral. The chapel was converted into a storehouse for fodder. (This will be discussed later, when we come to Falstaff.)

Did tragic heroes really roam these places? The little courtyards and low towers are infused with something peaceful, ordinary. Perhaps in those times the weather was different. Shakespeare's whirlwind tore the roofs from houses; squares were fettered in glacial frost, and waves heaved to the stars. The symbolist poet Aleksandr Blok wrote that life is hard when the "black wind" visits the house. The black wind was playing about the walls when a murdered man emerged from its stones and looked at Macbeth.

Now a special breed of inhabitants sometimes take shelter in the castles. Themselves the owners of ancestral lands, it is not rare for them to live out their days showing guests through their estates for a fee. The world still has its Earls of Warwick. If you buy a ticket, you can look at his towers, armory, picture gallery. . . . This part of the excursion calls forth some amazement: Vandyke is next to Victorian watercolors, and a Holbein hangs beside a modern salon daub. It seems that the latter is there by reason of the theme: the portraits of kinsmen. It is Anthony Eden, who married a Warwick. But even the most successful matches cannot guarantee the same quality in a canvas; a special dowry is needed here.

In Shakespeare, too, genealogy has a particular outlook. Queen Margaret spoke of what had occurred in this castle:

> I had an Edward—till a Richard killed him.
> I had a Harry—till a Richard killed him.
> Thou hadst an Edward—till a Richard killed him.
> Thou hadst a Richard—till a Richard killed him.[5]

The branches of the genealogical tree have spread to our day. The little heads of well-bred brides and respectable grooms bloom on fresh shoots. They say that, after the visitors have gone and the receipts have been taken from the till and counted, the masters of the house issue from distant rooms. In their great hall hung with armor, banners, and hunting trophies, they sit around the table for

[5] *Richard III,* IV, iv.

supper. I hardly think that whole roasted venison is still served, nor is it probable that anyone drinks wine from a horn anymore.

The stones that comprise these walls do not seem gray or bloody at all, although they were hewn in the eleventh or twelfth century. Actually, quite a few corpses fell against them. A situation of no small import reveals itself here: in art, a wall will change according to whose shadow falls on it. Even in their day, these towers were not so very big, nor did the gate seem high beyond measure. But if the people Shakespeare created were to appear in this castle, everything would change. Its scale does not derive from the stones, but from the characters. They have been established by the poetry, and do not lose their vital force. The stones, kept intact, adjusted to other times. Men of ordinary stature set foot within these walls, and everything seemed commonplace. The grandeur had gone.

The verse proved more durable than the stones. It was surely Shakespeare's prerogative to write:

> When wasteful war shall statues overturn,
> And broils root out the work of masonry,
> Nor Mars his sword nor war's quick fire shall burn
> The living record of your memory.[6]

Sluttish time is powerless to erase this record—not because the author had it engraved for all time, nor because it passes unchanging through changing life. But, to the contrary, the whole point is that his figures have the faculty of acquiring new traits, of changing with the realities of a new century. The generations who admire classic art find in it not the fossil of an ideal, but the interests and feelings of their own time. Even today, Pushkin's lines are permeated with a vital energy. Rembrandt's paintings do not have to be explained by the dates of their composition.

The phantom of Richard III retains its full range of foreboding evil. His shadow has appeared on the concrete walls of death camps; it was cast by those who preached the insignificance of man, who called for the oppression of peoples and the annihilation of nations. The image of the humped shadow looms large even till now. It has been chiselled into the memory of generations by poetry, while the historied castles already seem unimpressive and

6 Sonnet 55.

reduced in size. The old uniforms of the Tower guards look like costumes for a masquerade, hardly appropriate for such elderly people.

But listen! Thunder of drawbridge chains, guards are saluting with their halberds. King Richard III of England enters the Tower once more. We are seeing Sir Laurence Olivier's movie.

One more "landscape" gives ground for thought: the absence of sets in the Globe. The bare stage of Shakespeare's theatre was not in any way due either to poverty or to an impoverished imagination. Shakespeare's contemporaries applauded luxury in stage finery, and the performances of masques (court spectacles) gave evidence of resourcefulness enough. Burbage's troupe did not skimp on costumes, and was not unacquainted with the devices of stage technique. It was not a question of meagerness of theatre equipment, but one of poetic excellence. Future years have indicated that technical innovation and increased expenditures have, in themselves, contributed little to Shakespeare. The magnificent spectacles of the past century, like Charles Kean's productions, which had crowds of extras pacing about against a panoramic background of ancient London, only interfered with the poetry. Even the archeologically oriented naturalism of the Duke of Meiningen did not improve an audience's ability to grasp the poetry. The props for *Julius Caesar* were made according to specifications dictated by evidence from excavations. They tried to substitute archeological accuracy for poetic truth. Fretting over the cuirass, they forgot about the heart under it. And it stopped beating.

The winged goddess of victory was transferred to the Louvre many years ago. No longer does she have a backdrop of blue Hellenic skies, but one of black velvet. She flies nonetheless. This flight over centuries still astounds the men of new centuries, but the scale has still not been invented which can weigh the sculptor's artistic intention. Unity of poetic movement does not lend itself to segmentation; it cannot be articulated into fixed and separate parts. Its secret is contained in its very movement, in the flight. Even the folds of the tunic fly. Of course, it is possible to master the art of the ancient tailors, and even to make a tunic like this, but it will not resemble the clothing of a Victory of Samothrace.

The events of the tragedy took place in castles: its heroes left by castle gates to join battle in a woods. It is easy to depict castle, gates, and woods on the modern stage. It is not difficult to re-create a dawn; but it is more complicated to have it echo a Shakespearean one. Throwing rose lights on the backdrop and intensifying their brightness will not get your effect across as will:

> . . . the morn, in russet mantle clad,
> Walks o'er the dew of yon high eastward hill.[7]

They built huge sets for *Richard III*. Skilled designers restored period furnishings. But the historical did not become history, nor did the dimensions on the screen give scale.

In the poetry of Shakespeare, the Tower appears not only as a place for action but also as an actor. It is an epic image, capable of changing and springing up with new qualities and new corre-spondences. When Gloucester put her children into the dungeon, Queen Elizabeth turned neither to the courtiers nor to the jailers, but to the fortress, entreating it as she might entreat a human being:

> Pity, you ancient stones, those tender babes
> Whom envy hath immured within your walls!
> Rough cradle for such little pretty ones!
> Rude ragged nurse, old sullen playfellow
> For tender Princes, use my babies well![8]

The historical Tower, which the film probably reproduced with accuracy, was small and ordinary beside the immensity of the tragic poetry, beside the symbol it evoked of the ruthless power of the state.

But can the speculative become visual? Let us recall the stone lions in *The Battleship "Potemkin"*[9]: here we see what cinematog-raphy is capable of. The designers of *Richard III* could reproduce ancient masonry. Eisenstein could make stones leap and begin to roar. The Moscow Art Theatre dictum is well known: "One does not play a king. Kings are played by their surroundings." This does not suffice for Shakespeare. Even stones must play the king.

---

[7] *Hamlet*, I, i.
[8] *Richard III*, IV, i.
[9] A 1925 Eisenstein film [trans.].

Sir Laurence Olivier is one of England's finest actors. Employing superb restraint, he expresses depth of thought and emotional tension. In his work in the cinema, he has shown us many things unknown to the theatre. The heart of the Shakespearean monologue was bared in his *Henry V* for perhaps the first time. The young commander-in-chief made the rounds of his camp before the battle. The actor's lips were compressed, but words—very quietly —were heard in an interior monologue. The mouth being closed, his thoughts rose to his eyes. This was shown in close-ups, and a microphone seemed to catch the sound of inner speech. In *Richard III,* Olivier returned to the traditional delivery of the monologue. His hunchback stumped through the halls of the palace and meditated aloud on the laws of politics. He formulated a theory of power, addressing himself not only to us but also, rhetoricianwise, to heaven and earth. Loudly, he mocked law, human and divine. He would have liked to challenge humanity to single combat, to threaten the sun. Savagery of brigandage was combined with daring of thought and energy of character. In certain moments, this daring and energy made Olivier fascinating, but suddenly he would stand stock still, under the weight of his hump. Then, thrusting his dead face out from under a protuberance on a Gothic cathedral, a chimera looked out at the world with eyes of stone.

I do not know how Olivier, slender and handsome as he is, turned himself not only into a monstrosity but into a dwarf.

The film begins with a close-up of the crown. Richard is looking at it. Unfortunately, the crown does not look particularly impressive. This is not a designer's blunder. In castles that have been converted into museums, the original crowns of England and Scotland may be seen. In spite of references to their gold content and the value of the precious stones set in them, these symbols of power invariably look like props. What is so special about these things? In order to grasp their significance, they must be perceived not as objects, but as symbols, the sinister associations of which were compounded from iron, fire, and blood by the history of a people.

One would like the figure created with such force by Sir Laurence to leave the set for the larger stage of history. For this to have happened on the screen, they would have needed the iron, fire, and blood. And the stones would have had to be gray and bloody.

For some time, Shakespeare has been much in demand as a script-writer. According to the statistical calculations of world film libraries, *Hamlet* has been filmed more than thirty times, *Macbeth* eighteen times, *Romeo and Juliet* thirty, and *Othello* twenty-three. I am speaking of various kinds of movies, including those of scenes from theatrical performances and reels from the great silent screen, as well as the modern sound film.

In a French film museum, there is shown a poster advertising the first experiment: a lady, in a huge hat and wearing leg-of-mutton sleeves, stands leaning on one elbow against a wooden chest fixed on a tripod. Film dangles out of the chest. A phonograph, complete with horn, is at the lady's feet. This is a poster for the "victor-phone" theatre.

In 1900, a critic wrote for *Le Figaro,* "Thanks to the complete union of two contemporary wonders—the cinematograph and the phonograph—the results that have been achieved are striking in their perfection." A copy of the film has been preserved, and we can return to this first year of our century. But it looks like some other century; the spectacle on the screen seems to be of incredible antiquity. Courtiers, dressed à l'opéra, bustle around an elderly woman who is costumed like a man and brandishes a sword. This is the Hamlet of Sarah Bernhardt. The "miracle of the twentieth century" looks archaic, but no more so than the same kind of theatre.

In a 1913 film, a huge bearded man cowers convulsively at the sight of a skull. Good lord, but isn't this the legendary Mounet-Sully?[10] How our views have changed! You know, his acting was greatly admired. People queued up all night at the box office. They wept at his performances. Could it be that it's hard to judge by only one performance, and a mute one at that? No; the very appearance of the actors, their manner of movement, and their exaggerated gestures are all impossible by today's standards. Like a microscope, the screen will show up corruption of style in even a sliver.

Neither does the cause lie in the inexperience of stage per-

[10] Jean Mounet-Sully (1841–1916), French tragedian [trans.].

formers before a camera. In a 1920 film, the celebrated screen star Asta Nielsen played the Danish Prince. The director and scenarist for the Swedish movie, both men of this century, were convinced that their idea of life and art was superior to that of Shakespeare. They corrected the motives and made the action more natural. A prehistory was introduced: Hamlet and Laertes are students in Wittenberg; they play youthful tricks, throw bits of feather at one another, and anger their aged teacher. An entirely lifelike and practicable motive was supplied, so that the plot would not depend on the tale of a ghost. The Prince finds the dagger that killed his father. This dagger, as Hamlet well knows, belongs to Claudius. On the screen, literally everything seems unnatural and meaningless.

In 1959, a modern version of Hamlet was filmed—*The Rest Is Silence*. John Claudius, the son of a Düsseldorf manufacturer who was killed during a bomb raid, returns to his homeland after studying at an American university. Each of the Shakespearean situations is made topical. The uncle is the murderer; he takes over the factories that had belonged to John's father, and marries John's mother. The father's spirit reveals the secret of his death by long-distance telephone. The story is corroborated by the sequences of a documentary film taken during the bombing and now kept in the company safe. The wandering players are replaced by an American ballet troupe on tour in West Germany. John-Hamlet stages a dance (the death of his father) to programatic music and the howling of sirens. Everything is as Shakespeare has it, only brought up to date. Helmut Keitner is an experienced director. The camera was skillfully used and several situations (within the limits of the set task) were clever. Nevertheless, despite jet planes, steelrolling mills, and fascism, the shallow ideas and superficial emotions were far less modern than Shakespeare's. There was no need to have had Shakespeare write the script; Agatha Christie would have done it with more flair.

One should not conclude from all this that classic plays should only be produced in full, without any change. I saw a *Macbeth* in which there was no verse and no Scotland. Instead of the witches, one little old man unravelled the fateful thread. But, in my opinion, Akira Kurosawa's 1957 film, *Throne of Blood,* is the finest of Shakespearean movies. There were fortress enclosures put together from huge logs, the military ritual of the samurai, the bannered badges woven on their backs, the bloody dance of their duels—and these plastic images of feudal Japan all seemed closely bound with the tragic poetry of Shakespeare's images. Of course, the first thing to be mentioned should be the vital power which permeated the plastic forms, and the force of the passion conveyed by the Japanese actors. This passion is unknown in European theatre and cinema. The face of Toshiro Mifune, with its rabid slanting eyes, was an immobile mask which cannot be forgotten after one has seen the film. There was no external verisimilitude in the performance of the actors, but their conventions were animated by a tension of both thought and emotion. Not only was the inner life of these people authentic, but it possessed Shakespearean strength. The scene of the murder serves as an example.

At night, in an empty room, two people sleep on mats: Washizu (Macbeth) and Madame Washizu (Lady Macbeth). Their forms are motionless; only their eyes are alive. Quiet. The King is asleep in the next room. A pause that seems to have no end. Lady Macbeth (I shall use the Shakespearean names) rises and, walking like a ceremonial doll, goes to her husband. She sits down beside him on the mat and slowly opens the fingers of his fists. In the same ceremonial step, she leaves the room to bring back a lance. She sits down by her husband and places the lance in his hands.

Macbeth goes out of the room. An immense pause, impossible on the screen. Macbeth returns with the lance and sits on the mat, assuming the same position that he had taken in the beginning of the scene. Silence. His wife slowly unclasps his fingers and removes the lance. Blood trickles down from his hands.

In the English quarterly Sight and Sound, I read an article by G. Blumenthal about this film. The critic asserts that the success of Throne of Blood lies in its cinematic sense.

Kurosawa is one of the world's best film directors. His plastic forms and his montage are excellent film art. Yet the traditions of theatre are evident in every sequence. For the UNESCO Shakespeare Jubilee in Paris, Kurosawa mounted several episodes, each of which began with a close-up of a mask from no theatre. It turned out that these masks were the key to the style of his film.

Kurosawa has said that Machiko Kyo[11] played the mad scene

[11] According to a feature article in Sight and Sound (Spring, 1957, pp. 196–197), Izuzu Yamada played Madame Washizu [trans.].

precisely according to this theatrical tradition. Dressed in a white kimono and with a white masklike face, she sat beside a bronze vase and ceaselessly washed invisible blood from her fingers. Only her hands moved, like white moths in an ominous dance.

This most cinematic film proved to be closely linked to the most ancient traditions. Any discussion of the "specific character of the various arts" will be extremely complicated. Of course, every aspect of creative work has its specific character, but the boundaries between one art and another frequently shift, and a success will refute earlier notions. There is nothing stable about the theses—which are true, for the most part—on "convention" as the medium of theatre and "the natural" as the generic trait of the film. Charlie Chaplin's walk is conventional enough, and the naturalistic set has not been a stage rarity for a long time. Shakespeare can be produced in various ways on the screen, but it is my belief that Shakespeare and naturalism are as incompatible on the screen as they are on the stage. The quest for the measure of convention and the measure of the natural is still going on in contemporary art. In Japanese art, the fusion of the two is almost Shakespearean. But this degree of passion and this degree of convention are not known to the European artist.

The Royal Shakespeare Theatre is also occupied in a search for the measures of convention and of the natural. The aesthetic of Bertolt Brecht reigned triumphant in Stratford. There was no realistic living environment in Peter Brook's production of *King Lear*. Flat pieces of iron were hung over a stage covered with bare canvas. People wore costumes made of leather. History knew no such palaces, nor any such costumes. Yet the interrelations of the characters, and their behavior, were far more lifelike than in many productions which set the stage with authentic palace apartments and costume the actors in the fashions of the period. Paul Scofield's performance as Lear was resonant with inner life; the ideas were profound and the emotions genuine. His leather costume looked natural on him, and the metal of the oval forcefully recalled the iron age. This was not a copy of life but, if you will, its algebraic formula.

I find Peter Brook the most interesting director in Europe. He brushes off the Victorian clichés from the tragedy. However, in order to break from these clichés, he sometimes veers too far in the other direction. In his *Hamlet,* for example, the mad Ophelia was a frightened, ragged Mary Ure with matted gray hair. The actress did not sing the songs, but twanged them through her nose. I don't think there would be any sense in reminding Brook that, as Shakespeare's Laertes said, "Thought and affliction, passion, Hell itself,/She turns to favor and to prettiness." I am sure that he has read these lines. But how many times have actresses come on like a Gretchen with little flowers in their prettily unbound hair? So there was some necessity for an antidote, for breaking away from sentimentality.

Brook also wants to do away with Lear's revolt. In his production, Lear's knights really run riot in the castle, and Goneril has her reasons for evicting a suite like that. The only truth in this world is suffering, and this order of things is immutable. According to Brook, the most powerful passage in the tragedy is not Lear's cry: "Howl, howl, howl, howl! Oh, you are men of stones, . . ." but Kent's words, forcefully and loudly addressed to those surrounding Lear: "Oh, let him pass! He hates him/That would upon the rack of this tough world/Stretch him out longer."

This is how the English director read *King Lear.* Later, I will talk about Mikhoels's performance of the role, and the reader will also become acquainted with my ideas on the tragedy. It is not a question of "the correct" or "the erroneous" understanding of Shakespeare, but of the possibility for each artist to find his own meaning in the playwright's art. Theatre audiences will make their own choice. And time will have its say.

There is an experimental workshop connected with the Shakespeare Theatre in London. Peter Brook invited me to see one of its rehearsals. Upon opening the door, I fell from a London street straight into our 1920's. It is a smallish room, with a steeply raked amphitheatre and unplastered walls. There is no curtain, just a platform with white screens. The sound panel is brought out into the house, and the director's assistant sits with a prompt copy of the play and switches on sounds reminiscent of Chinese theatre.

Masked players were rehearsing *The Screens* by Jean Genet. During the course of the action, a capitalist, a French general who has come to Algeria for a while, and a prostitute (whose appearance recalled a type from the posters of ROSTA) had an unhurried discussion. Meanwhile, far upstage, darkly tanned Algerians appeared in white burnooses. In a rapid-fire tempo, using pieces of red chalk, the latter scribbled tongues of flame onto the white screens. Toward the end of the episode, the white platform was covered from top to bottom with whirling fiery spots, but the colonialists had not noticed anything, or, more accurately, had not understood any of the events around them. They merely continued their conversation.

The day before, I had seen the movie *Lawrence of Arabia.* Infinite caravans of camels passed by on the screen; though they were filmed in a real desert, there was no feeling of heat. I felt heat in the combination of light and color of Peter Brook's production. I understood why the experimental workshop was attached to the Shakespeare Theatre: here they are seeking the white heat of passion and the color of folk theatre. Somehow, the art of the sixteenth century proves closer to the twentieth century than are the naturalism, archeological conglomeration, and the "de luxe" productions of the Victorian era.

Several years before seeing these new productions, I saw *A Midsummer Night's Dream* in Stratford-upon-Avon. Knowing that only this play was being staged, I was chagrined. Only with difficulty was I able to picture its fantastic figures coming concretely to life. Various theatrical traditions interfered. So did memories of illustrated editions, Mendelssohn's music, pastoral sweethearts, and ballet elves.

The director, Peter Hall, and the designer, Lila de Nobili, did without romanticism. I do not know whether or not they had considered the Tate Gallery portraits that I described earlier, but one glance at the stage brought to mind the barefoot gentleman. Bare feet seemed to play no small role in the production plan. Oberon and Titania strolled about in court attire, but without shoes and stockings. The stage was strewn with straw, and the fairies walked barefoot. It was explained in the program that "The scene is Athens—or an Elizabethan version of it."

Of course, it is not easy to create the vision of an epoch long past, but the director was able to communicate this kind of visual quality. Hall's fairies wandered through the hay. They were totally believable fairies, such as a child might picture them in his serious approach to fantasy, his belief that he really sees the unreal. The wood spirits began to live on the stage in a poetic and, at the same time, real world. They were not phantoms flying about in a vacuum, but house spirits. Sorcery did not seem to be their métier; they exuded odors of domesticity. Elves were no strangers on the farm, but were fellow villagers. With a crash, Puck opened a hatch and climbed out onto the stage. The imp wore little horns, but nonetheless he breathed garlic and his habits recalled those of a playful watchdog. The world under the trap was hardly an underground kingdom, but rather resembled a cellar for storing vegetables and grain. The Queen of the Amazons wore a cuirass instead of a bodice. Since her mode of life necessitated riding and fighting, her skirt was slit for greater comfort; under it you could see powerful thighs and calves. Hippolyta bestrode the throne like a saddle, with her arms akimbo. Naturally, the notion that classical heroes might look like this would not occur to a learned gentleman, but the tellers of folk tales probably saw them this way.

The laughter never died down in the audience. Students, who had come from many countries to see how Shakespeare was played in his home town, were thoroughly enjoying themselves. There was no evening dress here, no prim or blasé satiety.

I went out on the balcony during intermission. Under the roof hung a spotlit yellow pennant emblazoned with a lance and raven. This was Shakespeare's coat-of-arms, and is now the symbol of the Memorial Theatre. Not long ago, this flag had hung at the entrances to Moscow and Leningrad theatres. It was also not long ago that the curtain with the seagull[12] rose in London. Happily there can be a rapprochement of peoples under the banner of art, a banner that bears both Shakespeare's raven and Chekhov's seagull.

On the far bank of the Avon, electric lights shine from within their leafy hiding places in the trees. White swans swim in the dark water. . . . I must leave early tomorrow morning.

"Goodbye, swans of Avon!"

Hearing my accented English, the swans keep on swimming without even turning their heads.

[12] The symbol of the Moscow Art Theatre [trans.].

Wingéd Realism

NOT ONLY DO REAL SOUNDS BEGET ECHOES in empty space, but art forms also reverberate, in their own way, in the souls of men. If, moreover, these men are artists, image responds to image. The creation of one art continues, as it were, in another. Sound echoes in spectacle; creation in color can give birth to music.

The heroes of famous tragedies and comedies have long since become incarnate in the sketch, the painting, and the sculpture. If an exhibit of all the paintings on Shakespearean subjects were to be assembled, it would probably fill a sizable museum. Anyone who wandered through such an exhibit would be stunned by the variety of interpretation of even the external features of the characters. There is little affinity between the paintings of English artists of the end of the eighteenth century (Boydell's *Shakespeare Gallery*) and the romantic etchings of Delacroix, or between the quick-flowing line of Blake's visions and the genre sketches of Gilbert. Are the Hamlet and Ophelia of Dante Gabriel Rossetti really at all reminiscent of the man and maiden portrayed by Vrubel?[1]

Almost every artistic current has responded to the images of Shakespeare. A remarkable phenomenon, however, has resulted: the venerable plays have proved far more durable than their reflections in the work of artists more contemporary to us. Techniques of reproduction have improved, but illustrations of Shakespeare's works have become quickly antiquated. Now it tries our patience to look at de luxe editions of Shakespeare. Artistic thought has long regarded historical illustrations and genre

[1] Mikhail Aleksandrovich Vrubel (1856–1910), Russian artist [trans.].

sketches on subjects from *Macbeth* or *King Lear* as old-fashioned and outmoded, while the plays themselves invariably seem contemporary and vitally significant. In the theatre, matters have improved. More than once, set designers of this century have found effective stage settings and appointments for Shakespearean productions.

Among our designers, there is one man who is uniquely connected with Shakespeare. I speak of Aleksandr Grigorievich Tyshler. Aleksandr Grigorievich has designed for *Richard III, King Lear,* and *Twelfth Night* (sometimes the sets and costumes were the best parts of the productions), and his work has been particularly influenced by Shakespeare's poetry. Motifs begun in Tyshler's theatrical work were developed for years in his paintings.

In discussing Tyshler, the common theatre term "design" seems inadequate. This artist does not design a play, but, rather, expresses it as the poetry of the plastic arts. Instead of an exposition, he fashions a kind of reincarnation. He does not construct a background for action nor does he create a lifelike milieu for the production, but somehow continues verse line by pure line, stanza by plastic form, poetic movement by color.

The curtain rises: not a word has yet been heard, but verses already dominate the stage. From the stage platform springs a house, in poetry; wooden sculptures are placed in the stern harmony of an ancient ballad. The Fool runs in, his costume covered with the imprints of widespread fingers: the designs are puns.[2]

---

[2] The pun concerns a fool's coxcomb that resembled spread fingers and was in fact sometimes fashioned from a stuffed glove. The Fool's first lines make reference to his coxcomb:

Enter Fool

Fool: Let me hire him too. Here's my coxcomb. (Offering Kent his cap.)
Lear: How now, my pretty knave! How dost thou?
Kent: Why, fool?
Fool: Why, for taking one's part that's out of favor. Nay, an thou canst not smile as the wind sits, thou'lt catch cold shortly. There, take my coxcomb. Why, this fellow hath banished two on's daughters, and done the third a blessing against his will. If thou follow him, thou must needs wear my coxcomb. How now, Nuncle! Would I had two coxcombs and two daughters!
Lear: Why, my boy?
Fool: If I gave them all my living, I'd keep my coxcombs myself. There's mine, beg another of thy daughters.

King Lear, I, iv [trans.].

In the theatrical city-poems of Tyshler, medieval architecture gives rise to new proportions. Fantastic statues bear palace halls or torture chambers on their heads. Townsfolk are arrayed in costumes sewn from unfamiliar fabrics that do not resemble taffeta, velvet, or silk, but that are like sounds created by nuance, like the modulation of color, like the play of glossy and dull surfaces. Even the air here is permeated with a special shimmering light. On the stage, the poetic atmosphere of the production is itself the plastic impression.

The personality of the visual image is sometimes condensed almost to a single trait. In *Richard III,* at Leningrad's Bolshoi Dramatic Theatre in 1935, not only did the designer build castles in masonry, but the curtains also appeared to be of stone. Stones filled the stage: human chests were constricted by stones—costumes seemed to be made of brick; people entered resembling stone towers; stone hands wielded swords; collars, hacked out of cobblestones, propped up heads.

These words are not to be taken as literary exaggeration. The artist really designed costumes reminiscent of walls, little brick squares crowding a canvas, a flower recalling stone. . . . Cold solitary walls surrounding cruel soulless people who were more like humanoid bastions and bunkers. . . .

In one scene, the director proposed masquerade figures. The plan was later dropped, but sketches for the costumes remain. Designers have often concocted fantastic costumes, hitting upon many original combinations of themes and motifs. The most daring of their inventions, however, could hardly rival one of these masques by Tyshler. The one I mean is the costume for a "lady-prison": it has the head in an iron cage, the skirt is a stone sack, curved knives are in the hair, and instead of a hat is a hangman's face.

The sketches had lain unused in the artist's briefcase. Later, however, reflections of his theatrical visions often appeared in his paintings. In one of his canvases, a light blue bull rushes across the sky over a darker blue city; seated on a tall chair on the back of the animal is an amazon playing a mandolin. Gay flags flutter between the horns of the bull and are stuck into the hair of the lady. The artist enjoys painting female portraits with whimsical constructs instead of hair, sometimes using towers, sometimes baskets of fruit. What is this? An actress in an unknown production? Are these indeed sketches for some play? No, these are the images of folk festival masques, theatrical poetry.

Theatre can be understood in a variety of ways. For Tyshler, a performance is a sort of holiday; it is a happy day when nothing resembles weekdays. In this festive theatre, both comedy and drama can be performed. The sketches for *Richard III* show both the harshness of the age and the savagery of the grotesque. But the tragic itself is not inherent in this designer's work. His art is buoyant in origin, and even the stone world of *Richard III* is, after all, built on a stage platform. For Tyshler, even a tragedy is colored by the essential delight to be taken in a theatrical performance. Bitterness and anger are muted by lyricism. The artist should hardly be reproached for this: such is his creative world. There is joy in his world for the spectator as well.

When it comes to comedy, Tyshler is unwilling to recognize even a shadow of melancholy. Under a cloudless sky skims so gay a round dance that one is carried away by it. This is not only a carnival where people playfully get dressed up and make themselves look funny; the very houses masquerade. Merriment penetrates under every roof and changes all ordinary appearances; that which had been stolid breaks into a dance. Human hearts are borne like fruit on the branches of trees. The architect-inventor lines up a whole street on the backs of merry-go-round horses.

Are stone costumes and spirited merrymaking the only correct methods for the theatrical expression of tragedy and comedy? This kind of question is sometimes heard, but hardly merits consideration as reasonable. There are innumerable modes of expression. The author of *Twelfth Night* is a genius in this regard. The word "correct," at any rate, is meaningless here.

"Shakespeare belongs to humanity." This sort of aphorism has been pronounced more than once, and it has a solemn ring. To speak plainly, however, it only means that he belongs to every man. If, moreover, the man is an artist, he must find his own meaning for Shakespeare's poetry. And if all an artist can see in the famous plays is what has already been done with them, should he bother to undertake a production? . . .

Performance of Shakespeare differs in the various theatres of the world. He is played in evening dress and among bare canvas drops, in naturalistic sets and in Victorian costumes; there have been restorations of the Globe and park productions. Are there, perhaps, groups for saying that all these scenic forms are equally interesting, that they invariably bring classical works closer to the contemporary audience? . . . Not at all, for, as the argument goes, it is not bold device nor the fever of originality which prevails, but depth of understanding, force of expression, and the discovery of new elements of creativity.

There is no prescribed approach to classical works, nor is any-one given the right to erect guideposts and "no trespassing" signs. Of course, every era knows its obscurantist practices: they have tried to turn Shakespeare into a mystic, even into a bard of Nordic ideals. What, indeed, has not been tried! But in such cases, it is not the originality of the undertaking that counts, but the modes of distortion.

Shakespearean figures appear in Tyshler's work: it is difficult not to recognize Richard III, Lear, or the Fool at first glance—in fact, not only does recognition occur but so does the discovery of characteristics formerly unnoticed. Shakespeare's characters are bathed in a new light, in Tyshler's vision of them.

This original vision is the essential quality of his talent. Al-though Tyshler worked with many directors, there are no traces of their plans in his sketches. All of the drawings express, rather, a single understanding of the plays. And the resulting visual holiday is the work of the artist himself.

When he designed the sets, Tyshler also sketched the characters. He was least occupied with the future show as spectacle; sketches for it were done on scraps of writing paper and on the backs of other sketches. His drawings are perhaps the most notable part of his work on Shakespeare. Both the sets and the sketches were done by one hand, of course, but there is much to differentiate the one form of work from the other. At first glance, there seems to be a strange contradiction. His sets, for example, for a *Hamlet* or a *Lear* are variants of one and the same platform: a stage is supported by sculptures—carousel horses, maybe, for comedy, or weeping angels for tragedy; a system of curtains turns the stage into the court of a castle or a public square. Here, in this theatrical world, the story of the characters must be told.

How does Tyshler see these characters? Only as masquers in a charade? Surely such external theatricality, this interplay of convention, is a phase through which our theatre passed long ago. To whom would aesthetic stylization be attractive, especially when applied to Shakespeare's works? Tyshler offers a most interesting solution; the characters he depicts are both masquers and nontheatrical creations of the designer's artistic imagination. For one thing, their execution is quite distinct from the set drawings, since the artist is not at all involved in problems of staging. The character himself is treated, not just his stage image. *King Lear* and *Richard III* are particularly interesting in this respect. In first conceiving his characters, the artist is not preoccupied with problems of make-up or costume design but with their spiritual life and their personal idiosyncrasies and, what is most intriguing, with the basic idea absorbing their entire being.

In Tyshler's figures, the harsh and somber power of an inhuman era is softened by spirituality and his concentration on the personal. The designer, however, is not eager to romanticize: he sketches Othello as absorbed only by sorrow, and how unusual this image is! This is not a typical illustration of a black man. The costume is not exotic, nor does Othello seem dominated by the fury usually endowed him by old-school tragedians. Rather, this man no longer has the strength to look on life. He has covered his face with his hands and is immersed in grief. Of course, one can speak of the Negro admiral in other terms, but it is perhaps worth remembering that the first actor to play Othello portrayed him, in the words of a contemporary, as a "grieved Moor."

There is a large number of sketches that are superficially similar to one another, yet that offer clues as to Tyshler's path of inquiry. For among the drawings there is a subtle but crucial artistic difference. Line imperceptibly changes its movement. A stroke is added, vague shadows gather, and the ideas become sharper, the vision keener, character traits more vivid.

In his sketches of Richard III, Tyshler urgently seeks the spiritual core of the philosopher-murderer, the man who despised not only people but the very concept of humanity. On these pages, the artist searches gesture, expression, and attitude until it seems that the figures will move and come to life. Line is absolute, taut.

A character's inner state is expressed with such force that his body becomes distorted, and he is made both man and chimera. It is not hard to see the influence of Goya in these drawings. The sinister grotesqueries of the rites of the Inquisition, the horror of human carnage, and the inhumanity of his age all reverberated in the Spaniard's etchings. But every century knows its own inhumanity, and the grotesque thereof. In every century, people sometimes feel that they dream a waking nightmare.

The drawings, however, are intended for theatrical productions. Can any actor play a character as portrayed by Tyshler? Will a figure given such traits not seem cold and improbable on the stage? I recall my encounter with one actor who could have played such a Richard. Shortly before his death, Solomon Mikhailovich Mikhoels suggested that I produce *Richard III* with his assistance. We were only able to meet a few times, but it would be hard for me to forget his description of the role as he conceived it. "Richard has a perpetual collocutor," said Solomon Mikhailovich, "a pal, a crony with whom he likes to consult and share his thoughts—his hump. The aim of this freak is to force people to bow to his friend the hump, to make it their idol. After each success, Richard turns to a new crime, and winks at the growth on his back."

Mikhoels not only discussed all this, but rising from his chair, he played whole scenes. His rumpled jacket, the tousled hair fringing his baldness, all this was forgotten, and it seemed that there could be no one in any way more suitable for the role. This short man gained stature, some kind of diabolical arrogance caught fire in his eyes. . . . An awesome and tragic myth sprang suddenly to life in a small Moscow room.

The fate of an actor is sad. Applause dies away; the last act is long finished. What then remains of his remarkable artistry? Reviews, a packet of uninspired posed photographs (the photographer was arranging the lighting, took a time exposure—and all this after a performance as well). Mikhoels, however, is luckier than many of his colleagues: the Tyshler sketches remain. Thus Mikhoel's image of Lear endures to some extent.

A traditional king of Britain, with huge beard and pathetic gesture, is shown in some other rough drafts. A series of completely different sketches follow: Lear and the Fool, Lear and Cordelia. In the relationships of the figures rests Tyshler's main theme: wisdom, bought with life. The Lear of these drawings appeared on the stage of the Jewish Theatre. The curtain rose: an ancient world, the most profound level of the play came to life. Wooden sculptures, under the spotlights, seemed to have been carved from antique ivory. A coffer lay on them; servants opened the leaves of its cover with gaffs; courtiers gathered; the heiress sisters entered. After the sets, nothing seemed surprising nor even strongly stated; the actors' movements and the blocking of the directors seemed perfectly normal. But then Lear's face appeared from behind a curtain. It was an undistinguished profile, with a protruding lower lip, a startling and tenacious gaze—the ancient and bitter wisdom of an old person who is conversant with the world and watches life.

In reference to a man's knowledge of the world, Mikhoels liked to note that in the Bible the verb "to know" meant both to understand the relationships of things and to become intimate with a woman. At the time, we were talking about great consuming passion, but Mikhoels's observation also seems relevant to his interpretation of Lear.

By his performance, Mikhoels opened up the mythological stratum of the tragedy. He acted with apparent calm, rarely raising his voice. When I got backstage somehow during the intermission, Mikhoels lay on a shabby oilcloth sofa in his small dressing room. He was breathing with difficulty, and the sweat streamed down his face. "You know," he said to me, "acting with restraint is a very difficult thing. I do not agree with the director; he wants a storm on stage—they project a little cloud onto the curtain; they make noises in the wings. . . . I would like to show the storm only in the soul, but to do that you need to act with restraint, with complete restraint. . . . "

The spiritual storm of Mikhoels's Lear has stamped Tyshler's drawings.

Lear, Richard III, the Fool, Cordelia—looking at them in the sketches, one contemplates the ways of reflecting life in art. Anatomy is often distorted on these pages, individual features are exaggerated, proportions are changed. Is this realism? . . . Do you ever meet people who can see things like that?

Only Shakespearean figures are under discussion here, however. Clearly, the exaggeration in the drawings is a Shakespearean one;

disruption of normal proportion is also Shakespearean. It was the author of *Richard III* who created a prince-freak, a villain untimely born yet superior to all who surround him in both scope of purpose and daring of thought. Perhaps even his adamantine costume seems less strange when one recalls that the author was fond of metaphors like "stone-hard heart" and "gravel heart." The poetic realism of Shakespeare's characters does not lie in any superficial verisimilitude, but in their solidity and historical truth.

If one retells, in prose, the verse description of Ophelia's destruction, its physiological improbability becomes apparent. Is it really likely that someone would sing a song while gradually sinking "to muddy death"? Yet the essence of spiritual activity and its processes was uniquely elucidated by Shakespeare's poetry. Hyperbole, the displacement of time and space, the volitional transition from lofty to commonplace accents, all these are characteristic of the poet's creative method. Tyshler's artistic strength lies in his awareness of the nature of such poetics. In no way does this interfere with concrete expression of a period. His scenic forms derive from medieval wood carvings, feudal towers, the houses along the sides of old London Bridge. The stage itself is a variant of the platforms of the market-place theatre.

One last trait distinguishes Tyshler's ideas; it is found in his carnival figures, his painted curtains, and his flags on their tall poles. Here the effervescence of folk theatre lives on, with its passion for bright colors and its synthesis of real and fantastic.

And so, like the echo of poetry, a visual imagery was born.

King Lear

STORM[1]

AS OF THE PAST CENTURY, playwrights have become fond of itemizing everything that relates to the place of action. Compared to their long descriptions of sets, Shakespeare's remarks are striking by their brevity. Only one or two words are needed, and they are repeated without change through most of his plays: a street, a hall of state, a plain, the court of a castle. . . .

These directions were probably not written by the author. It is general knowledge that the theatres of those times were innocent of scenery. In the open, under daylit skies, one saw simply an unadorned stage. From time to time, an armchair might be brought out, or perhaps a table. The audience understood convention perfectly and did not find that it interfered in any way with their understanding of a play. It was as though a pact had been concluded between the theatre company and its public from time immemorial. If the actor crossed the stage, the place of action changed, and returning, he would already find himself on another street or perhaps even in another kingdom. A background of dark carpeting placed the action under cover of night, while a light

---

[1] In 1941, my article on *King Lear* was published in the Soviet magazine *Theatre*. I worked on it in preparation for a production of this tragedy at Leningrad's Bolshoi Dramatic Theatre. Seeing my ideas become stage realities, I could test my theories as they arose. Some were verified; others proved farfetched. I wanted to continue this work; this is the effect Shakespeare usually has. The images which once arose consciously become part of life. Years pass: associations grow in scope and complexity; definitions which had seemed adequate lose their cogency, and it becomes evident that they only explain separate, and often not the most significant, aspects of a work.

curtain designated day. When three swordsmen ran onto the stage, there was a bloody battle between armies. The authors themselves frequently chuckled at all this.

Although a performance would be given in space defined by convention, the dramatic poetry approached realism by dint of its attempt at a precise reproduction of the circumstances of life. Rereading these pages, we now find less in the line of convention. And so, there arose a curious contradiction: the eye saw three naked, nonrepresentational platforms, and the ear heard a detailed narration concerning the hues of a dawn, a buffeting wind, fields traced in flowers and grass. Nature bloomed and withered, snows whirled, and there were scenes of human life as lived in palaces and ruined hovels.

The flat light of day touched the same boards and carpets, while poetry transferred the action into the midst of life, varying the milieu according to the play. The scenery, then, was not built with canvas, wood, and paint, but was invisibly constructed of words arising in the course of poetic development. These unseen pictures appeared only in the imagination and possessed the ability to extend the limits of the theatre into infinity, to turn the real into the fantastic, and to unite nature and human emotion.

Scenery born of verse is to be perceived not by the eye, but by the ear. Sometimes the author will interrupt the action to ask his audience to imagine all those things without which any stage event would be, to put it plainly, unintelligible. So he asks the listeners to conceive of foreign cities and ancient battles. The audience is addressed in his name by a conventional character who takes no part in the plot—a character usually called Chorus or Prologue. This was the simplest method: narration. The description of the night of Duncan's murder or of the appearance of the ghost in *Hamlet* were more complicated. Landscapes arose in conversation. The characters described the cold of night and the gusts of wind which were ripping chimneys from their roofs. They mentioned that the moon had set. All this not only has specified time and place but has also established the mood of the scene and exerted an emotional influence on the protagonists.

The landscape of *King Lear* is distinctive and quite different. The pictures of nature found here are in constant motion and ceaselessly change character. They are correlated both with the inner worlds of the heroes and with the development of the theme. The underlying causes of the very principles of *Lear*'s poetic structure ordained the storm that is unseen on the stage but that rages through the whole imagic pattern of the tragedy.

From antiquity, popular poetry has described the phenomena of nature, translating them into fantastic images. The causes of natural occurrences were unknown; man's struggle to master nature had not begun. The power of the elements seemed unlimited. Man was surrounded and ruled by omnipotent deities.

This earliest stratum of art—the religious and poetic imagery of myths—later provided a unique treasury. More than once, artists turned to the wealth of popular imagination. Old images were revived, were filled with new meaning, changed their forms. But the glow of the myths could be seen through the multiples of later formations.

Sinister—these images of thunder and storm. They betokened the punishments inflicted on people by the gods; they meant death and desolation. A wild chariot roared and sped through the skies while fire bedazzled the earth. The hoofs of its horses beat the clouds and struck sparks. A thousand-tailed whip of flame lashed forests and villages; fires broke out; people were consumed with a thirst for murder and destruction. Chaos ruled, and everything turned to dust. Folk art strove to express the awesome grandeur of the powers that threatened man. Its images brimmed with violent movement, evil power, belligerence. Amid rolls of thunder and the blaze of fire, the storm entered art as a symbol of destruction, disaster, calamity.

In his introduction to *Retribution,* the symbolist poet Blok wrote that it was his custom to compare all the facts of the times that his glance could absorb, and to cull these facts, be they crucial or insignificant, from the most varied spheres of life. In this comparison, the poet found "a single musical pressure." Mayakovsky, the futurist, spoke about rhythm "passing through the whole poetic thing with a rumble." Of course, the discussion hardly concerned meter, the mere relationship of stressed and unstressed syllables. By "musical pressure," "rumble," is understood an inner movement, a rhythm like the heavy beat of history's

subterranean tremors. Poetry echoes the low roars uttered by the
rumbling of events.

A storm rumbles through the tragedy of Lear. Events move and
alternate in the sensation of its single musical pressure. But what
does this whirlwind mean?

THE PLOT

An avalanche can start with the almost imperceptible movement of
a single stone. And yet this slight movement is the result of much
effort: a gust of wind rocked and pushed what it had already
loosened; the destructive work of many years was complete. One
last puff shifts the stone's center of gravity and makes the stone
roll. Other stones are knocked down by it, and roll. Small ones
fall on larger ones; boulders so huge as to seem inseparable from
the earth begin to stagger.

A mountain comes crumbling down, uprooting and upending
trees, splintering dwellings. All that had been immovable for years
becomes movement itself. There seems to be no force capable of
holding back this cataclysmic pressure. . . .

Many theories have been advanced concerning the causes of the
tragic events of *King Lear*. They claim to be unique, or even
conclusive; they include filial ingratitude, the petty tyranny of age,
the fatal decision to divide the kingdom. Many pages have been
written in explanation of Cordelia's unfortunate reply, which had
led to so much adversity. However successful any of these theories
and explanations, they only exist in the name of conclusive
motion, that last puff—but here powerless to budge even a smallish stone. Only in uniting the conflicting efforts of that epoch, in
the clash of many of its aspirations can one understand the imagic
level of *Lear,* or the "single musical pressure" of the storm.

It has often been noted before this that it is not easy to correlate
the indications of time in each of the scenes. Several names force
one to assume that the action takes place some eight centuries
before our time, but the titles of count, duke, and lord transfer it to
another era. Oaths to Apollo and Juno do not tie up with a rank of
captain, nor with a herald's summoning of a knight to a tourney.
Each of these peculiarities is separated from the next by centuries,
and efforts to unite them can, somehow, only lead to a tangle of

centuries and customs. However, all these are mere externals. If one but looks into the heart of the action, the outlines of its time come into focus.

The major chessmen are immediately placed on the board. The king, the dukes and earls who vie among themselves, the courtiers who follow them. A government now united, now disintegrating. "I thought the King had more affected the Duke of Albany than Cornwall," says the Earl of Kent to the Earl of Gloucester.

Beyond the walls of the royal palace is a landscape: plains, poverty-ridden villages, and stone towers on the more elevated hilltops. This castle dominates the less well-fortified strongholds of feudal robbers. They are surrounded by emptiness and the rotting thatch of huts. The gallows and quartering block are necessary props in the scenery.

The people gathering in the court are concerned. Edmund, the Earl of Gloucester's natural son, has been by law deprived of his rights of inheritance; the family property went by primogeniture to Edgar, the eldest son. The younger brother had been gone nine years, and has returned full of envy and malice. He intends to destroy the lawful heir and thus come into all his father's possessions. As to the father, he only inspired contempt in Edmund.

The Duke of Cornwall, fearing the rise of the latter, harbors plans for the destruction of the Duke of Albany. From the conversation between Gloucester and Kent, it is already known that the King regards Albany with more favor than he does Cornwall. The ducal discord, presaging war, is already ripe.

Of the three heiresses to the throne, two—Regan and Goneril—despise the third, their youngest sister, Cordelia. They envy her, who is the King's favorite daughter. They fear one another; they are rivals in the division of the kingdom.

The King of France and the Duke of Burgundy have arrived to ask for the youngest daughter's hand in marriage. Love is the last consideration; the proposed marriage is a dynastic event. The poetry expresses an argument between the possessors of great domains, not between rivals in love. "The vines of France and milk of Burgundy" contend for Cordelia. A new balance of power depends on the marriage. But until the King has spoken, all these people are prepared by the course of events to clash in war.

The strained quiet preceding the advent of a storm recalls this beginning. The next scene is that of the partition of the kingdom, which has called forth so many charges of improbability.

L. N. Tolstoy, a most severe critic of Shakespeare, began his censure with the plot of *King Lear,* which he considered particularly absurd. In his essay *Of Shakespeare and of Drama,* Lev Nikolaevich retells the scene in his own words:

. . . trumpets sound, and King Lear enters with his daughters and sons-in-law and gives a speech about how he, in his old age, would like to retire from his duties and divide the kingdom among his daughters. In order to know how much to give each daughter, he announces that he will give the most to the daughter who will tell him that she loves him more than the others do. The eldest, Goneril, says that no words can express her love, that she loves her father more than sight, space, or liberty, loves him so that it interferes with her breathing. On the map, King Lear immediately sections off her part, with its fields, forests, rivers, and meadows, and then asks the second daughter. She, Regan, so loves her father that all save his love is repugnant to her. The King also bestows a grant upon this daughter, and then asks the youngest, the favorite. Cordelia, . . . as though to anger her father on purpose, says that although she both loves and honors her father and is grateful to him, all of her love would not belong to her father should she marry, for she would also love her husband.

Hearing these words, the King flies into a rage and that very minute curses his favorite daughter with the most strange and fearful imprecations. . . .

This exposition seems unbiased at first glance, but a typically Tolstoyan satiric device lies in the manner of narration and in its apparent precision and clarity. The divine service is similarly ridiculed in *Resurrection,* as is the opera in *War and Peace:*

Smooth boards formed the center of the stage, at the sides stood painted canvases representing trees, and in the background was a cloth stretched over boards. In the middle of the stage sat some girls in red bodices and white petticoats. One extremely fat girl in a white silk dress was sitting apart on a low bench, to the back of which a piece of green cardboard was glued. They were all singing something. When they had finished their chorus, the girl in white advanced towards the prompter's box, and a man with stout legs encased in silk tights, a plume in his cap, and a dagger at his waist, went up to her and began to sing and wave his arms about.

The aim of the satire is clear; the author has stated his ideas plainly. Only in an idle society could people consider such art essential to man. As a matter of fact, it was not even art, but some kind of senseless spectacle. Everything happening on the stage is parodied with the aid of the author's device: he carefully lists the materials from which the costumes and sets are made, describes the appearance and gestures of the performers. He forgets only the music—which is, however, the basis of this particular art and which gives meaning and life to it. One had only to plug one's ears, and the singers and dancers promptly turned into masked fools, stupidly opening their mouths, gesturing for some unknown reason, and idiotically pawing the ground. Art has disappeared, leaving only painted cardboard, a fat damsel, a man in a ridiculous hat with a feather in it, and a little prompt box.

Tolstoy dealt with the scene from *Lear* in the same way. In the language of inventory, he enumerated metaphor and hyperbole, maintaining the unruffled intonation of protocol. It is particularly inappropriate language for the dynamism of Shakespeare. Setting forth the external action in detail, he omitted everything that gave any sense to the scene, as though he had neither noticed its inner development nor cared to hear its poetic subtext. The thoughts and feeling of the characters remained beyond the bounds of Tolstoy's exposition, and only words and bare events remained. The words of poetry lost their meaning in the prose retelling, and the action became incidents, and improbable ones at that.

Tolstoy, who well understood music, feigned deafness only to demonstrate that art deprived of an ethicoreligious idea is not necessary to people. In a period of passionate enthusiasm for his notion, Tolstoy compared a man who wrote verse to a ploughman who had decided to follow his plough dancing childishly. At this time, poetry struck the novelist as no more than unprincipled mischief-making. The tale of *King Lear* was retold from this point of view. Poetry proved beyond the scope of his discussion. There remained only the grimaces of the dancer trying to plough.

Expression of filial love was not to have determined the measure of inheritance given each daughter. Shakespeare grudged no detail to make it clear that the allotment of property had been concluded long before the court ceremony began. The scene with his daughters is a final rite. For Gloucester, having met Kent on the way to the festivities, says to him: ". . . in the division of the kingdom, it appears not which of the Dukes he values most; for equalities are so weighed that curiosity in neither can make choice of either's moiety." Although Lear invites Cordelia so to describe her love that her words will move him to award his favorite daughter "a third more opulent than your sisters'," it must not be taken literally. We know that two of the three parts are already given to the older sisters. In what way, then, can Cordelia's reply earn a better share?

The division is determined not only by the answers of the heiresses but by considerations of an entirely different sort. In the beginning of the ceremony, Lear does not address his daughters, but their husbands:

> . . . Our son of Cornwall,
> And you, our no less loving son of Albany,
> We have this hour a constant will to publish
> Our daughters' several dowers, that future strife
> May be prevented now. . . .

The prevention of strife—of civil war, in other words—is the reason for the equality of the patrimonial dividends; the King was not even influenced by his partiality for the Duke of Albany. Cordelia's portion was known beforehand; her Burgundian suitor asks as dowry only that which had been promised, ". . . no more . . . /Nor will you tender less."

The deed is done. The ceremony is to conclude with the gratitude of each of the heiresses. Their words are for Lear the fulfillment of one of the most ancient customs: it ordains that the daughters shall solemnly declare their love for their father. And the King, even having stepped down from power, cannot exist without his suite of one hundred knights. But this is only part of the scene's import. For Lear, all this ceremony is filled with sublime poetry and deep significance. At eighty, he no longer has the strength to rule. That he gave his kingdom to his daughters before his death is wise and just. He sees the avowals of these daughters not as mere ceremonial, but as the expressions of a genuine relationship: the declarations of love are deserved.

Goneril readily performs the rite. The whole point is that she performs it with too much diligence. Her elevated style is so exaggerated that its very form betrays an absence of feeling. This

is the way it usually is in life; emptiness is mostly expressed in high-sounding words, while pathos screens itself with indifference.

This is important in terms of understanding not only the spiritual mold of the Duchess of Albany but also the character of Lear. Tyranny has led him to blindness. Even crudely gilded tin could easily be palmed off on him as pure gold. Attitudes toward this counterfeiting serve as a touchstone for all the characters.

Lear notices nothing strange in the speeches of his first two daughters. Cordelia really loves her father and understands that a similar speech is expected of her. Her answer is frequently thought to be unnatural:

> . . . I love your Majesty
> According to my bond, nor more nor less.

And really, forgetting what preceded this statement, this sort of treatment of one's father does not seem normal. However, it is not an account of her love, but rather a rebuke to flattery and a withdrawal from the competition. If stubbornness and strength of will, as well as candor, are seen as part of Cordelia's nature, if she is recognized as one of Shakespeare's "fair warriors," it becomes clear that her words are a protest. She deliberately opposes dry words to grandiose declarations. Not only does she not wish to use her love for profit, she is repulsed by the custom itself if it can be followed in such a way.

The insignificant becomes meaningful. The ceremony now expresses more than form; it now expresses the heart of vital relationships. Everything brought forth in the tragedy previously was no more than a deceptive façade. Now the underlying meaning of the action begins to show itself. The ceremony of trial by filial love turns on a multitude of significance.

Shakespeare's works continued the labor of generations. The centuries had loosened the literary soil. Tales, legends, old chronicles, plays of anonymous composition—all this prepared the frameworks of plots and the contours of characters. Most important, it brought him the tradition of folk creation. This tradition, the artistic work of the people as expressed in the generalization of myth and folk tale, reappears in the tragedies, but with fresh meaning and force.

It is interesting that, in working on venerable stories, Shakespeare's attention was usually arrested by the older elements of the plot, rather than by the more recent ones, which would seem closer to professional playwriting. He adopted poetic tradition rather than "eternal" themes. Instead of amending the plots of old plays, he filled them with new vital substance. The content breathed reality. Its life shattered the system of performances-with-a-moral and gave new meaning to artless legends.

The tale of an old King and his ungrateful daughters was the work of generations. European folklore knows many variants of this legend. Many nations liked to tell of a King who resolves to test the love of his daughters. He invites each of them to say how she loves him and to find comparisons for her love. In one version, the eldest claims to love her father like the sweetest of dainties; the second compares her feeling for him with love for a beautiful dress. The youngest answers, like salt. The King is outraged by this reply. In anger, he exiles the youngest daughter and divides his property between the other two. But the time comes when he is himself banished from his kingdom. He suffers dire hunger, and is brought some very simple food. It is unsalted, and he cannot eat it. It is then that he appreciates the value of salt.

This tale came to appear in chronicles. In the twelfth-century *Historia Regum Britanniae* by Geoffrey of Monmouth, we find a legendary Leir, son of King Bladud. Having decided to abdicate in favor of his three daughters, Leir subjects them to "trial by love." This time the answers of the sisters resemble those of the Shakespearean heroines. Gonorilla says that her father is dearer to her than her soul. Regan loves him more than everything on earth. The youngest daughter gives the King a riddle: "Is there a daughter who loves her father more than a father? I do not believe that any daughter would claim this even in jest. I have ever loved and will ever love you as a father. If you wish to force more from me, attend: as much as you have, so much are you worth." The incensed King banishes Cordeilla and apportions his kingdom between the other two daughters. Having subsequently lost all his possessions, he becomes convinced of the truth of Cordeilla's words. Now he has nothing, and is already unloved. He understands that they loved not him, but his wealth. Exiled by Gonorilla and Regan, he finds refuge with Cordeilla, who has married the Frankish King. Her love proves genuine.

Literary historians have counted more than fifty treatments of this plot. It came to Shakespeare in Holinshed's *Chronicles,* in John Higgins's *The Mirrour for Magistrates,* in Spenser's poetry— and finally in the so-called "old drama" *The True Chronicle of King Leir and His Three Daughters,* which was performed at the Rose Theatre in 1594. In this play, the folk motif of "trial by love" came to the end of its childhood, the play being neither legend nor parable but a literary composition with some plausibility. This pertains to the plot in particular. Tolstoy considered it, and most especially its first scene, significantly more artistic than Shakespeare's version:

In the old drama, Leir relinquishes his throne because, being widowed, he thinks only of the salvation of his soul. He questions his daughters about their love for him in order to keep his youngest daughter on his island by means of this ruse, which he has devised himself. The elder two have been asked in marriage, but the youngest does not wish to marry, as she loves none of the nearby suitors whom Leir suggests to her, and he fears that she may marry some far-distant king.

This sort of psychological justification was not necessary to Shakespeare. More than superfluous, it was contrary to his artistic intention. He did not create kings who thought only of saving their souls. Even the old motif underwent change: the kingdom was divided among the sisters even before the beginning of the "trial by love." The "trial" itself reverted to the fabular tradition, but another role was assigned to it and a different meaning imparted to it. The motif came to symbolize the concept of a man's true value. The reply of the youngest daughter found in the chronicle of Geoffrey of Monmouth—"as much as you have, so much are you worth"—was brought out in its deepest sense, replete with folk wisdom.

What exactly defines a man's real value—his possessions or his spiritual qualities? Does it depend on his position in life? Or is he this value in and of himself, even though he possesses nothing? And what is the relationship between wealth and the genuine worth of a man?

The inner movement of the entire tragedy provides the test by which this worth is measured. Trial by love is but a small part of the test. The bold contrast of sugar, the beautiful dress, and salt is revived in the philosophy of the tragedy, although in a completely different way. The social forces behind the heroines come into view. As regards psychological justification, a realistic environment relieves the unusualness of Goneril's lie. The inability of the old King to recognize deceit no longer seems improbable.

The action is explained by life. The exceptional only expresses the ordinary. All sorts of flattery thrived as part of this ordinary. In servility, Lear's elder daughters could not hold a candle to the literary dedications that haloed the names of patrons of art. Besides an omnipotent sovereign, there certainly were those who were ready to make an idol of tyranny, fawning on the tyrant with all their might. And those to whom all this was directed almost always listened to it with pleasure. Even if a statesman were intelligent and practiced, neither his wit nor his experience would prevent blindness to insincerity, and a credulous acceptance of enthusiastic appraisals of his person. This phenomenon had for so long assumed such magnitude, that Dante willingly allotted flatterers a whole ditch in hell, where, squealing and grunting, they were cast into sewage and stinking refuse.

The events of the tragedy should be perceived as taking place in a real world of tyranny, rather than in the vacuum of fabular convention. Then the behavior of Goneril, Regan, and Lear seems lifelike.

The way time is portrayed in *Lear* has little in common with the usual historical sense of realistic dramatic composition. Shakespeare frequently expressed the heart of an action in a form that appears to contradict it. Sometimes the narrative concerns one era but refers to another in the process. His plots deal with reality, but historical fact is interlarded with legend. He made mistakes in geography, was shaky in chronology. It is rash to contend that all his anachronisms are intentional, but it is no less frivolous to consider them mere by-products of Elizabethan playwriting or the results of haste. The reasons for this meshing of centuries and kingdoms frequently lie within the poetry itself.

It is general knowledge that, whatever he named his protagonists, and no matter what he called the place of action, Shakespeare's characters and plots concern the England contemporary to him. This statement, however, though fundamentally correct, does not mean that one and the same milieu is described in every tragedy and is merely masked by the matters of centuries past. No one has yet tried to set *Hamlet* into the world of *Romeo and Juliet,* or to play *Othello* in costumes from *Macbeth.* In short, the times and places ascribed to events by the play are not so very non-existent. It is more accurate to assert that the action takes place both in Elizabethan England and in some other country (specified in the play), that it happens in Shakespeare's time, to which era are fused the traits of another time (specified in the play).

What necessitated this displacement of times and tenors of life? Shakespeare's attempt to comprehend life by seeking the roots of a given phenomenon. Going far into the past, he reconciled legend and reality, the spirit of antiquity and the passions of his own times. By blending periods and locales, he was able to compare, emphasize, generalize.

Similarly, the mixture of times in *King Lear* was not accidental. The legendary names of the King and his daughters were not retained simply because these characters had been so named in ancient times, nor were they retained by chance. Other characters similar by plot situation to those of the old variants were renamed. In order to bring contemporary processes into full relief, the shadow of another epoch was cast on the principals and on the course of events. The story of the olden hero was repeated in a new time and with a totally different quality.

Lear is distinguished from those who surround him by several of the traits in his character. It is precisely because he is different from them that both great delusion and equally great insight are possible to him. But what exactly distinguishes Lear from the other personae? First of all, importance. Lear is given the poetic force of legendary heroes. Each movement expressing his character is filled with immense power. This man is not one of the Elizabethan breed. Although Regan is his daughter and he is eighty, he seems older by several millennia than she. The light of patriarchal fires illuminates his figure.

Sometimes he seems to have come from prehistoric times, when legend has it that the earth was inhabited by a people sublime in good and evil alike. The oldest, wisest member of the clan held power.

Sometimes he appears as a fated elder, an Old Testament figure. Neither simplicity nor madness is contained in his certitude that he is right, but poetic grandeur. His figure is bound up with legends of times when only gold had its price and people had not learned cunning and perfidy. There is an abundance of biblical imagery in *King Lear*. The poetry is full of the thunder of Old Testament curses. The despair of laments and the ecstasy of prophecy adds strength and passion to the rhythms. Powerful simile derives from ancient symbol and allegory.

The pathos of Renaissance oratory was often bound up with the tonal richness of those images. What is more relevant, the biblical words became rebellious. When Luther set the forty-sixth psalm to music, it turned out, Heine wrote, to be the "Marseillaise of the Reformation." The prophets Jeremiah, Daniel, and Ezekiel provided the dicta of Thomas Münzer.

But the image of Lear is not only defined by these "loud and ironclad old words" (*Heine*) heard through the strata of legend. Other qualities exist, indissoluble from those of antiquity but changing their essence and form. The living traits of a despotic ruler show through the legendary figure. One can hear how he judged, minted money, and recruited soldiers. The mad scenes contain a number of details relating to the time of his reign. Coercion, blood, and war are part of these pictures of the past. The royal warrior himself taught soldiers to draw a bow correctly; the royal hand grasped the sword powerfully.

> I have seen the day, with my good biting falchion
> I would have made them skip. . . .

His mind is occupied not only with thoughts of justice trampled but also with reminiscences of military matters:

> It were a delicate stratagem, to shoe
> A troop of horse with felt. I'll put't in proof,
> And when I have stol'n upon these sons-in-law,
> Then kill, kill, kill, kill, kill, kill!

If all the legendary elements are omitted, the poetry and the magnitude of the figure collapse. But if only these elements are seen without any understanding of everything reflecting reality, the figure loses both its meaning and its tragic force. Lear perceives the injustice dominant in the world, yet one of the outward signs of this injustice was his rule. He was himself a king.

In the scenes that reach the heights of tragedy, Lear condemns not only the abstract concept of power but also the real power, which he himself possessed. Such power now strikes him as criminal and irrational. Hideous scenes of popular woe reflect the real relationships of the period. This woe is the corollary of Lear's dominion.

The tragedy of Lear is more than that of an old father who has ungrateful daughters. The whole edifice of his royal grandeur proved flimsy, like any power that takes its strength from oppression and fear and harkens only to flattery. Real life was hidden from the King. He saw only externals, be they of things, attitudes, or people. The world was replaced by a little lying sphere. This worldlet was mirrored in the conscious, and overshadowed reality. Flattery blinded the old King, so that his thinking ceased to reflect actuality, and he took fantastic notions for fact. The microcosm of man, a favorite philosophic and psychological concept of the Elizabethan, was substituted for the macrocosm of life. The poetic expression of this great human delusion amounts to a sixteenth-century tradition. Bacon recalled with pleasure the words of Heraclitus: "Men sought truth in their own little worlds, and not in the great and common world."

Lear wanted to find truth in his own small world. He idolized his own identity. He began to believe that his place in life was not determined by power, which he possessed in full, but by the intrinsic and immutable value of his human qualities. In Lear's mind were gradually formed distorted impressions of real relationships, impressions based on external appearance. Everything surrounding the King was artificial and ostentatious. The mirror of apprehension became tarnished and crooked. The world changed, but the tarnished and crooked worldlet of the consciousness of the man screening himself from life remained the same. The images of these two worlds appear in the very beginning.

Ever stronger subterranean tremors shake the great world. One more shock, and everything will be destroyed. There is nothing that is not already rotted through; any appearance of human relationships is only barely retained. More force, and it will not just be the government which disintegrates into three parts; everything will tumble down and be smashed into smithereens.

Lear does not notice this. He sees gilt, smiles, finery, hears only rapturous words. There is not a cloud to shadow his little world; it is ruled by idyllic peace. Everything that happens is perfect: the just and wise King carries out his most recent decision. He removes the crown from his head and, amid the love he has merited from everyone, gives his power to his heiresses. Now they are the guardians of justice. The sere patriarch legislates for the last time. The trial by love begins. It is not only Lear who puts questions to his daughters; life itself asks the old King a riddle: What is more important—sugar, a beautiful dress, or salt?

The fog of lies shuts Lear off from the meaning of the trial. He still seeks truth only in his small world. He lives through the last minutes of his day of happiness. He answers: sugar and a beautiful dress are more important to a man than salt.

The youngest daughter is cursed and exiled. For Cordelia and for aged truth stands Kent, the last of the guardians of ancient honor. But Gloucester is silent; he remains a courtier unable to gainsay his sovereign, even though the latter be wrong.

A puff of wind has moved the stone. Everything that time had shaken loose begins to sway, to move, to collapse. The dead glow of lightning shines on their faces: there is nothing human in them. Rapacity has made them over into bestial snouts. The sky is cleft by a long and heavy clap of thunder. The storm has begun.

In his article on Mochalov's Hamlet, Belinski described the Prince's temper of mind—it could be said of the majority of Shakespeare's heroes: "For the present, he is content and happy with life, because reality has not yet diverged from his dreams. . . . This mood is that of moral infancy, from which moral disintegration necessarily follows. . . ." According to Belinski, disintegration is a "transition from infantile and instinctive harmony and the spirit's delight in itself, to discord and struggle, which are essential conditions for a transition into courageous and deliberate harmony. . . ."

This is how the figure of Lear is developed. At first, there is moral infancy, spiritual self-gratification. The regular historical development of such phantasmal harmonies is dissipated by the very first onslaught of reality. There is no iron railing that can protect awareness from actuality. Thus the storm, annihilating its illusions, bursts into the microcosm. Disintegration and disharmony will follow. Then the time will come when the hero will see the great world of social injustice. He will learn of it so that he may later curse injustice and challenge it, even though he does not know how to struggle with it. This is the scheme of the development of most of Shakespeare's tragedies. In *King Lear,* the situation is further complicated by the fact that in his coming to know reality, the hero discovers the essence of his own being and that of his little world.

Lear errs in his idea not only of life but of his own significance therein. He believes that his importance is unchanging. He can relinquish power, but a train of one hundred knights must still accompany him, who is "every inch a king." His intrinsic worth gave him the right to primacy of place, and the inviolability of his position is the basis for the existence of everything else in the kingdom. The place of each man is established by his proximity to the sovereign. So Lear thought. The mistake was not only his; it was the opinion of his time.

The huge concretion which is government hierarchy appears in the scene of the division of Lear's possessions. Everything is firmly placed, immovable, and subordinated to an unchanging order. The King occupies the highest position; after him are ranged the heiresses to the throne and their husbands, and then the top state dignitaries: Kent and the Earl of Gloucester. They all stand stock still, as though eternally glued in place. Lear takes off his crown. To him, nothing seems to have changed. He is sure that the world is stable.

DAME AVARICE

The world of feudal hierarchy found its expression in the dogmas and degrees of subordination of the strata dictated by Scholasticism. There were artificial levels in which all things had to be stationary and isolated one from another. Everything in existence adhered to its place, meaning, and rank. All things were defined and did not change; they related either to good or to evil, to virtue or to vice. The earthly order continued in the order of the other world (Dante describes nine circles of hell, purgatory, and nine spheres of paradise). Each sinner was assigned to a torment appropriate for him: one torment could not replace another. There was a hierarchy of suffering, just as there was a hierarchy of redemption and a hierarchy of sanctity.

The symbols of faith were unfathomable. Power was incontestable. Class relationships were to exist eternally.

Firm against the wind, directing their eyes not toward one another but toward eternity, there stood on the protuberances of Gothic cathedrals statues of emperors, warriors, monks, and women with stone babes in their stone arms—the human race eternal occupied its place. Every member of it had its own significance. No one, nor any thing, was able to move them from their places or to alter the meaning given them and sanctified by centuries. So thus they will stand summer and winter, spring and fall.

As the stone statues rise one above the other over stone portals, so emperors, dukes, squires, and peasants would stand in ascendancy, one over the other. And nothing changes or can change until the heavens burst into flame and the trumpets of the Last Judgment thunder over the world. Meanwhile, soldiers pass through, and people grow fewer. An epidemic sets in and the Black Death carries people off, but more soldiers will be born—and peasants and priests and kings. Everything constantly moves in the same closed circle, always returning to its place.

Shakespeare's poetry reflects the fire of the lightning that struck that immovable order. Moving with great speed through the tragedy of Lear, the storm is the figurative expression of the fall of the old order, and of the transformation of the solid into splinters, of the worshipped into the despised. Everything in *King Lear*— events, characters, thoughts, feelings—seems to have been introduced only to later transform itself impetuously into its own contradiction and to refute its former self.

In a tract on painting, Leonardo da Vinci described the likeness of a battle: crazed human faces, blood mixed with dust, runaway horses dragging their dead riders, the rolling eyes of the dying. Selecting only that which is most powerfully expressive, he concluded with the advice: "Indeed there must not be a single level place, only footprints filled with blood."

The tragedy of King Lear is written this way. The structure of its imagery is expressed by the poetic generalization of the storm, and reflects in a "single musical pressure" the processes of the time of the initial accumulation of capital.

At that time, the earth rocked under the terrible blows of

underground violence. Everything was shuffled—the groan of
death with the cry of birth. The lash whistled in medieval torture
chambers, but the click of abacus balls was heard all the louder.
Feudal outlaws discussed the price of wool, and rumors about the
success of Flemish textiles were intermingled with authentic details
of the witches' Sabbath.

Unrestrained by its ancient limits, avidity burst into the world.
The prologue to a new era began. People's minds were governed
by the norms of Scholasticism, which conceived the new epoch as
a frightening figure dressed in medieval allegory. From their
pulpits, preachers wailed about the rule of this scarecrow. It was
called "Dame Avarice." The approach of her kingdom was proclaimed, and they prophesied in horror that she would devour
everything, that if her triumphal procession did not come to an
end, the earth would be depopulated.

One form of oppression succeeded another. Scattered resources,
scraps of small land holdings, primitive equipment for working the
soil, wretched shacks—all this was doomed to annihilation. The
naïve era of feudalism and the guilds was over. New rulers cut
down medieval detention stocks in the name of the free development of new forms of production, and the free (though already
unlimited) oppression of man by man. Dame Avarice burst into
thousands of hovels. Arable land became sheep pasture. A frequently met image, from Thomas More's *Utopia* to anonymous
ballads, is that of sheep eating people. Land became a commodity,
money. Those who tilled it were driven off and reduced to beggary.

Hordes of vagabonds, terrible caravans of human grief, roamed
the country. They were ragged, exhausted from hunger, and vainly
sought work. They dragged themselves along the roads, leaving by
its edge the corpses of those who did not have the strength to go
farther. So went the future army of hired labor. It had already
begun to be disciplined to the new order. Executioners fired iron to
white heat and ground their knives. The citizens of merry old
England will brand these people and cut off their ears; the law will
command them to deal thus with "vagabonds." Such the epoch.
There was not a single level place to be seen, "only footprints filled
with blood."

The audience is introduced to the new century in the very
beginning of *King Lear*. Onto the stage proceed all the most

seemingly stable relationships of people: these are the most substantial human bonds, sanctified by custom and legitimatized by
legal and moral concepts. They are introduced only so that the
progress of later events may demonstrate that these bonds are no
more. There is nothing that still unites people, not one of the forms
of social existence. Everything had abandoned its place, and was
destroyed. There remained only the lying façades which covered
mildew, wormholes, and decay.

There are no more notions about the sanctity of kingly power;
there is no royal mediator between heaven and earth. The heiresses
to the throne mock the very idea of the intrinsic worth of the
King's person. Deprived of his troops, the King is only a senile old
man with idiotic whims. Only military force or wealth possess any
measure of sanctity.

The foundation of the family is overthrown. In the night, the
daughters cast the old man out of their castles into the storm; in
the downpour, he goes into fields where there is not a shrub for
shelter. A son condemns his father to death. Brother is ready to
execute brother. Sisters despise each other, and finally one kills
another. The younger son rises against the elder. Kin kills kin.
Nothing unites people anymore, nothing—not family, not creed,
not country. This is the realm of Dame Avarice.

Like a titanic cave-in, there begins in *King Lear* an uncontrol-
lable avalanche of the fragments of structures, attitudes, ties, all
intermingled in frenzied movement. The social organization
crashes. Ugly formless slivers are all that is left of what was once
whole and stable. The government disintegrates; revolts flare up;
foreign troops burst into a country mutilated by discord. Smoke
from the conflagration creeps over the ravaged earth.

A bloody dawn casts its light on migrating crowds of beggars,
on trees weighed down with the bodies of the hanged. The stumps
of human bodies putrefy on the wheel on which their owners had
been broken. Poisonous fumes rise over the earth and gather into
thunderclouds. A storm rumbles over the world.

The diminutive figure of the exiled King summons all the forces
of his little human world to argue with the violence of the forces of
destruction which have just broken free.

Trial by love has become trial by iron and blood.

THE CLOTHES AND THE MAN

Both East and West have a legend about the Emperor and his imperial garb.[2] The Emperor goes for a swim; he comes to a river, undresses, leaves his clothes on the shore, and dives into the water. While he is swimming, thieves steal his clothes. The Emperor has to go home naked. When he approaches the palace and orders the gates to be opened, the guard will not admit him. Without his imperial regalia, he is not recognized. He claims to be Emperor, but no one believes him. Soldiers come and lead the naked man off to prison. Later he is tried and sentenced to be whipped in the public square for calling himself the Emperor. And thus it is that the Emperor ceased to be the Emperor when his clothes were stolen. Majesty consisted in clothes, not in the man.

The shoulders of the British sovereign were draped in an ermine-trimmed mantle of velvet. But once he gave up his power, they stole the mantle. And Lear immediately ceased to resemble a king. A scene in Goneril's castle is devoted to this theme. Staying with his daughter, Lear begins to notice that he is served somehow differently than he had been before. He senses a new attitude toward himself, but he still cannot grasp what the essence of this change is. The Duchess's steward, Oswald, catches his eye. Lear beckons to him, but Oswald does not even turn and just continues past. Lear—only recently the master of the life and death of every subject—looks after the lackey in bewilderment. It does not enter his head that the man exists who would dare insult him. Oswald, feigning not to notice him, passes Lear again. Lear orders him to stop and to come nearer: he is sure that the steward, having understood his negligence, will fall to his knees in horror, begging pardon. But the lackey's face is calm; his bearing loses none of its ease. Lear asks: Does the contemptible servant know who stands before him? The answer comes: Yes, he knows. Before him stands the Duchess's father. The lackey sees Lear only as the parent of her who wears the imperial garb.

The grandeur of him who was "every inch a king" proved not to be a quality of his particular nature at all, but a mere consequence

---

[2] I first learned about the application of this legend (in its Russian variant) to Shakespeare's tragedy from N. Berkovski's article *"King Lear* at the Bolshoi Dramatic Theatre."

of his power. Only the clothes he wore distinguished him from other people and raised him above them. It was not Lear who was worshipped and flattered. When they stole the clothes, the lackey no longer recognized the King. So it was that Lear stopped being a king. He even ceased to be Lear; as the Fool said to him, he was but "Lear's shadow."

The old King sets out on a long road. He tells everyone he was King, but no one believes him. They laugh at him and then want to kill him, and he complains, falls silent, and finally curses.

Later he understood, and he did not need the stolen clothes; he would not wear them anyway. He had come to the end of his journey. Now he no longer claimed to be different from all other men: he had come to know that he was not. He was a simple human being.

The story has a moral: In order to discover the true worth of things, one must understand ordinary life. Lear began to learn all those things that he had not known. Beginning with the immediate and simple, he later progressed to more remote things, to the general. He began to learn the connection between the simple and the complex.

The obstinate answer of his youngest daughter had shaken the infantile harmony of his existence. Lear raged because Cordelia dared to not carry out his wishes. Subsequently, when the real feelings of his older daughters were unmasked, he repented of his utter injustice. He began to consider Cordelia's answer but a negligible fault and saw himself guilty in its exaggeration. But in his opinion, a fault was nonetheless committed:

> . . . O most small fault,
> How ugly didst thou in Cordelia show!

He had not yet understood the meaning of her words. He still did not see that Cordelia's answer was not a blunder, but a mutiny.

Lear was convinced that his error had only been partial—that of the father, not of the King. The action remained for the present in the family. The dramatis personae included only a father and his daughters. However, the action had already assumed a totally different scope. Messengers were galloping by night from castle to castle, bearing calls to revolution. The King's suite and those of the dukes had already been drawn into these events. Supporters had been recruited; the factions had formed. War was imminent.

For Lear, however, no events were taking place save in the limited area of family relations. The same drama could be staged on a squire's farm or in a peasant's hovel—wherever there is a family with older and younger, parents and children.

Filial ingratitude was the first thing Lear saw in the real world. It was with this that his road began.

Lear considered state sovereignty and power over others to be his personal property. He presented his children with it much the same as a landed gentleman wills the house, fields, and herd to his heirs. He gave his daughters an enormous patrimony, and they begrudged him his suite—a paltry one hundred knights, all told. Ingratitude—the original vice. And it is nowhere more horrible than in one's children.

As the most violent punishment he can devise, Lear wishes Goneril to go through the same thing he has experienced: Should the Duchess of Albany bear a child, let him forget the cares of his mother when he is grown.

> . . . that she may feel
> How sharper than a serpent's tooth it is
> To have a thankless child! . . .

An insulting unnaturalness is inferred in the very combination of these words. They deny laws sacred to all men:

> Is it not as this mouth should tear this hand
> For lifting food to 't? . . .

The ingratitude of children is the rankest injustice. And it is thus that the theme of injustice first appears in the tragedy.

Lear now saw that he had accepted gilt for precious metal. The real value of sweets and pretty dresses proved insignificant. He had not yet learned the price of salt. The king of the tale understood the worth of salt when he experienced need and, being painfully hungry, was forced to try the food of the poor.

He had forfeited power, refuge, the love of his children. There was no roof over his head to shelter him from inclement weather. The King found himself in no better condition than that of his lowliest subjects. Then the King, apparently drinking the dregs of life, saw the figure of another injustice. Deprived of everything, exhausted, and despairing, he became aware of the gravity of his situation—now that he saw a number of others going through the same things in life as he was experiencing. From his own immediate existence, Lear's thoughts turned to the more removed general question.

His eyes rested on the Fool. No longer a thing of amusement, the clown is a man in no way differing from the King, and sharing the same feelings. Lear already knew the measure of what that man felt. When Kent suggested taking cover from the weather in a hut, the King let the Fool go ahead of him:

> In boy, go first. You houseless poverty—

His thoughts went deeper. The conscious reflected life more distinctly. It was not only Lear and not only the Fool who dragged out a miserable existence. Thousands of pictures of wretchedness appeared in front of him. His country rose before him ragged, hungry, and humiliated. His subjects passed before him, falling from exhaustion and worn out by deprivation. The real world burst into the little world of man, and it filled every corner of Lear's awareness. The infantile harmony was shattered. The reality that had dealt the blow to Lear's mind was the world of disharmony and of sorrow.

Offended paternal ego and wounded royal pride are already forgotten. The action now takes place in the family of all men, on the boundless stage of history. Incalculable, unbearably cruel, injustice showed itself to Lear. It rose to its full gigantic stature and covered all new phenomena with its shadow. The injustice of children was but a small part of this creature. Lear had come to realize that social injustice was the basis of all relationships. He saw "the very age and body of the time."

In a moment of greatest sorrow, he already thought of others beside himself:

> Poor naked wretches, wheresoe'er you are,
> That bide the pelting of this pitiless storm,
> How shall your houseless heads and unfed sides,
> Your looped and windowed raggedness, defend you
> From seasons such as these? Oh, I have ta'en
> Too little care of this! . . .

There is no law, no right, no morals; they are false concepts. They only serve him whose shoulders bear the velvet mantle. Once the supreme guardian of these notions, Lear scoffs at each of them. He speaks of the nature of power and turns concept about to look at each of its facets.

Here is the law of the kingdom. You see what this law is: "Look with thine ears. See how yond Justice rails upon yond simple thief. Hark, in thine ear. Change places and, handy-dandy, which is the Justice, which is the thief?" So the judge and the thief are indistinguishable one from the other.

A dog breaks from his chain and attacks a poorly dressed man with the intention of badly biting him. The vagabond bolts from the ferocious animal. The cur becomes a symbol for Lear. "There," he says to Gloucester, "thou mightst behold the great image of authority. A dog's obeyed in office." The animal represents an official about his duties.

The term "a law" is particularly deceiving. The lawgiver holds converse with an agent of law enforcement:

> Thou rascal beadle, hold thy bloody hand!
> Why dost thou lash that whore? Strip thine own back.
> Thou hotly lust'st to use her in that kind
> For which thou whip'st her. . . .

Morality is the servant of him whose shoulders bear the mantle. Adultery? Lear forgives adulterers—"for I lack soldiers."

These pictures, one clearer than the next, reflected happenings in the kingdom. Nothing more separated Lear from life—neither walls, nor guards, nor cajolery. He not only had an opportune vantage point from which to observe reality; he found himself in its midst. From the highest rung, he had descended to the bottom of the ladder. And now his feet were on the ground.

Lear learned the price of salt. He did not acquire this knowledge because hunger had forced him to taste bland food. Its price came to him in another way: he knew it because he had known the taste of tears. He was not only familiar with the salty taste of his own sorrow, but with that of the grief of all those whose existence he had once not suspected.

In the lives of almost all the heroes of Shakespeare, there is a moment when each of them begins to realize that his suffering was not caused by an evil man or by coincidence of circumstances, but by another thing, something that lies concealed in the very roots of life. The evil that comes to a man is only a part of a greater evil that affects most people. Its causes are secreted in the heart of social relations. From this moment, a new passion enters the hero's life. Everything that has happened before this, all the tormenting thoughts and outbursts of feeling, is but a preparation for the birth of this passion. The wounded trustfulness of Othello, the shock of Hamlet when he learns of his father's murder, the despair of Lear when he recognizes the error of his attitude toward his daughters—these are but the first steps of these heroes on the road that is opening before them.

A sole passion now possesses them; it is the same for all and scorches them with its flame. It is the passion of knowledge, the desire to seek out the meaning of events. Man begins to think not of himself alone, but of humanity. He does not see evildoers, but communal evil, and you cannot make short work of it with a stroke of the sword. Claudius dies, but his death does not re-establish the continuity of time. The death of the criminal does not destroy social iniquity. The injustice does not stop when they lead Iago away to a horrible torture. It does not resurrect Desdemona, nor does it restore the faith that a love like that of Othello and Desdemona, or of Romeo and Juliet, could exist in this century.

The sufferings of Lear can not be alleviated by the execution of his daughters and the return of his crown. The passion that has taken hold of his being demands other satisfaction. He must know that which had been concealed from him, and must comprehend the reasons for injustice.

The blindness had lasted too long, but he had recovered his sight. Instantly, a startlingly brilliant light penetrated life. The depths of abysses and the horizons in the distance all became visible. The light was so clear that every new picture reverberated in the conscious, causing pain. The pictures change with ever-increasing speed, opening up new forms of injustice in life.

Into his understanding of reality, Lear inserts such passion that his mind becomes too weak to endure the impetuous pressure of his thoughts. They wound, stab, burn; the suffering becomes unbearable. The pain sears through his whole being. Lear cries out, "I am cut to the brains."

When he wakes in the tent of Cordelia, he implores them not to rouse him; should he awaken from this dream, he would prove still attached to "a wheel of fire." Kent permits no one to address the dying man; the words would return him to reality. One would have to be heartless to want to restore him to the "rack of this tough world."

Metaphors of trial and torment permeate the tragedy. Life is a rack, and here on this rack is stretched him who once gave the orders.

The human heart cannot contain the sorrow of humanity. But this little muscle in the chest responds, with each flickering beat, to the pain suffered by the many people of whose existence their sovereign had not dreamed earlier.

In this way, there appears a feeling of the bond between one man and humanity, an impression of the unity of his sorrow and the sorrow of millions of people. Lear feels this; he has seen the real picture of life. He goes mad, and becomes wise.

MOTHER FOLLY

Finished works of art contained images that expressed the predominant elements of the firmest social contradictions. Centuries changed the forms of these contradictions, but they remained essentially unresolved. Poetry created a clot, as it were, of this essence by the "poetic idea." Images and ideas outgrew their times, and a new era would recognize its own time in them.

In Gogol's poem, the verbal combination "dead souls" was itself a poetic idea, with the possibility of grand generalization. It embraced not only the matter of serfdom under Nicholas I but also the whole world of predatory acquisition—inimical to the development of human progress and to the world of "living souls."

The poetic idea crystallizing the substance of events also appears in *King Lear*. Shakespeare saw reality as a realm of deception and fraud. He perceived social attitudes as mad and inhuman. In what way did these relations exist and possess their evident strength? Obviously they could seem human and reasonable only to unseeing eyes and to an obscured intellect. It is this thought and these images which are the source of his poetic idea. We shall attempt to follow its origin and development.

In the beginning of the play, the stage is occupied by statesmen, advisors to the King, those who are close to the throne. Yet none of them, clever and experienced though they are, understands that the division of the kingdom entails the ruin of the aged King and the collapse of the country. Neither Kent nor Gloucester nor the King himself has grasped this. Nevertheless, there is a man who foresees it all, everything that the wiser men cannot comprehend. This one sensible man is a fool, a clown. In his first words, he immediately predicts what the future holds.

The King of Britain was eighty years old, but his experience had brought him only to naïveté. Everything he had accomplished in sound mind . . . was madness. The condemnation of Cordelia and the exile of Kent were the deeds of a madman. Yet Lear had performed them in sound mind. There was nothing in which the King was not mistaken: he did not understand his children; the life of his people was unknown to him.

He had but to lose his reason, and he began to grasp the real meaning of events. The only wise man was the Fool; reasonable men were lunatics. The lunatic became a man of wisdom.

These contrasts are possessed of a most profound significance. The poetic idea, expressing the poet's appraisal of happenings in the real world, carried the bases of the system of government to an extreme and pointed to the irrationality of social attitudes.

In what way could this be said? Who had any opportunity to express such thoughts without paying for them with his head? Only one man had this kind of privilege: the Fool. He was generally recognized to be an idiot, and could speak the truth with impunity. This was his unique right.

The melancholic Jaques in *As You Like It* dreamed of becoming such a man:

> Invest me in my motley, give me leave
> To speak my mind, and I will through and through
> Cleanse the foul body of the infected world,

From antiquity, people have been accustomed to the idea that the man they considered most foolish should express wise ideas. A fool without rights was an accuser. Foolish fun frequently became mockery of everything that people were ordered to hold in reverence.

In the womb of the Middle Ages was formed an allegorical Mother Folly, who ruled the world. She crowned princes, popes, and knights with her fool's cap. Revolutionary humor suggested that the tinkle of merry-andrew bells could be heard in important speeches, and that asses' ears protruded from under elegant head-dresses. In churches, they arranged fools' holidays: a she-ass was dragged into the cathedral, a fool-bishop was chosen, incensing was done with putrid smoke, and the service was made into buffoonery. Theatre history recalls the order of the French King to shackle and imprison the Basoche clerks who portrayed the rule of Mother Folly at his court, how she stole and humiliated the people. Fools' unions arose everywhere; there was a "Guild of Fools," as well as an "Order of Fools."

At the end of the fifteenth century, Sebastian Brant published his *Ship of Fools,* in German. In his book, he described how idiots gathered from all over the world to sail for Narragonia, the country of fools. They included dandies, doctors, bribe takers, pedants, astrologers, and cardsharps. The cover of the book bore a painted ship crammed with people and sailing on a sea. A flag with a fool's head in a jester's cap fluttered over the head of the seafarers.

What called forth this world of asses' ears? Self-interest, which induced man to forget about the common good. From then on, Master Pfennig ruled the world. The medieval doctrine of original sin had already ceased to explain the ugliness of life, and reason subjected the social order to its own judgment.

In the sixteenth century, the number of books glorifying folly increased. The most foolish mother ascended the rostrum and announced in the hearing of all: "Folly creates kingdoms, and supports power, religion, government, and the courts. Indeed, what is all human life, if not the concern of Folly." This was said by Erasmus of Rotterdam in the *Praise of Folly,* a militant work of Humanism. The idea was stated without subterfuge. It was argued with all cogency that the contemporary social organization existed only because the majority of people were evidently fools, who did not perceive the nature of government institutions, which seem to be a fundamental mockery of common sense. If all this continued to exist, folly would obviously rule the world.

Rabelais wrote, "In this world, everything is upside down. We entrust the salvation of our souls to theologians, who are—for the most part—heretics; we entrust our bodies to doctors, who despise medicines and never take them, and our property we trust to lawyers, who are never at law with one another."

Folly and madness: these are the bases of society. "Foolery, sir, does walk about the orb like the sun. It shines everywhere," says the clown in *Twelfth Night*.

Under the sun of folly, everything comes out topsy-turvy. For the time being, the whole world walks on its hands, head bottommost. The Fool sings of this in *King Lear*. His couplets are original comic echoes of the tragic representations of Sonnet 66. These jokes are anything but a game of gay absurdities. Such witticism and puns are introduced into the most dramatic scenes of the play, and their force consists in their showing all the consequences of an "upside down" life in scenes which are full of pain and anger.

The figure of wise folly was strengthened by another which made it more precise: the image of blind vision. Deprived of sight, Gloucester says that he does not need vision:

I stumbled when I saw. . . .

He had had mistaken notions about his sons and about affairs of state. Later events forced him to an understanding of his error; he came to have another, correct appraisal of that which had happened. In such situations it is said that a man's eyes are opened. However, if he recovered his sight now, he must have been blind before. The poetic idea of the discrepancy between eyesight and vision permeates the imagic development of Gloucester. When Lear's advisor had good eyes but saw nothing, all his actions were compared to those of a blind man. He blindly believed Edmund, blindly obeyed the Duke of Cornwall. He glanced, peered, stared but saw nothing. Then they blinded him and he saw. Suffering helped him to perceive the world.

The crux of Shakespeare's poetic idea is stated by Gloucester:

'Tis the times' plague, when madmen lead the blind.

Madmen rule, and those who voluntarily obey them are blind not to see the insanity of society. The situation is confirmed by a number of contrasts that serve to make it more precise. They show law, morality, and right to exist "topsy-turvy," "head bottommost."

The storm swept away all familiar concepts and situations in one powerful gust. The King becomes a beggar, the Fool a wise man. The blind see. The clever speak insanity in delirium. A madman becomes a philosopher.

"Denmark's a prison," asserted Hamlet. His statement refers not only to the Denmark of Claudius but to all places where tragic action takes place. Life in a nation-prison is the greatest affliction for any man, but if that is the situation, perhaps happiness is best sought in a real house of detention. Lear pleads that they quickly jail him and Cordelia; he describes life in a prison as a blithe holiday:

> No, no, no, no! Come, let's away to prison.
> We two alone will sing like birds i' the cage.

In the realm of Dame Avarice, prison is not the worst place for a man. He is deprived of liberty behind locks and bars no more than he is in his daily life, where any freedom in his life is purely imaginary. The dominant injustice fetters his best aspirations, feelings, and thoughts, anyway.

Each of three different figures expresses the chaos of social relations in its own way. Sometimes these three form a single group: they become bound up with one another, and their thoughts converge on the same thing. They complement one another, so that, despite all their differences, some inner resemblance emerges. They are Lear, the Fool, and Edgar. Each express the theme of madness in a particular way. The madness of Lear is a real malady. Presenting himself as crazy in order to escape persecution, Edgar is a portrayal of madness. The third plays the role of an idiot in order to entertain under the guise of a jester; the Fool is a form of humor.

All three speak nonsense. It is, nevertheless, worth pondering their apparently senseless gusts of verbiage to seek out the meaning in it all. All three are thinkers. Their interrelation is complex.

It is difficult to define the relationship of Lear and the Fool, whether you take the living relations of the two as people, or their corelation as poetic images.

The Fool's human character traits, formed as they are by real circumstances, are not hard to perceive. His biography can be reconstructed, and you can understand what has happened to him even before he first appears on the stage. He was probably a manor peasant who was obliged to entertain the master from day to day. He had to summon a smile to Lear's face and to disperse sad thoughts. One of the pastimes of the age was a fool's conversations with his sovereign, which resembled banter between friends even to the point of nuances of disparagement. This was most amusing clownery, and only omnipotent monarchs were able to provide it for themselves. They laughed from their souls, and the fools earned their living from this sort of fun.

Shakespeare's Fool accomplished this especially well. Thus they were accustomed to address one another as equals, the most powerful man in the kingdom and the least significant. But the Fool was a clever man. He looked at life from other vantage points as well as through the embrasures of the palace, and he saw a great deal. Insignificant though he was, he knew much about which the sovereign had no notion. In the nonsense with which he entertained, there were grains of wisdom. He had been taken from the manor peasantry, and his wisdom was the bitter stuff of poverty-ridden people.

So the ancient folk image of the sham fool, who possessed a quantity of wisdom and sagacity, entered the plot of *King Lear*.

Events complicated the Fool's conduct. From halls of state, he found himself in a plain. He had once had a powerful master, but the master was now a wretched exile. Yet this did not alter his relationship with Lear; he was sincerely attached to him, and continued to serve him as honestly as before, despite the many changes in the old King's life. He tried to fulfill his obligations; for him this meant to amuse. But he had been thrown out of the life to which he was accustomed. He was exhausted by deprivation. His jokes took on a new manner. Unnoticeably to him, a smile turned into a grimace of grief. His merriment became saturated with bitterness. Still, he did not stop playing the fool. Like a soldier who cannot walk in a nonmilitary gait, the Fool could not forget how to jest. His complaints turned into puns, and sorrow unwittingly manifested itself in clownish faces.

Though the Fool has his life story and human character, it does not make up the entire content of the role. Poetic generalization is inextricably bound up with his real traits and involves the folk artistry that deals in satiric apotheosis of Folly and Madness. The

Fool is their ambassador plenipotentiary on the stage, and it his business to accompany events with his comments. He views events from the vantage point of a wise man; when everyone else's brains are added, the only intelligent man about is he whom everyone deems the most foolish.

His cap and bells are familiar to everyone; he has but to appear and everyone knows who he is and what he represents. He is more than one of the participants in tragic action. He stands for an image that exists outside the play and that all men know from childhood. He has been depicted many times as pestering kings, rich men, and even death itself, with his rattle. The audience is used to taking the familiar figure both as man and as allegory.

The Fool's complex relationship to Lear is determined not only by individual links forged in the daily round but also by poetic reciprocity. The characteristics of one object come to light by comparing that object with another, and consequently inner similarities are revealed in externally dissimilar phenomena. The Fool amuses the King and exposes the meaning of the King's actions. He accompanies him when Lear acts the fool. The jester becomes a sort of shadow to the King, save that the shadow wears asses' ears. Behind Lear trails the Fool with his unpleasant memories of the absurdities performed by the King.

None of this is a permanent definition of symbols. As the poetic idea develops, new connections arise and new facets of reality are reflected.

The shadow is not merely something cast by the bulk of a man, but something that joins with that bulk in a unique affinity. The man laughs, hearing the jokes of his own shadow. Time passes and the man stops laughing. The shadow had told him of things that he had already begun to suspect, but that he was still afraid to admit to himself. The shadow becomes conscience. The Fool has begun to give utterance to Lear's most secret thoughts.

The light shifts. The shadow now shortens, now grows longer. It becomes a parody on the contours of the body that casts it. But it is still thrown by a body and is inseparable from it.

The Fool does not leave Lear for any reason other than that of devotion. He accompanies the King because the King is acting like a fool:

"That lord that counseled thee
To give away thy land,
Come place him here by me,
Do thou for him stand.
The sweet and bitter fool
Will presently appear—
The one in motley here,
The other found out there."

The Fool ends his stage life in the third act. He vanishes without a trace, and neither his closing words nor the speeches of the other characters give us to understand why one of the major personae disappears in the middle of the play.

Aside from the unusual finish of the role, there is another peculiarity in the development of this figure. It has attracted the attention of scholars more than once. The Fool and Cordelia never meet. Yet in some puzzling way, they are dependent on one another. As soon as Cordelia leaves, the Fool appears: Cordelia has only to return, and the Fool vanishes. In several studies, evidence that both roles were played by the same actor is cited. Poetic complexity is replaced by commonplace misunderstanding. The question can certainly not be solved in such a simple way. The personnel of Burbage's troupe have little to do with the reasons for the Fool's disappearance. The solution lies in the poetic idea; the idea came to its conclusion and then it, and the figure representing it, came to an end.

The Fool disappeared as soon as Lear came to understand the meaning of things. The sound of jester's bells immediately subsided, and the fool's rattle was still. When the King became a sage, the shadow with ass's ears wasted away; Lear no longer needed to equate himself with an idiot. Mother Folly had lost a subject. The epithet abandoned the man, for the comparison had lost its meaning.

Here lies the reason for the impossibility of a meeting between the Fool and Cordelia. The French Queen must not have a fool's cap pulled over her eyes. The Order of Fools had no jurisdiction over a father and daughter who had finally found one another.

Madness got along by the side of folly. The Fool's couplets could turn into the babble of the crazed. In those times, it was not only fools that entertained but also madmen. The fashionable often visited insane asylums, much as they might go to a theatre, to laugh at the grimaces of the mentally ill.

Clowns and madmen were outcasts. They were not even considered human and had no place in society. They found themselves outside the gates of life. Only foolishness could sustain them; it was an amusing form of the disease.

The inhabitants of Bedlam roamed about, begging and earning a living from their madness. These were the poorest of beggars. A man could sink no lower; these people were deprived not only of all human rights but also of their reason. It was this kind of a mask that was adopted by the legitimate heir of Gloucester.

The extreme poles of the human condition come together in the part of Edgar: the rich man becomes poor, the courtier turns into a vagabond. The transformation takes place with staggering speed and lack of subtlety. The ease of transition from one mode of existence into another is expressed in the scene of the flight. One has only to rip up expensive clothes, smear up the face, churn the curls of well-barbered hair into tangles, and in the place of a court fop stands a half-witted ragamuffin. Exit Edgar; enter Poor Tom.

As always in Shakespeare, the figure turns on many meanings and shows many sides. Its connection with the fundamental character is complex.

Lear's mind first perceived social injustice as a picture seen from a great distance. The life of the people appeared before him in outlines still shrouded in fog. He cannot see it distinctly, but he soon guesses what it is like. It is the faceless crowd that appears in the monologue about "poor naked wretches." The sorrows of thousands merge into one immense whole. Look not for an isolated fate in the crowd of faces and the general woe.

This fate becomes known: its face will sit next to you and you see it with all its details. Tom darts out of the hut after pigs. Howling and wailing and shouting nonsense, he stands before Lear. Now they have finally met and stand side by side—the King and his subject.

Two men.

Two figures of madness.

Lear loses his reason because he has begun to understand life.

Edgar imitates madness: it is his only chance to live.

The scene begins full of meaningless words and the deepest significance. The inflamed consciousness of the King is completely occupied with the unhappy vagabond, who is trembling and delirious. Lear thinks that only the cruelty of daughters could reduce the man to such a condition.

The audience has seen the transformation of my lord Gloucester's son into a beggar. Now the opposite happens: Poor Tom reverts to Edgar.

The beggar tells of a lordly life. While the tale seems wild and preposterous, the whole point of it is that it is perfectly truthful.

"What hast thou been?" asks Lear.

". . . proud in heart and mind," answers the dirty outcast, "that curled my hair, wore gloves in my cap; served the lust of my mistress's heart and did the act of darkness with her, swore as many oaths as I spake words and broke them in the sweet face of Heaven."

Thus Edgar had lived, but these words are spoken now by an almost naked man, his whole body pricked by sticklebacks and thorns, and more thorns stuck into his hands. This man does not speak, but howls and stammers:

"One that slept in the contriving of lust and waked to do it. Wine I loved deeply, dice dearly, and in women outparamoured the Turk."

This is the one pole of human life, and here is the other: no more pictures of Edgar's life; instead, now Poor Tom the Bedlamite speaks of his life:

"Poor Tom, that eats the swimming frog, the toad, the tadpole, the wallnewt, and the water; that in the fury of his heart, when the foul fiend rages, eats cow dung for sallets; swallows the old rat and the ditch dog; drinks the green mantle of the standing pool. . . ."

This is the delirium of one dying from hunger. Edgar is describing the life of those who are banished from society, those who have become beggars and vagabonds, all those whose name is Mad Tom. His destiny is now the main route: ". . . who is whipped from tithing to tithing, and stock-punished, and imprisoned. . . ."

But, really, aren't these real pictures just as unnatural as the visions conjured up by disease?

Lear stares intently at his subject. He looks at the dirty mutilated body, the face mangled by suffering. All his spiritual forces are now subordinated to the one in which his thoughts are fully absorbed. Forgetting all else, he studies the vagabond with particular attention, as though there were hidden in the beggar a secret which Lear must find.

Lear is now sure that he sees the basic thing, the thing that contains the definition of the essence of all events. He looks, and does not see Poor Tom or Edgar, nor anyone else with a particular name. He sees before him—man. Lear's thoughts converge on the very heart of this concept. It seems to him that it is visible to his naked eye. Here he is—man.

Shakespeare looks with Lear at man, this demigod to whom Humanists wrote their inspired hymns. Here he is, born to create wonders, discover new lands, revel in the treasures of Greece and Rome; here he is, wise, holding the key to all the sciences, seeing the depths of the earth, and hearing the music of heavenly spheres. Pico della Mirandola once wrote him a panegyric: "O highest and most marvelous felicity of man! To him it is granted to have whatever he chooses, to be whatever he wills." Here he is: Lear bends over the spasmodically writhing beggar.

"Is man no more than this? Consider him well. Thou owest the worm no silk, the beast no hide, the sheep no wool, the cat no perfume. Ha! Here's three on's are sophisticated. Thou art the thing itself."

This is what man is, free of any debts, having no more than his own inalienable property. Money is acquired by fraud, and creates a fine exterior; it hides the substance of man under velvets and silks. All comeliness is mere dress. Gold buys law, which stands guard over these semblances. Neither judges, nor soldiers, nor hangmen permit the theft of rich clothes, of that which distinguishes the few from the many. Love, esteem, devotion, and gratitude all belong to the clothes, not to their owner. This is the value of dress.

Only attire has real worth. Everything else is counterfeit. Everything is bought: people's looks, their words, their feelings. Philosophers have devised a lying wisdom for money; it explains the greatness of clothes, but not of man. Poets weave beautiful words in praise of dress. A daughter kisses her father's hand; she kisses the sleeve of his garment. A vassal falls to his knees before his king; he worships the mantle.

All is deceit and sham; everything serves only to hide the substance. In what regard is this essence a true evaluation of the qualities of man and not of dress? Here is the evaluation: "Unaccommodated man is no more but such a poor, bare, forked animal as thou art."

Lear has the opportunity to make an estimate because his criterion for evaluating existence has become the life lived by most people. This majority is deprived of owning even a diminutive particle of any kind of property. Poor Tom does not even have rags enough to cover his body, only a dirty bit of frayed linen to wrap about his loins. The narrowest straw in the hands of the least significant judge could pierce this man's skin. And Lear now understands the most important fact: nothing distinguished him, once an omnipotent ruler, from this poor forked animal.

The storm ripped the King's robe from him, and he became like the rest of mankind. And most of mankind resembled this creature lying before him—Tom, an inmate of Bedlam.

A poor forked animal, this is the degree to which Dame Avarice has reduced man.

The images of clothing and the naked body frequently meet in *King Lear*. In this confrontation of images can be heard echoes of the medieval debate of naked Truth with velvet-gowned Vice. But the echo is distant; the tragedy is not a morality play. Shakespearean metaphors express not the dispute of granite concepts but, rather, sudden shifts in condition, abrupt transitions from one situation to another. The motif of changing clothes, frequent in the play, is important not only for the dramatic art but also as an expression of the instability of vital relationships.

The storm has burst into a little human world, and raged in its undefended space. The chaos of nature blends with the chaos of ideas. Lear loses his reason. The rhythm of the storm permeates the external action, the tread of thought, the evolution of feeling. The whirlwind sweeps everything in the scene into motion, as it roars through each part of it. It is not easy to find another scene in world literature as expressive as Act III of *Lear*. Everything in the act is strained almost beyond the limit of human endurance. Those who are caught in the storm are no less tormented by the mighty spiritual tempest raging inside each one of them than they are by the rain and cold. In this field, where there is not the shelter of a bush for miles, are gathered only those who have been driven out of life, stripped of names and hopes, sentenced to death.

In these scenes, all relationships are twisted inside out. Everything changes its appearance, so that it does not resemble its earlier self. The hidden Edgar speaks with the hiding Kent; they are both masquers. Sentenced to death, Gloucester tries to save a Lear doomed to ruin. The father does not know the son standing beside him. Friends speak to one another like strangers. There is not one reasonable man here. The madman philosophizes with the fool, and into the argument enters an idiot. It is hard to grasp who is really mad and who feigns it, who is the real sage and who is crazed. Natural situations, ordinary words, and normal thought are absent here. There is no level place in this scene, only footprints filled with blood.

The end of these scenes: for the last time, the sovereign of Britain summons a King's Court. It is not accidental that a trial ends the episode. It had been devoted to the theme of injustice, and the image of a court of justice is a natural conclusion of it. Lear will pass judgment on his daughters. He will pass judgment on injustice. He appoints his judges: the Fool and the madman. The foolish and the insane will try injustice. The royal tribunal sits at night in a swine-hut. The madman states the indictment; the Fool conducts the questioning; the lunatic is appointed juror.

The pain of the protagonists is depicted with particular force in this scene. Lear, who has lost his reason, Edgar, who can no longer pretend even from necessity, the Fool, who is tortured with exhaustion—they all approach the limits of their vital energies. In this mad court, words lose meaning and thoughts are scattered. Foolish song alternates with lamentation, and shouts with howls. As though this were not odd and unnatural delirium, there is heard through its wild combinations of words one all-penetrating sound —the groan of pain and despair.

The jingling of the bells on the Fool's cap merges with the heavy tolling of a death knell. Everything heads toward destruction. The mad lead the blind.

If the social structure that destroys the best in man is promised a long life, it is better to let the whirlwind flatten the globe into a cookie, and the sea rise up on end, and the stars be extinguished by its waves.

The storm acquires ever new meanings. It becomes an immense epithet for the whole tragedy.

The difficulty of determining the implications of this image lies in the fact that themes and poetic attributes are found in constant development and abrupt change. The energy of the verse movement is such that the real, described with prosaic clarity, will become mythological hyperbole in several lines. Theme and simile are often not confronted, but collide, rather; they penetrate one another and change places. The storm is now a natural phenomenon, now a cosmic flight of apocalpytic visions, now an expression of the spiritual experiences of the hero. It is both his collocutor and his conscience. It is the chaos of human spirit and the chaos of the social conditions surrounding him.

STONE HEARTS

Goneril, Regan, Edmund, and Cornwall lack humanity. They have no hearts.

In his *Lives,* Plutarch told how Caesar, while making sacrifice, suddenly discovered with horror that the animal he had sacrificed had no heart. Plutarch wrote that this was a fearful omen since an animal without a heart does not exist in nature.

The world inimical to Shakespeare is expressed by the poetic image of stone hearts. Lear's elder daughters have hearts "more harder than the stones." Their souls are hewn from stone. The most horrible example of ingratitude is called "marble-hearted fiend."

As always in Shakespeare, the image becomes solid; it can be weighed, measured, and touched. Lear demands that the physicians perform an autopsy on Regan: ". . . see what breeds about her heart. Is there any cause in nature that makes these hard hearts?" Shylock and Richard had hard hearts; knives could be honed on their souls. When Othello is convinced of Desdemona's infidelity, his heart becomes stony. He says that when he strikes his chest with his hand, the hand hurts. Lear, closing a speech with a shriek, cries to all men, ". . . Oh, you are men of stones."

Only the heartless could permit the death of Cordelia, and then look impassively at her corpse.

They are not people who make forked animals out of most of the human race. They are imitations of people. Were an anatomist to open the chest of one of these counterfeits, he would find cold stone in it. Their human exterior is deceptive; in reality, they are beasts. Shakespeare likens them to beasts of prey who hunt men down. Catching sight of their prey, they conceal themselves, wait for the proper minute to pounce. They snap at the throat with their fangs, tear the breast with their claws, lap up the blood, and gorge themselves on human flesh.

Metaphors involving wild animals abound in *King Lear*. In malicious faces, there appear the snarling snouts of boars, the blooded muzzles of bears and wolves. Behind these bestial snouts crawl incredible scarecrows, vampires, and werewolves, mysterious monsters of the seas and oceans. These are neither beasts nor demons, but the hideous results of fear and despair, ominous signs of chaos challenging reason and humanity.

With tragic power, the poetry shows how a system of social madness drags mankind back to the savagery and horror of centuries, to plunge everything back into the turbid chaos of primitive existence. The stone hearts want to destroy the work of prehistory.

Many species of carnivorous beasts are brought into the tragedy. Some of them had retained their ancient customs, and others had already developed new habits.

In analyzing the characters of Goneril, Edmund, and Regan, it is difficult to place them in categories such as feudalism or capitalism. These characters are the result of a complicated crossing of breeds. They are full of the spark of the period of primary accumulation of capital. Their souls overflow with anxiety. Thirst for activity strangles them. Their passion for gain leads them to insanity. They do not know any moral norms, nor do they profess any religion. All these are characteristics of the new period, but the goals these people pursue are, for the most part, old ones.

They destroy their time from within. They are the leprosy and vice of the age, the corruption of the body of time. The fever of disease rages within them; the unslakable thirst of an envenomed organism possesses them.

Albany
Well, you may fear too far.
Goneril
                    Safer than trust too far.
Let me still take away the harms I fear,
Not fear still to be taken. . . .

Thus runs a conversation between Goneril and her husband, who does not understand the cruelty of her treatment of her father.

Macbeth feared too far. He murdered, at first, to eliminate his rivals and then to destroy the witnesses. However, each murder became more than a step to power; it was also a step to ruin. The crime committed for deliverance from fear evoked horror. The murdered shattered not only Duncan's sleep but also his own.

He that steeps his safety in true blood
Shall find but bloody safety.

Goneril deals in poison. Watching the writhing of Regan and hearing her moan, "Sick, oh, sick!" Goneril whispers an aside: "If not, I'll ne'er trust medicine." Evidently, she was given the opportunity to test her skill not only in the murder of her sister but also elsewhere. There is a convulsiveness to most of her displays, something on the order of the frenzied expressiveness of the Gothic. In paintings of this style, there are strange combinations of paroxysmally distorted hands and feet, twisted against the laws of anatomy. There are also representations of everything connected with torture and punishment; this is executed with frightening naturalism.

The Duke of Albany calls his wife a gilded serpent.

Probably her appearance reflected the barbaric luxury of the age, which could turn a woman into a fantastic idol wrapped up in heavy velvets and costly brocades. The figure of Goneril is linked to one of the allegories. Kent is indignant that Oswald serves her, this doll called Vanity. One of the figures of the morality plays is so named, and the fact that Goneril compares herself with the personification of this particular vice says something about Lear's eldest daughter.

The sisters do not resemble one another. Goneril is impetuous, not always in control of herself. Regan is quiet and reserved. Each of them has a suite, her own constellation.

At Goneril's side is Oswald, an important figure. The Duchess

of Albany's steward occupies a sort of intermediate degree between people and animals. He is the fine borderline separating man
from the grimacing apes who repulsively parody human manners.
His similarity to man evokes the special fury of Kent, who is a real
human being. The curses that Kent confers upon him are interesting: "A knave, a rascal, . . . a lily-livered, action-taking
knave; a whoreson, glass-gazing, superserviceable, finical rogue;
. . . one that wouldst be a bawd in way of good service, and art
nothing but the composition of a knave, beggar, coward, pander.
. . ." Also, "you whoreson cullionly barber-monger. . . ."

In these sobriquets, a sizable place is occupied by the external
signs of civilization. In *Henry IV,* Hotspur speaks of a courtier
who appeared on the battlefield dressed up as though for a
wedding. Sniffing perfume from a phial, the Lord had ordered
soldiers to carry the corpses to one side so that the smell of
corruption should not poison the air. He was sleek, fragrant, and
bore some resemblance to a parrot. Another such figure makes an
appearance before the death of Hamlet; Osric "did comply with
his dug before he sucked it."

Part of the new era is reflected in these images. In the midst of
blood and sorrow, there existed a breed of beauticians' curl-
papers, careerists prepared to prostitute themselves. The tribe
multiplied with surprising fecundity. Facile villains, ready to take
part in any infamy, began to fill the antechambers of houses from
which they could expect reward. Like mangy lap dogs, they were
prepared to stand on their hind legs to serve any ruler, and to tear
anyone in disfavor into little pieces.

Oswald belongs to one of the first litters. The traits of the
species are already clear, but the subspecies are not yet well
defined. There is neither palace foppery nor euphemistic affectation in Goneril's underling; he was reared and trained on a feudal
estate, not in the ballrooms of the capital. Kent claims that Oswald
was not contrived by nature, but by a tailor of some sort. If a
king's stature was in the mantle, then this kind of people found the
meaning of its existence in the livery.

In his hatred for this breed, Shakespeare reaches the bounds of
fury. There is no doubt as to this; he himself says this of them
through the lips of Kent. He devises a special torment for Oswald:
"I will tread this unbolted villain into mortar, and daub the walls
of a jakes with him."

Oswald is the basest creature in this world of sham; he is a coop of flattery, servility, and effrontery. Wherever there are lies, wherever they wish to finish off the fallen, wherever they need people who find their greatness in infamy, there is Oswald. Through this retainer of Goneril, her reign can be understood; it was a creation not of honest labor like masonry or carpentry, but of the contrivances of tailors and hairdressers who strained themselves to accommodate the loathsome tastes of a client.

They do their killing with a cane, not a weapon.

If Goneril eliminates the people in her way with a pinch of poison, Regan uses more usual means. She is in no way inferior to a man. Her weapon is the sword—not a light rapier, but a sword like that of the castle guard. The mistress can wrench a weapon from the hands of a servant and can stab a mutinous villain. She knows not only how to kill but how to torture. She obtains Gloucester's confession herself, pulls out his gray hairs, and gives the orders in the torture chamber.

With the Duke of Cornwall, she gallops along the roads at night—black horsemen bound for castles. They recruit supporters and confuse vassals and urge one on against the other. Evil princelings, they divide the kingdom into tatters by their interminable intrigues. In this pair is contained all the savage cruelty of an iron age, the sullen brigandage of diminutive lords. They only know how to ram people into stocks, pull out their eyes, and break their bones. Medieval hangmen, they entered the world from a torture chamber; the rack and other refined instruments of torture stand behind them. There is nothing human to be discovered in their heavy gaze.

Cruelty is not the only quality which defines Lear's second daughter. Another trait is no less important: Regan is stingy and small-minded. When her father is about to die from grief, she argues about the lack of supplies in the castle storerooms, about the difficulty of feeding Lear's suite, about the house being so small that the servants would spat. Is this a desire to humiliate her father still further? No, this is merely the sphere of interests of this duchess who keeps at her belt a dagger in the folds of her dress.

Ancient forms of baseness are replaced by new ones. Next to the Cornwalls stands Edmund.

In connection with the word "Renaissance," people are usually fond of recalling the Humanist who bows before ancient pergaments, the discoverer of unknown lands, the poet who sings of the greatness of man. But the epoch also had other equally characteristic units: the soldier of fortune, who sells his sword arm to the highest bidder, today fights against one enemy and tomorrow with that enemy against yesterday's allies, and the piratical merchant, who feels sure that nature endowed him with strength so that he might rob the weak.

Humanist aspirations were oddly interwoven with unrestrained cynicism. The declaration of the freedom of the individual did not have an idyllic stamp. Politics were freed from illusion. Bracciolini wrote that the strong held laws in contempt, inasmuch as they were created for the weak, lazy, and cowardly. In his *Dialogues,* he asserted that outstanding deeds always seemed to be violating the concept of law; power seemed to be their only justification. Guicciardini vindicated fraud and hypocrisy. He considered people's real incentives to be thirst for money and power, not the striving for social justice. Machiavelli praised the strong personality, the man of blood and iron who was capable of achieving power by any means.

Along with theological morality, other moral concepts were destroyed. A new human type appeared in all fields: the fortune seeker, prepared to do anything in the name of success. He is an active and enterprising character, a true hero of the era of primary accumulation. He destroyed religious beliefs not from any desire to free man's reason from the bonds of Scholasticism, but to eliminate superstitions that might interfere with the enrichment of the individual at the expense of the majority.

Literary figures of this destruction were complex and contradictory. In Shakespeare's plays, these men were reflected in different ways. Richard III is a political agent along the lines of Marlowe's heroes; he is a great force of negation. Machiavellianism is shown here in the scale of historical phenomena. The law and power of the state comprise the author's range in investigation.

Iago is a thinker. The evil he contemplates has no practical meaning. His only motives are jealousy and offended ambition, and these are not convincing enough. He is an experimenter, as it were, testing a hypothesis concerning the immutability of man's animal nature. Despising everyone else, he asserts the strength of his personality.

Edmund is a businessman. His aims are obvious: to get the inheritance and title and to advance himself by playing on feudal intrigue. Not only a medieval brigand, he is also a poet who praises the greatness of brigandage. He is, in this, a worthy hero of the Renaissance. He mocks all that could limit the will of man; everything depends on human will, and success depends on nothing but will. Nothing is sacred, neither God, nor king, nor father. The illegitimate son of the Earl of Gloucester is a legitimate child of the new age. He despises superstition and religious belief. He laughs at astrology. He is amused by ideas of fidelity to sovereign and attachment to family.

Nature and time, which usually are conflicting concepts in Shakespearean poetics, form a distinctive unity in Edmund's philosophy. Edmund glorifies both the stormy lawlessness of nature and the demands of the iron age.

He is an old-fashioned actor, skillfully changing masks. For Gloucester he plays the obedient son who is ready to betray his brother for love of the father. He betrays his father to Cornwall, acting the role of staunch ally. He is ardently in love with Goneril, but no less passionately loves Regan.

An adventurer who earns his way at the juncture of centuries, he stands on the crooked crossroads of the times and waits for sacrificial lambs. He does not let a chance at plunder pass him by; he considers booty to be anything that is possessed by the spineless fools who are still bound to ancient superstition.

These are people without family or clan, people strong in that nothing can hold them back. And their time has come.

Shakespeare saw both the evil of the old order and the savagery of the new. He knew that to the medal struck by the Renaissance there are two sides; on one are the faces of Hamlet and Romeo, on the other Iago and Edmund.

In speaking of individual characters, one must not forget that a theme implied in one image is not exhausted by it, but continues and finds its completion in another. The officer who kills Cordelia is not to be distinguished from Edmund. The size of his role is limited to two lines, but they are sufficient. The man is portrayed with comprehensive clarity.

After the battle, the victorious Edmund suggests to one soldier recently elevated in rank that he set off for the prison where Lear and Cordelia are held, and carry out the orders contained in a letter. Giving him the note, Edmund tells this officer that, should he consent, Edmund would open the road to further successes:

> . . . Know thou this, that men
> Are as the time is . . .

The note contains an order to hang Cordelia. Without a moment's pause, the officer nods his consent. His answer is stated somewhat unusually:

> I cannot draw a cart, nor eat dried oats.
> If it be man's work, I'll do 't.

The century has already taught this soldier everything. The only thing he has not yet mastered is gorging himself on the fodder put out for cattle and pulling in harness. But all the rest, any brutish act, he can do without the slightest hesitation. The moral norms and social instincts worked out by man through the centuries have no hold on this murderer.

The time demands that men resemble this mercenary.

These are the times. If they continue, people will learn to eat oats. The strong will harness the weaker to carriages, and the latter will pull loads and draw gentry.

The theme of the destruction of not only feudal restrictions but all social bonds begins in the complex nature of Edmund and comes to a conclusion with the figure of the executioner, in only two lines.

Two Ways Out

The world of stone hearts is frightening. Wherever their domain extends, there can be no love; affection seems silly, friendship absurd. Life loses the warmth of human relations. Unbearably cold, its frost constricts the heart. How is man to be warmed? Where can he find a warm place? Sounding from inside the hut, Poor Tom's first words tell where to find this place: "Fathom and half, fathom and half!" Graves are dug a fathom and a half into the ground. Tom advises: "Hum! Go to thy cold bed and warm thee."

Throughout his confused tale is heard one and the same complaint: "Tom's a-cold." . . . People are not strong enough to endure the cold of the iron age. Perhaps exhausted man rests there, in the depths of the earth; there is no prison there, nor hunger, nor the hangman. There, the head is not besieged by thoughts that injure the brain. You need not look for a way out there, but of course you will not find it.

Thus Hamlet puts his famous question, "To be or not to be." Is there any sense in existing when injustice reigns and the worst of men are in power, when virtue is trampled in the mud? For him to whom has fallen the misfortune of knowing all this, perhaps the best exit is that which takes him from this life. Perhaps death is the only way to assuage the unbearable pain of head wounds.

Pursuant to this line of thought, the theme of suicide appears in the tragedy. In his delirium, Edgar speaks of the possibility of just such an exit. Evidently he has felt his weakness more than once, and despair has taken hold of him. The devil laid a knife under Tom's pillow, hung nooses over his chair, dribbled poison into his soup. But Edgar rejected these thoughts. To lie in a cold bed and warm himself became the urgent wish of his father.

The parallel plot of *King Lear,* the tale of the Earl of Gloucester and his two sons, is known to be taken from Philip Sidney's *Arcadia.* The borrowing, however, consists of only external plot characteristics. The content and characters acquired a totally different significance.

The fate of Lear and his daughters is echoed by the fate of Gloucester's family. The exceptional is bound up with the ordinary. The moral picture of the times becomes all-inclusive. However, this is not the sole meaning and place of the parallel intrigue; the stories are not only connected, they are confronted. Both Lear and Gloucester are mistaken in their children. It has befallen both of them to suffer from those to whom they had shown favor, and to be saved by those they had repudiated. Yet the circumstantial similarities underscore even more strongly the depth of inner divergences.

Gloucester's basic quality is submissiveness. Hot-tempered and despotic in family affairs, he is silent in palace halls. He is a vassal; the term implies his attitude. For Gloucester, the order of subordination is the basis of the universe and is not humanly indictable. He is honest and kind, in his own way, but these qualities are restricted by the philosophy of a feudal seigneur. He is a medium-size star, shining only by grace of the reflected light of the main sun. He is of one flesh with the social system; in order not to be, he would have to infringe upon the customary order of things, and to Gloucester that means insubordination. There are irregularities, and there is evident tyranny, but power is power. And Gloucester is silent. He holds his tongue when they partition the country, does not utter a word when Kent is banished, and is mute when they clap the King's envoy into the stocks. When Lear himself, the recent sun, is insulted by Cornwall, now one of the more important planets, Gloucester comforts the King and explains the complexity of the situation to him:

> My dear lord,
> You know the fiery quality of the Duke,
> How unremovable and fixed he is
> In his own course.

A new luminary had risen in the sky; Cornwall has become the sun. Now he is lord and noble sovereign, and the vassal can only be silent.

In several older studies, it is claimed that Gloucester's downfall is an act of supreme revenge. Edmund, born out of wedlock, destroys his profligate father. The fruit of the sin punishes the sinner. This moral is not relevant at all. The fundamental idea of the figure is expressed quite clearly a number of times. The blind Gloucester has the sympathy of his guide, the old man:

> Alack, sir, you cannot see your way.

> *Gloucester*

> I have no way and therefore want no eyes.
> I stumbled when I saw. Full oft 'tis seen,
> Our means secure us, and our mere defects
> Prove our commodities. . . .

He is blind. He must experience the depths of privation in order to recover his sight. When he sees the situation as it is, he decides to make an end by suicide. Submissiveness to circumstances simultaneously takes on a new form and reaches its final expression.

What arguments can make him retract his decision? Edgar finds one: he persuades his father that the notion of suicide is inspired by the fiend and that a violent death would strike the higher powers as opposition. The son brings his father back to the idea that it is necessary to submit to that which is higher than the vassal, Gloucester. And the blind old man resigns himself once more:

> . . . Henceforth I'll bear
> Affliction till it do cry out itself
> "Enough, enough," and die. . . .

The concept of man's powerlessness in his struggle with social evil, and hence of suicide as, perhaps, the only result, is stated both in *King Lear* and in *Hamlet*. The statement is made, however, only in order to be rejected. The very spirit of the poetry, filled with conflict and movement, disproves it. It is also denied by the actions of the protagonists. The tragedy indicated a totally different way out.

The hearts of this world are not only made of stone. There are also living hearts, which are capable of more than love. We find in *Richard III:*

> Every man's conscience is a thousand swords,
> To fight against that bloody homicide.

The conscience, or heart, here becomes the image of terrible power.

When Gloucester finally dared raise his voice in defense of Lear, he did not find himself alone. Cornwall's servant interceded for him. This man could not watch the torture of the old man with indifference. He drew his sword, intending to strike his hereditary master. The significance of this brief episode is immense: the peasant lifted his weapon not only against a cruel duke, but also against the law that the lowly shall be humble before the exalted.

The storm is met by the anger of Lear, as well as by the submission of Gloucester. The elements of evil collide with the energy of human indignation.

A gentleman tells Kent about Lear's behavior in the plain. The whole force of his insubordination is conveyed by the poetry:

Kent

. . . Where's the King?

Gentleman

Contending with the fretful elements.
Bids the wind blow the earth into the sea,
Or swell the curlèd waters 'bove the main,
That things might change or cease; . . .

.   .   .   .   .

Strives in his little world of man to outscorn
The to-and-fro-conflicting wind and rain.

The eighty-year-old man throws a challenge in the face of destruction. Even if the means of opposition are unknown, the struggle has already begun with his unwillingness to reconcile himself and yield. The force itself of internal resistance establishes the scale of the personality that advances alone against the madness of the social order.

Lear revolts. Deprived of power and alone in the plain, he rises against injustice. He who has no rights demands a trial; he who has no audience addresses the world. He preaches a sermon to the lightning, summons the wind and the thunder to revolution. Not only does he not try to put an end to his life, but he demands that life be altered, that all existing attitudes change. He states it as a condition: "That things might change or cease."

In these scenes, Lear again resembles the heroes of ancient legends. But now it is a totally different myth. Centuries have passed. Instead of the unknown forces of nature, opposing man are new threatening elements, elements that are still as unknown to him as the forces of nature once were. These new threats are those of social relations. They beckon a destruction more dreadful still then earthquake or drought.

Lear curses this force. And those who submitted to it and who tried to live with it are ingloriously ruined. Gloucester has been paid for his silence; the disposition of the Duke of Albany was too gentle; how many disasters were caused by his mildness?

The storm has blown over the world. . . .

Nothing was left whole on the surface of the earth; nothing had escaped destruction. It seemed as though everything had died, and only a few last fugitives, crazed with sorrow and fear, were still trying to be saved, by flattening themselves against the ruins in the darkness, haze, and ashes.

Night came to an end. Morning dawned, and it became apparent that not everything was destroyed. Only those things that had existed solely on the surface had perished. Anything that had had roots stretching into the bowels of the earth had withstood the storm.

Lear returned to life. Cordelia's soldiers found the King in the plain and carried him into the camp. The doctor gave him a sedative. After a profound sleep, the exhausted old man woke up. His youngest daughter stood before him; and so Lear and Cordelia found one another.

When Iago tried to ruin Othello and Desdemona, he set himself a goal. As well as to defile their love, he had to destroy the harmony that had arisen so unexpectedly out of chaos.

But I'll set down the pegs that make this music. . . .

In order to save her father, Cordelia had to restore "his bereaved sense." With Cordelia, the theme of harmony enters the tragedy. Lear's return to life begins with music. A musician is placed by the side of the tent where Lear lies; the doctor orders him to begin playing. In the harmony of sound, a feeling of possibility of a sane and happy existence appears for the first time. The presentiment is still vague, and music is more capable of communicating it than are the other arts.

When Shakespeare turns to a concept more noble in his opinion, music appears among his images. A noble person has music in his soul, and he who is called to harmony cannot merit confidence (*The Merchant of Venice*). Cassius does not like music; such people are most dangerous (*Julius Caesar*).

The music comes from an unknown place. Lear opens his eyes. He begins to recover.

He is unaccustomed to all those things that are seen and heard by a man who returns to the living. They had brought him into an unknown country where nothing resembles what he had known till now. He thinks that this is a dream and that everything he sees does not really exist, save in his dream. What is unusual about what has happened to him? Why do his daughter's simple words seem to come to him in some strange dream?

Human kindness stands before him. All events are defined by that concept. The King knew the artificial world of flattery, bestial spite, and animal greed, but he did not know humanity. Now there are human faces before him, and human eyes full of kind tears. All this seemed impossible; it had seemed absent from life. So Lear thought that he was still asleep.

Lyrical elements pervade the poetry of the stage. It is a special lyricism, and its nature must be defined. The figure of Cordelia lacks susceptible softness or incorporeal dreaminess. She lives in a tent; her breast is protected by chain mail. She is a French queen at war, and she fights. Her poetry is close to folk balladry in its tension; the rhythm is severe, the colors subdued, the images often cruel. The lyricism of Cordelia is indivisible from the ring of the verse, its energy of expression, its sense of inner strength. None of this resembles the singing of the angels with whom this youngest sister is frequently compared.

The theme of Cordelia expresses more than filial love, it speaks of the struggle of man with the inhuman. She is not only an heiress to the crown (a symbol of power which did not strike Shakespeare as attractive), she is heiress to the infinitely greater treasure of the values earned by humanity for man.

The Duke of Albany tells Goneril that a daughter who repudiates her father is comparable to a "rude wind" that lacks the sap of life. The branch is broken from the trunk; she is fated to ruin. Nothing can live when it is torn from its roots.

Man is obliged to know his roots. They grow deep into the bowels of the centuries, gain in strength, grow along with the development of progress in history. The path of mankind is not an aimless circle for Shakespeare, but a noble road. Nor was the word "humanity" an empty noise. This expresses a concept born of the work, suffering, and courage of generations.

Shakespeare compares the social order under which the triumph of humanity will be achieved with a liberal profusion of flowering nature. The smallest pockets of harmony appear for an instant as prototypes of the dream world. Two magnificent human beings find one another; human nobility is here expressed, as in the relationships of Romeo and Juliet, Othello and Desdemona, Lear and Cordelia. Their love is more than the passion of lovers, or the affection between father and daughter; it is an illustration of wisdom. In Shakespeare's poetry, love is a martial concept, a challenge addressed to the ideas of the iron age.

An instant of harmony is so beautiful that the rest of life is like utter darkness beside it. The optimism of *King Lear* does not only lie in the idea that evil men either are punished or kill one another; it lies mainly in the feeling of victory of the worthy over the unworthy, even though their moral victory be a factual defeat at the same time. This is evinced in the last scene between Lear and Cordelia. Edmund, Goneril, and Regan have achieved their goal; the French forces are defeated. Lear and his youngest daughter are captive. It seems that their enemies have won a sweeping victory. Their enemies have but two adversaries left, a helpless old man and a young woman. Unarmed prisoners, they are alone in the midst of a hostile army. A small effort from any of the soldiers around them would suffice to destroy this defenseless pair. Nevertheless these vulnerable two are the victors. They prevail because they know happiness.

They have found one another, and their instant of harmony is more powerful than iron. No matter how much more time he has to live, Lear spends these few moments as a wise man. He has come to know what is counterfeit and what is real. Now he understands the comparative values of candy, smart dresses, and salt. All Goneril and Regan win are mere glittering shards. But at the end of his life, Lear finds true wealth.

Moral victory, however, cannot become a real gain; harmony can exist but a minute. It exists for Lear until he listens to Cordelia's heartbeat. When that fades away, the world falls silent and seems to be dead.

The old King has come to the end of his road. He learned human unhappiness, heard the sorrow of others with his own, and it became his own. He came to know the community of man and to understand the responsibility of one for all.

He withstood the pressure of the storm and did not yield.

This man remains in our memory lit by bursts of lightning, a sere rebel who accuses injustice and demands that the world change or cease.

Hamlet,
Prince of Denmark

"Hamlet" and Hamletism

*Even when we return to works of the past (different periods
never select the same work from the great storehouse of the
past: yesterday it was Beethoven and Wagner, today Bach and
Mozart), it is not the past which revives in us; it is we our-
selves who cast our shadows into the past—our desires, our
questions, our order, and our confusion.*
        —Romain Rolland, *Goethe and Beethoven*

Dostoevski wrote that even the shyest of bride-
grooms is hardly likely to jump out of a small window from sheer
fright; it just doesn't happen that way in ordinary life. But Gogol
had only to write his *Marriage,* and people began to recognize
Podkolësin, the unlikely bridgroom, in one another. Shyness,
uncertainty, fear of any change whatsoever—these common human traits now had a single name. Everything that in the real
world, according to Dostoevski, existed in a somewhat diluted
form was suddenly condensed into clarity; it was invested with a
more expressive form and became an appellative. Art had succeeded in stating the very essence of a living phenomenon. The
figure became a type.

The phenomenon of a given time lived; Podkolësin survived this
century and became representative of new generations of lie-abeds
and milksops, whose character had been defined by quite another
reality.

The nineteenth-century radical critic Dobroliubov was pleased
by the appearance of a literary nickname which united and ex-

plained a number of the characteristics of prereform[1] Russian life.

This word is oblomovism.[2]

Now, when I hear a country squire talking about the rights of man and urging the necessity of developing individuality, I know from the first words he utters that he is an Oblomov.

When I hear a government official complain that the system of administration is too confused and cumbersome, I know that he is an Oblomov. . . .

When, in the journals, I read liberal denunciations of abuses and expressions of joy over the fact that at last something has been done for which we had so long been waiting and hoping, I think to myself that all this has been written from Oblomovka.

Dobroliubov's article "What Is Oblomovism?" was published in *The Contemporary* in the late 1850's, but his initial list of Oblomovs found new entries after the critic's death. The "brothers of the Oblomov family" had no intention of dying off, and continued to exist in subsequent years.

"Oblomovs remain," wrote Lenin, "since Oblomov was not only a landed gentleman but a peasant, and not only a peasant but a member of the intelligentsia, and not only a member of the intelligentsia but a worker and a communist, . . . *the old Oblomov remains, and he must be thoroughly laundered, cleaned, tousled and thrashed to make some sort of sense emerge.*"[3]

The world has a new tenant: the figure who has become a literary type. It is "the nickname for many objects, expressed, however, by a proper noun" (*Belinski*). This tenant proved much longer-lived than an ordinary mortal. In him were not only the qualities of a man who lives in a specific place at a specific time, but also those human characteristics that have a particular stability and a tenacity to life. These characteristics survive the centuries and cross national boundaries. They change form, but keep the family name.

Everyone is familiar with these figures from youth. These are

[1] That is, the period preceding the decade of reforms under Aleksandr II. This period of reform begins with the emancipation of the serfs in 1861 [trans.].

[2] Sluggishness, inertia, apathy, as in Oblomov, the principal character in I. A. Goncharov's novel of the same name [trans.].

[3] V. I. Lenin, *Works,* XXXVIII, 197.

Don Quixote, Tartuffe, Oblomov, Khlestakov,[4] and other such hero-types. They accompany men's lives for many generations.

And this is Hamlet.

Each of these characters has not only a name but a nickname. The interrelation of the two is complex. In the history of culture, this sort of nickname often separates from the character to acquire a movement and development of its own. It is attributed by new eras to new real phenomena.

It is taken up by various social groups as a weapon, and is sometimes used for ends that contradict one another.

This often resembles the correspondence of legend to biography. A warrior or statesman will live out his time, his life divided between personal affairs and matters of more general significance. He will have been a man of a particular stamp, but when both he and those close to him die, no one remaining will have known him well. Then biography begins to be lost, and legend to emerge.

The legend originates with factual events and those incidental traits that struck his contemporaries as important. These latter elements are subsequently exaggerated, and the rest forgotten. Later generations know only the legend and amplify it in turn with new, fabricated details. They introduce their ideals into it in a desire to make it fulfill their own aspirations. The burial mound settles and is overgrown with grass, and the legend preserves nothing of the man save his name. It now reflects the thoughts and feelings of new generations.

Something along this line also happens with literary characters. A play was written three centuries ago. The name of its hero, a Wittenberg student and Crown Prince of Denmark came to be known not only as that of a character in a play but also as an appellative for certain human types. Its dissemination took on a scale unique in the history of culture. A number of eminent people saw it as a generalization that embodied the characteristics not only of individual men but sometimes of whole nations at certain moments in their development. Vast concepts broke away from the small figure in mourning, and the mourner participated in mighty clashes of ideology.

As the clashes grew more violent, the concept itself was by far

[4] The main character of Gogol's play *The Inspector General* [trans.].

the more frequently discussed, and the actual figure of the Danish Prince receded into the background. "Hamletism" became the topic for debate. Its author was not only Shakespeare but a great number of others as well. Among the co-authors were great minds and empty ones, ardent progressives and arch conservatives.

The rise and development of hamletism is only partially related to the study of the play or to that of the hero taken separately. Furthermore, the very concept has changed and has frequently been used to describe complete opposites. Today, hamletism involves doubt, vacillation, split personality, and the predominance of reflection over will to action. This is how the encyclopedia interprets it and how we customarily understand it unless we go deeply into its real meaning. But the entire idea, and everything included in it, has been evoked in different times by different social phenomena, and the concept has had a specific character in relation to each era.

In Shakespeare's day, many united under the flag of "melancholy." Philosophic treatises were written about it, and dandies struck a pose of disillusionment with life. The subject occasioned a good many jokes, and Hamlet implies that the affectation of melancholy was common stage business. Yet suicide increased, and particular attention was drawn by certain Stoic teachings concerning the wisdom of voluntary departure from this life. Many of Shakespeare's characters, from Jaques (*As You Like It*) to Antonio (*Merchant of Venice*), had caught the "Elizabethan disease," as the condition is called in English scholarship.

The conflict between Renaissance ideals and the reality of the epoch of primary accumulation of capital was evident enough. This is the germ that sickened those who had the misfortune to realize the depth of the rift.

Did early seventeenth-century audiences note these precise qualities in Hamlet's spiritual life? The evidence provided by contemporary sources is too meager to give an answer, and any conclusions would be purely arbitrary. *Hamlet* had a variety of audiences, and it is probable that the play was seen differently by London apprentices than by the habitués of literary taverns, and again differently by court patrons. It could, however, be suggested that the above-mentioned were not the only qualities in Hamlet which attracted attention, even though they were uniquely expressed. Hamlet's clash with life was evidently perceived through the steamy heat of rhetoric, and the duel with rapiers had much to do with the success of a performance. Neither the theme of split personality nor that of reflection, as we now understand them, could have had much influence on the play's success, but a contemporary assures us that it pleased "all," and had "come home to the vulgars Element" (Anthony Scoloker).

The popularity of the play in its first year of existence is indicated by its performance by sailors on the deck of a ship anchored off the coast of Africa. The captain recorded the event in the ship's log and noted that the performance should distract his men from idleness and licentiousness. It is hard to picture the production, but it could be suggested that the unruly crew of the "Dragon" was little interested in Hamlet's doubts and hesitations.

Almost nothing is known of the acting of Richard Burbage (1567–1619), the first actor to play Hamlet. In an elegy written in his memory, it can be read that he played "young Hamlet" half as a man crazed with love, half as "a sad lover." The role passed to Taylor, then to Betterton (1635–1710). Richard Steele remarked that Betterton played a "young man of great expectation, vivacity, and enterprise." These are, of course, general descriptions, but none of them bears any resemblance to what is now called "hamletism."

The acting of the famous English tragedian David Garrick (1717–1779) has been described by many of those who saw him. In *Tom Jones,* Fielding mocks a simplehearted spectator who considered the actor playing Claudius to be better than Garrick: he spoke louder and more clearly, so that "anyone may see he is an actor." Garrick's Hamlet was afraid of a ghost, as anyone would be, and was completely natural in his anger with the Queen, which was no surprise: "Any man, that is, any good man, that had such a mother, would have done exactly the same." Mister Partridge would hardly have thought Hamlet an utterly ordinary man —in fact, would have found him disappointing in the naturalness of his behavior—if he had recognized the tragedy of the split personality.

Mid-eighteenth-century audiences were not so much interested in the play as in the actor playing the main role. The actor played his own version; he altered the play, both cutting and expanding the text. George Winchester Stone calls Garrick's rewrite extraordinarily dynamic and "effective." The dynamism and effectiveness were achieved by cutting Hamlet's meditations. Most performers cut the monologue spoken by Hamlet after the scene with Fortinbras and the Norwegian troops. Thomas Sheridan was the first to restore it, but not from an interest in the contrast of strong and weak will. The monologue provided an opportunity for making topical allusions: there was a war in Canada. A few words in praise of shedding blood for glory and a diminutive patch of land called forth patriotic ovations. Could one imagine a treatment more alien to the idea of hamletism?

At the end of the eighteenth century, a young Russian nobleman, H. M. Karamzin, saw one of the London performances. "I saw Shakespeare's Hamlet for the first time," he wrote. "Guess which scene made the deepest impression on the audience? The one in which they dig a grave for Ophelia. . . ." Karamzin's comment was not occasioned by a poor performance. He had attended a summer production at the Haymarket Theatre, where the best actors from Drury Lane and Covent Garden were performing.

Neither in the memoirs nor in the correspondence of people of the time is there any trace of interest in the complexity of Hamlet's emotional experiences. Even passages like "To be or not to be" were oddly interpreted. That monologue was turned into a romance and set to music; it was performed with guitar accompaniment.

In his adaptation, Voltaire rewrote the monologue, substituting "religion" for "conscience." Thus, doubts as to the meaning of life were replaced by this quite lucid thought: religion does make cowards of us all. "The native hue of resolution" is sicklied o'er with the pale cast of Christian dogma.

In the second half of the eighteenth century, the play was distorted into several languages. These translations turned verse into prose, let the Prince live, and crowned Laertes in the finale. The adaptations not only did not bring out the tragedy of reflection but turned the play into a tale of revenge.

French academicians and critics were aroused by the play's destruction of the three unities and by its combination of comic with tragic. They abused its author for his lowly style and his disregard for decorum. Eventually, however, accusations of barbarism gave place to praise for naturalness.

A number of new questions arose, but the character of Hamlet was outside the general range of interest and did not inspire particular treatment. There also seemed to be no need to explain his actions within the limits of the accepted or rejected art of Shakespeare.

During this century, Hamlet was performed in French and German theatres. The success of its 1776 Hamburg première was so great that a medal was struck to commemorate it; the medal bore a portrait of Brockman as Hamlet. A sentimental, elegiac prince appeared on the stage, but not a word had yet been said in reference to hamletism in its modern sense.

Scholarship has accepted the opinion that Goethe gave new life to *Hamlet*. There are, by the way, scholars who maintain that the decisive word was pronounced by August von Schlegel in his lectures. Others refer to the letters of Friedrich von Schlegel as containing this new idea for the first time.

This word was said because the time had come to say it.

The nineteenth century revealed not only the artistic power of the play but also its depth of thought. From now on, this work was placed in another category of artistic phenomena. The Danish Prince ceased to be one of the characters of a Shakespearean tragedy, and became a uniquely significant figure.

German thinkers did not pay so much attention to the events depicted in the play as to the character of its hero. It was as though the center of action had shifted from the castle of Elsinore to the soul of Hamlet. The drama was acted out here, in the limited space of a human spirit. The work was born anew. Everything that had attracted attention before now seemed to be insignificant; other aspects suddenly proved not only interesting but vitally important.

The play acquired new meaning because the perception of the audience was new and quite different from that of previous audiences. The time was past when they put bearbaiting in the same category of entertainment as the theatre, when people stopped along the road to take in a public execution at the square as though it were some kind of performance. The violent, motley crowd that had surrounded the stage platform at the Globe had disappeared.

Hamlet was now being read by people who were of a different mold and had a new way of thinking and feeling. Their perception was different, and so was their concept of the figure of the Prince. Not only could this figure, as it now appeared, not have been portrayed by a sailor from the "dragon," but probably Richard Burbage himself would have found it difficult to understand this kind of role.

Goethe wrote of Hamlet, "A beautiful, pure, noble and most moral nature, without the strength of nerve which makes the hero, sinks beneath a burden which it can neither bear nor throw off." The elegiac Hamlet of the second half of the eighteenth century received new and highly important traits. He staggered under the weight of the burden that had fallen onto his shoulders. According to this new approach, the main point of the play was that Hamlet could neither refuse to fulfill his duty nor could he fulfill it. The story of the Danish Prince became that of a soul, beautiful and noble, but by nature incapable of action.

This understanding of the play was evinced not only by the stories about it but also by the way it was cut. Goethe put words in the mouth of Wilhelm Meister, saying that the tragedy consists of two parts, as it were. The first consists in "the grand internal relations of the persons and events"; the second, "the external relations of the persons, whereby they are taken from one place to another." He suggested that the external relations be abridged, as having little importance.

These external relations included Hamlet's struggle with Rosencrantz and Guildenstern, the banishment to England, Hamlet's study at the university. After Goethe had made his changes, the Prince was no longer a student and foreign to court life; he did not come to Elsinore only for the burial of his father, nor did he hope to return to Wittenberg. Horatio became the son of the vice-regent of Norway, instead of becoming Hamlet's university comrade. Whatever scenes mention the bravery and resolution of the hero were considered to have been written merely for "external relations" and were therefore cut. Anything that contradicted Goethe's approach was eliminated from the play.

It is difficult to attribute to weak will the theft and forgery of the

King's order. "A most moral nature, without strength of nerve" could not exult in sending childhood friends to the block. During the boarding, he was the first to leap onto the deck of the pirate ship. Of course, these scenes are not basic to the plot, but the "basic" and the "immaterial" are relative in Shakespeare's art, and the use of these terms usually characterizes the critic more than the work.

Abridgements were not only necessary to reduce the length of a performance, but equally so for the subordination of all events to the one theme: the contradiction between noble thought and inability to act heroically. For the first two centuries of its stage life, this concept of the tragedy had not arisen. Why did it come up now?

The eighteenth century came to an end. The Bastille burned; a glow of unprecedented power illuminated the skies of Europe, and went out. Nations remembered how the heads of aristocrats rocked on pikes, and how the Liberty Tree came into foliage. Populaces rose up, and the armies left. The greatest hopes gave place to the greatest disappointments. In the light of the new day, it became clear that manufacturers had erected walls more solid than those of the Bastille, and that children learned worse than feudal serfdom at factory machines. The smoke from mill chimneys swallowed up the horizon. Mores were undergoing alteration: the din of forced transition matched that of the quarries, never stopping.

Existence in the backyard of history was hideous. In cramped little German princedoms and poverty-ridden dukedoms, the structure already destroyed by history was maintained along with the junk of ancient orders. In this retarded social structure, everything had lost its meaning and became shameful and vile. Every thinking German was aware of the miserable plight of his country. The situation seemed hopeless. There was no strength in the people to enable them to revolt. Two ways out still remained to them: either great deeds or reconciliation. The latter was totally ignoble; the former demanded not only energy of thought but also a heroic will.

Engels wrote of Goethe: "There is a gradual struggle in him between the poet of genius, whom the surrounding squalor fills with loathing, and the cautious son of a Frankfurt patrician or a

Weimar secret councillor who sees that he must make peace with it and get used to it. Thus, Goethe is a colossus of greatness, and yet petty; he is now the insubordinate, derisive, contemptuous genius, now the careful, ingratiating, narrow Philistine."

These words dramatize the poet's position as a man who understands the evil of the contemporary social structure, but who is unable to strike out against its causes. And so there arose the theme of contradiction between intrepidity of thought and inability to struggle.

Goethe greeted the Danish Prince as a close friend whose mind was not only intelligible to the artist but also allied to his. The torments of the stage character could be taken as real. The life expressed in the tragedy was worthy of comparison with the Germany of the turn of the eighteenth and nineteenth centuries, rather than with sixteenth-century England. The contradiction Goethe saw in *Hamlet* was vital to most of his contemporaries, as well as to himself. The tragedy of Elizabethan Humanism was similar to this later drama. Those who aspired to the ideal of free and active man saw that their hopes could not be realized without revolt and the destruction of the bases of the present social order. But there was no real possibility of revolution yet, and furthermore, the thinkers did not have the pure strength of will necessary to rebels.

Into what, then, had the life of their noble but irresolute hero changed?

"How he winds, turns, agonizes, advances, and recoils, ever reminded, ever reminding himself, and at last almost loses his purpose from his thoughts. . . ." Thus Goethe described Hamlet. This was probably a confession as well as a literary study. The contrast of strength of mind and weakness of will was basic for whole generations in nineteenth-century Germany. The Crown Prince of Denmark became first cousin to all those who thought they had the same spiritual qualities. One moment of the play came to be a symbol—that moment when Hamlet raises his dagger over Claudius but does not find within himself the power to murder the murderer. The play became the drama of a thinker who could not effect deeds of greatness.

This definition of the play and its hero demonstrates how a proper noun can suddenly become a common one. One quality of

Hamlet proved capable of providing a name to everything that was happening in the Germany of that time, to all that existed "in a somewhat diluted form." One quality gradually became the only one. Thus, hamletism was born.

Now not only Shakespeare's *Hamlet* was matter for analysis, but also the hamletism derived by German thinkers from the reality of their day and from the individual traits of a figure that they themselves had made over.

August von Schlegel wrote, "The whole is intended to show that a consideration, which would exhaust all the relations and possible consequences of a deed to the very limits of human foresight, cripples the power of acting."

Hamletism became a designation for the reflection that substitutes argument for action.

There were periods in history when the antiquated language and costume of another era came into fashion. New ideas were then expressed in old forms. The mourning of the Danish Prince became a masquerade costume to be donned by all those who were both unable to recognize the reaction that had prevailed, and even more incapable of fighting it. They wrapped themselves up in hamletism as thought it were a raincoat, and thought themselves beautifully and becomingly dressed.

When the conversation turned to *Hamlet* (it was brought up more and more frequently), one comparison kept coming up. Comparison with a mirror. Not with the mirror of theatre which is mentioned in the play, but with a plain ordinary mirror, glass-backed with an amalgam that enables anyone who glances at it to see his own reflection. "We know this Hamlet," wrote Heine, "as well as we know our own faces from seeing them so often in the mirror. . . ."

"Had a German written *Hamlet,* I should not have wondered at the work," Boerne states in the conclusion of his article. "A German needs but a fair, legible hand. He makes a copy of himself, and *Hamlet* is done."

The idea became traditional. Gervinus analyzed the play in the name of a good number of people: "The picture that we Germans see in this mirror before us is capable of frightening us by its very resemblance. And I am not the only one to say so; thousands of people have come to an awareness of this."

The comparison sometimes smacked of hyperbole. "Yes, Germany is Hamlet!" wrote Freiligrath on the eve of the year 1848.

The simile was not only frightening because of its similarity but terrifying in its accusation. Nobility of soul gradually receded into the background, and left the forestage to the inability to do anything. All this bespoke not only one generation's vice but also the disease of a nation.

Hamletism seemed to have found a homeland and to have entered its heyday. But that's a mistake.

The other end of Europe, another time, another country. London, 1852.

"Tessié said that I have the nature of a Hamlet, and that this is very Slavic," writes Aleksandr Herzen. "Really, this is a remarkable vacillation, this inability to act from the force of thought, and these thoughts which are carried away by a desire for action before they themselves are completely formulated."[5] Here, hamletism is related to the Slavic race. It may be added that the Polish poet Mickiewicz wrote of Poland as a Hamlet.

Now the mirror reflected completely different features, although some of the Russian political journalist's terms recall those of the German critics ("vacillation," "inability to act"). In fact, the sentence as a whole does not have the German meaning, for Herzen is not concerned with thoughts that cannot be transformed into action, but with the energy of ideas and a desire to act which has raced ahead of the completion of the ideas. Vacillation—not from lack of will, but from the force of thought. But what evoked this "remarkable vacillation"?

Hamlet's name is frequently mentioned by Herzen. It is used in his correspondence and in various articles. The reminiscences in *My Past and Thoughts* are especially bound up with it: "For example, Hamlet's character is largely common to all men, particularly in an era of doubt and hesitation, in an era when they are conscious of some sort of black deeds taking place nearby, some betrayal of the great in order to serve the insignificant. . . ." Here is both a definition of the period in which *Hamlet* was written and

[5] Herzen's nickname remained in use. "My dear northern Hamlet," Tessié called Herzen, bidding him farewell at a railroad station in Paris in 1867 (A. I. Herzen, *Collected Works,* II, 511).

relative one, and Grigoriev's impartiality could be doubted. Perhaps Mochalov, in playing Hamlet, attached particular significance to that which other experts, in their turn, might consider "rags and bags."

Mochalov's Hamlet, according to this article, "was radically different from, say, the Goethe notion of Hamlet. The sad and sinister elements in Hamlet patently overwhelmed all other facets of his character. . . ." What exactly influenced such a condensation of these colors? What was it that made the sad and sinister elements become so basic?

The beginning of Russian hamletism was connected with particular characters and destinies. In the Russia of Nicholas I, men of genius did not take employment as secret counsellors, insubordination did not unite with prosperity, nor greatness with pettiness.

The première of *Hamlet* at Moscow's Petrovski Theatre took place on January 22, 1837, but the performance had been prepared long before that. It was shaped not only by the genius of the actor but by the time itself. The era had awaited its expression in art, and Shakespeare's tragedy was suitable for it.

Everything written about Mochalov should not be thought to relate only to him. He was Hamlet, and people looked at him as though into a mirror. According to descriptions written by those who saw him, Mochalov's acting could seem excessively theatrical, too stilted to be lifelike. This would be untrue. If these descriptions are compared with the artificial language of the diaries of the period, with the correspondence of a time in which people sent one another epistolary confessions long enough to fill several printed pages and replete with dramatic phraseology, then the Mochalov "vocal thunder," "sobbing," "hair standing on end," and so forth, do not seem to be entirely related to scenic space. At that time, like-minded people would hurl themselves into an embrace upon meeting, would weep on the breast of a friend, would kneel to make a vow, pale with dissatisfaction and faint from anger. There was no pose in all this. The tears were not superficial; the oaths were kept. They paid for the upsurge of feelings with consumption, and the walls of their prison hardly looked like a stage set.

Hamlet had been famous in Russia during the eighteenth century, but the spirit of those times could not be expressed in this play. The "betrayal of the great in order to serve the insignificant" could not yet have been felt with such force. But when the people who had defeated Napoleon and had freed Europe found themselves slaves once again, the betrayal became unbearable.

Five gibbets on the outworks of Petropavlovski Fortress marked the death of hopes for freedom. A time of mournful silence and angry reflection ensued. Then came interest in a character who expressed doubt and hesitation and consciousness "of some sort of black deeds, . . . some betrayal of the great in order to serve the insignificant."

It was the beginning of the 1830's.

In 1834, the journalist Polevoi wrote an unfavorable review of a performance at the Aleksandrinski Theatre in St. Petersburg. But the play, which failed to meet the critic's approval, pleased the Emperor, and his criticism was equated with rebellion. Freethinking was suppressed by the government. The *Moscow Telegraph* was shut down; its disrespect for the authorities had long been noted. They brought Polevoi from Moscow to St. Petersburg on a courier troika. The chief of the tsar's police directed the interrogation. On that day, a talented journalist perished, and a frightened and obsequious literary official, a cog in the machine of state, began his existence. Despair, disgust, and fear did not desert Polevoi until his death. Stories about selling souls to the devil are cheerful next to the tale of this man.

During those years, Polevoi began to translate *Hamlet*. He approached the Shakespearean tragedy as he would a mirror, and looked into it. What sort of face was reflected there?

"A pale man with a gloomy physiognomy," Nikitenko wrote in his diary, in description of Polevoi, "but energetic. There is something grotesque in his appearance. . . . In speech he is witty and has a sort of convulsive energy."

Both the pale gloomy face and a kind of convulsive power are manifest in the translation. The translation itself became an adaptation; not only the poetry was changed, but the very tone of the play. One of his phrases became famous:

> Afraid,
> I am afraid for man!

Belinski was enthusiastic over this cry. He wrote that, although these words were not written by Shakespeare, they were genuinely

Shakespearean, and that the author would probably not have repudiated them if he could have heard them. Nevertheless, Hamlet did not say them, nor could he have said them in his own time. They were spoken by the Russian hamletism of the 1830's.

Judging from descriptions, the force of negation and a profound sorrow were fundamental to Mochalov's acting. Sarcasm became heart-rending anguish. Mochalov's Hamlet jeered, damned, despised, and tormented himself. "In the first performances," Belinski wrote, "the interrelations of emotions had not been worked out: Independent of the poet, the actor gave Hamlet far more strength and energy than is possible for a man struggling with himself and dispirited by an unbearable burden of calamities, and he gave him far less sorrow and melancholy than Shakespeare's Hamlet ought to have." But finally, during the ninth performance, "the feeling of sorrow following from an awareness of his own weakness did not smother either bitter dissatisfaction or morbid distress, but was predominant."

The feeling of sadness had a special significance for Belinski. He wrote of melancholy as the basis of folk songs, of sorrow in the poetry of Lermontov, of the "invisible tears" of Gogol. In Belinski's opinion, this emotion was dominant in the best of contemporary Russian literature. Its prevalence was expressive of the lot of a great people whose spiritual forces were paralyzed and who could find a way out only through melancholy. But it was a particular melancholy, one which concealed the "wing-spread of an eagle" and a "proud enmity with heaven."

In Belinski's description, the scope of this melancholy was reduced by Mochalov to comedy even when his discussion concerned only gesture. In order to convey this impression more accurately, the critic had recourse to comparisons like these: ". . . making a motion with both hands as though he were pushing the weight of the entire world from himself by pure strength of will, without any physical exertion" and ". . . throwing both arms away from his body, as though he were heaving humanity from the breast to which he had once so strongly clasped it. . . ."

The sorrow of the Russian Hamlet of the 1830's was replete with somber poetry and angry power. Not only Mochalov and Belinski held this view. Much of what was written on Mochalov concerned his acting, of course, but it also concerned the concept of Hamlet which was prevalent in this generation.

In 1831, while still a youth, the poet Lermontov described to M. A. Shan-Girei Hamlet's conversation with Rosencrantz and Guildenstern about "the pipe." He concluded his letter with the words, ". . . you would wrench from me, a substance endowed with strong will, my secret thoughts, . . ." a quotation he ascribed to Hamlet. There are no such words in the tragedy. Nevertheless, Lermontov ascribed to Hamlet not only a will, but a "strong will." This is, of course, a slip of the pen, but it is not an accident. The idea was so vivid that Lermontov heard words that Hamlet did not say, but should have.

The letter was written six years before the Mochalov première.

The sense of Hamlet's energy and strength began independently of the performance. The feeling was such that when an actor of another type played the role, general opinion called him cold and stilted. Nevertheless, he was Hamlet. Under the influence of a Karatygin[6] performance, Herzen wrote in 1839: "I have just returned from *Hamlet,* and, believe it or not, not only did tears pour from my eyes, but I sobbed. . . . I came home thoroughly agitated. . . . Now I see a dark night, and a pale Hamlet displaying a skull on the tip of his sword and saying, 'Here hung those lips, and now ha-ha-ha!' You will be sick after this play." In this same letter to his wife, he called Hamlet a "frightening and great" man.

Laughter was now fundamental in the image of the Danish Prince—laughter in which hatred merged with despair. However, actors' performances had no influence on this at all. Two years before the Karatygin performance, Herzen had already heard this laughter. He wrote to N. A. Zakharina in 1837, ". . . I have read *Hamlet* ten times; each word of his breathes cold and fear. . . . And just what was the matter with him after his first despair? He began to laugh, and this laughter, hellish and horrible, continues through the whole play. The sorrow of man, laughing in a moment of sadness. . . ."

[6] Vasily Andreevich Karatygin (1802–1853), Russian tragedian. Whereas Mochalov was Moscow's most prominent tragedian at that time, Karatygin held a similar position in St. Petersburg Theatre [trans.].

The idea of a man who is able to laugh in a moment of sorrow revealed new characteristics in the image of Hamlet. His laughter echoes through the silence. This was particularly significant.

There are various kinds of silence. The silence of the thirties was imposed. Muteness betokened loyalty. They made a career out of meekness. The speechless memory, noiseless sorrow, and gagged anger were terrifying. Reason was replaced by instruction, conscience by ceremony. You were not supposed to think; just know the job. The police protected the silence, and it was guarded by sleuths; they oppressed by persecution if not by the noose, by despair if not by poverty. The governmental prison stupefied Gogol with incense, rammed a bullet into the barrel of Martynov's pistol,[7] and directed that Chaadaev be examined and recognized insane.[8]

Here, in a time of enforced muteness, a rebellious human voice began to sound with all its might, ranging from peals of thunder to a whistling whisper. There was nothing of the military command in it, nor of gallant shouts of enthusiasm, nor of the mellifluence of banal nightingales. A voice of surprising beauty said that it is useless to equate a man with a flute and that it is possible, in a state of helplessness, to laugh with startling energy at everything strong—to laugh from hatred and sorrow.

The element in this work which exercised such an unusual degree of influence during this period was the destruction of silence. Both the content of the play and its style were defiant. The gag had fallen out.

A smallish man on the stage of the Petrovski Theatre grew to an immense height. Belinski wrote that his gigantic shadow scaled the very ceiling of the auditorium. This man proved that it was possible to break away from the system, disobey the command, tear off the suffocating uniform, and refuse to be silent.

The enthusiam for Shakespeare proved to be of different kinds, and was by no means general.

Bulgarin wrote, "Now they speak only of Shakespeare, but I am of the belief that it is neither possible nor necessary to imitate

---

[7] Martynov killed the poet Lermontov in a duel [trans.].

[8] Pëtr Yakovlevich Chaadaev (c. 1794–1856), Russian intellectual leader [trans.].

Shakespeare. He should not be a pattern for our century, but only an historical relic."[9]

Pushkin urged the imitation of Shakespeare. His *Boris Godunov* was conceived "according to the system of our father Shakespeare." Pushkin thought his tragedy "genuinely romantic." There were, however, various notions of romanticism. In the "Partisan of Classicism," Shevyrëv praised Shakespeare in his own way. Here, only the Romantic props were important: daggers, serpents, the "gloom of a Gothic cathedral," etc.

> Dread Shakespeare's weapon, glazed
> In hues of deadly reptiles,
> This dagger fired in blood
> Before thee did not glitter.

In this style, the images did not reflect the phenomena of life; their associative force was destroyed. The daggers were blunted, the horrors quite safe. Romantic declamation could not end with blood from the throat, nor in a casemate. In the Russia that owned serfs, Shakespeare the "historical relic," the "romantic," was no more than a pretext for polite conversation. "That little fellow" Shakespeare was a contemporary author again, one who, in speaking of the prison that was Denmark, spoke against all states that were jails.

Five years have passed since the Mochalov première.

Polevoi's translation, which had delighted Belinski earlier ("Neither the drama nor Mochalov could have had such success with another translation"), now struck him as "a decided melodrama," "a weak reflection of Shakespeare's composition," "attracted to the myopic understanding of the crowd." Polevoi's apostasy was not the sole reason for this new attitude. Life had changed. The period of circles and their debates had come to an end; a new stage of social development had begun. It was to be an era of the commoner-intellectual, of journals, open readings. The social forces found another use for themselves. In his letters

---

[9] "Theatrical Reminiscences of Thaddeus Bulgarin," in *The Pantheon of Russian and European Theatres,* Part I (St. Petersburg, 1840).

Belinski was often dissatisfied now: "putrid reflection," stupid, weak reflection," "empty reflection."

". . . The time of Onegins and Pechorins[10] has passed," Herzen wrote in the 1850's. "Now there are no more superfluous people in Russia; to the contrary, there are not enough hands for all this tilling. Anyone now who can find nothing to do has no one to blame; in fact, he is an empty man, a nothing, or an idler. And that is why Onegin and Pechorin have become Oblomovs."

This was not the end of the process. Oblomovs began to make themselves out to be Hamlets.

The phenomenon was not only Russian. Freiligrath's verses were pamphleteering, of course, but Hamlet's name was, nevertheless, in the title. Evidently, his contemporaries found some sort of resemblance between the hero of the poem and the hero of the tragedy.

> It comes from loitering overmuch,
>> Lounging and reading—tired to death;
> Sloth holds him in its iron clutch,
>> He's grown too "fat and short of breath."
> His learning gives him little aid,
>> His boldest act is only thinking;
> Too long in Wittenberg he stayed
>> Attending lectures—maybe drinking.

From Shakespeare's abundance of detail, only one thing is retained: short-windedness. It is hard to recognize Hamlet in this hero fond of lolling in bed and holding forth in alehouses. The mirror reflects the German middle-class liberal on the eve of the Revolution of 1848.

In Russia during the 1850's, they served another drink instead of beer:

"It's evening already, and a sleepy servant is helping you on with your coat—you dress and wander round to see a friend, you smoke a pipe, you drink weak tea by the glassful and talk about German philosophy, love, the eternal sunshine of the spirit, and other abstruse topics."

This is "Hamlet of the Shchigrov District."

[10] Literary heroes who are largely characterized by egoistic and irresponsible self-indulgence [trans.].

A golden cup of sparkling wine, the poisoned cup of tragedy, is exchanged for the mug of beer, the glass of thin tea. The drink is tasteless and won't harm the health. The once exclusive character of the hero became common. It is said in Turgenev's story that "there are numbers of such Hamlets in every district, but it may be that you have not come across the others."

"Do you see, he was something on the order of Hamlet, a man whose only strength lay in fruitless reflection, but who was weak in deed by reason of his lack of will," wrote the radical critic N. G. Chernyshevski of Buerakin in Saltykov-Shchedrin's *Provincial Sketches*. "He is not the first Hamlet to appear in our literature, one of the earlier ones is even called by the name, 'Hamlet of the Shchigrov District.' By all the evidence, our Buerakin wants to be the 'Hamlet of Krutogor Province.' It seems clear that we must have more than a few Hamlets in our society, when they appear so frequently in literature. . . ."

Once rebels wrapped themselves up in Hamlet's cloak; now provincial and county Danish princes have appeared. There came to be even less similarity between Hamlet and hamletism. The nickname had totally diverged from the proper noun, taking on a development of its own. The two were united only by threads of external detail.

Neither Claudius nor any other character of the original tragedy was contrasted with Hamlet; he was compared to the hero of another work. But a like thing happened to this other one, Don Quixote. In his essay on Hamlet and Don Quixote, for example, Turgenev was really talking about hamletism and donquixotism in the forms given these concepts by contemporary reality. The dissimilarity between Hamlet and hamletism had become obvious.

Working on his *Ivanov* during the 1880's, Chekhov described his artistic intention: "I cherished a daring dream: to sum up everything that had been written up till now about whining and suffering people." Hamlet did not strike Chekhov as either whining or sniveling. While he was writing *Ivanov,* Chekhov recalled the Danish Prince frequently. His name is met in the correspondence of those months and in the play itself.

Ivanov said, "Shame at the thought that I, a strong, healthy man, have somehow become a sort of Hamlet, a Manfred, a superfluous man, is killing me. There are fools who are flattered when you call them Hamlet or a superfluous man, but to me it's an insult!" The insult lies not in resemblance to Hamlet but in toying with hamletism.

The tragedy of Elsinore could not repeat itself in the land-owners' Russia of the 1880's.

"It's time we came to our senses," Ivanov says to Sasha. "I've been playing Hamlet and you've been playing a noble-minded young girl, but I've had enough of that." Hamletism is now an act, a pose. Ivanov is an intelligent, noble person, and pretense is repulsive to him. Yet there are a number of people who, when they find themselves in an analogous position, have no objection to being "a sort of Hamlet, a Manfred, a superfluous man."

The vulgar begin to play the role exclusively; Grushnitskis give themselves out to be Pechorins.[11] Toward the end of the century, the breed of snivelers increased even further. Hamletism became a style of parody. N. Mikhailovski wrote "The Hamletized Suckling Pigs" in the 1890's. In his article, he spoke of real Hamlets and of people "who imagine themselves as such," and mocked those who thought that the whole of *Hamlet* is "a feather in the hat, velvet clothes, and beautiful melancholy." Toward the end of the article, the critic's anger spread to Hamlet himself: "Hamlet is an idler and a milquetoast, and from this angle, idlers and milquetoasts can recognize themselves in him." Anger at hamletism had turned on Hamlet.

Tragic acting had also become a subject for parody. In *Talents and Admirers*, the playwright Ostrovski presented a hard-drinking tragedian, Erast Gromilov, as he roared famous lines from *Hamlet*. The word "tragedian" had nothing to do with an actor's spiritual power: it meant preposterous overacting. The times had changed. People of the new generation could not have repeated the oath of Herzen and Ogarëv on the Vorobiëv mountains.[12] Recalling his youth in *My Past and Thoughts,* Herzen wrote that the elevation of their intellectual range saved them from vulgarity and the common life; "civic exaltation saved us." Now, civic-mindedness and exal-

[11] Both are characters of Lermontov's novel *A Hero of Our Times*. In contrast to Pechorin, Grushnitski is a fanatic for petty, cheap romanticism [trans.].

[12] Youthful vows to sacrifice their lives to their chosen struggle against forces they could not as yet fully define [trans.].

tation had nothing to do with one another. The era of vaulting words had come to an end. "No beautiful talk," growled Bazarov. This was their aesthetic program.

Once the whisper of Mochalov had shaken Belinski; now Chekhov wrote in a review: "Ivanov-Kozelski hisses like a silly country gander." The difference between these actors consisted not only in the degree of their talent but also in the relevance of their Hamlets to reality. A sibilant whisper and "vocal thunder" could no longer express the phenomena of life.

A feather in the hat, velvet clothes, and beautiful melancholy, all of which were so thoroughly treated by the critics of the second half of the nineteenth century, had nothing in common with Shakespearean description. Hamlet's doublet was unbraced, his stockings were fouled and falling about his ankles, his expression wild. The beautifying of the Prince was a product of French hamletism.

When it came to Hamlet even Arthur Rimbaud, who found poetry in a search for lice, called him "the pale cavalier." He appeared as such on the stage. Critics celebrated his beret with its ostrich plumes, the velvet of his costume, and even the silk handkerchief with which he wrapped his hand before picking up the skull from the ground. Elegance and picturesque posing had become a tradition.

Women began to play Hamlet.

Between 1834 and 1843, Eugène Delacroix published a series of illustrations to the tragedy. In the artist's portrayal of him, the Prince is young, delicate, beautiful in his pensiveness. His pale face is stamped with something impractical; it is not distorted with passion in either the closet scene or in the springing of the "mousetrap." He seems either hypnotized or lunatic, and caught in a moment of paroxysm. Shakespeare's Hamlet bantered with the gravedigger; the Hamlet of Delacroix passed the gravedigger in silence without so much as looking at him. Yorick's fate seemed to interest no one but Horatio; in the etching it was not Hamlet that examined the fool's skull, but his friend from the university. In the last pictures, executed during the 1850's, the hero's gestures became unnatural and pretentious. This was not a Shakespearean figure, but more like a concentration of sensations that were evoked by the tragedy, or more accurately by one of its aspects, the melancholy of the protagonist.

The influence of these illustrations was so great that Romantic critics did not judge performances by the text of the play, but by the representation of it by Delacroix. Baudelaire and Théophile Gautier wrote at more length about the correspondence of the actor Rouvière's Hamlet with the Delacroix version than they did about its relation to the Shakespearean one.

A concept of a certain role can be understood by what cuts were made in the character's lines. Figuratively speaking, Delacroix cut passion, sarcasm, coarseness, and even wit from the role of Hamlet. Only one quality remained. A generation was marked by it.

"It was a degeneration of all things of heaven and of earth that might be termed disenchantment, or if you preferred, despair," wrote Musset in *The Confession of a Child of the Century,* "as if humanity in lethargy had been pronounced dead by those who held its pulse, . . . the terrible despair paced quickly around the earth, . . . spirits who were too weak to struggle and suffer withered like broken flowers."

This was not only the death of old illusions, but also the affirmation of the impossibility of hope. Decadence ensued.

Hamlet, around 1890, was a familiar figure—so familiar, indeed, that he lived intimately with the artists and their public. The characters of the symbolist novels of that time always owe something to this melancholy figure. . . . Their meditations are Hamlet's meditations, and poets soliloquize in graveyards by the sea as he did during the Renaissance. In very long novels, as in very short lyrics, the men of today express their understanding of the world and their inability to change. . . . There is for modern man no reason for acting unless it be out of despair.[13]

Mighty historic events shook the world. Humanity did not forget the treachery of the Revolution of 1848, the rout at Sedan, the storm of heaven by the communards. The death bells groaned heavily once more, and for many years the blood did not dry on the walls of the cemetery of Père Lachaise. The betrayal of the great in order to serve the insignificant took on an unprecedented

[13] René Taupin, "The Myth of Hamlet in Mallarmé's Generation," *Modern Language Quarterly,* XIV, 439.

scale. For those who were inimical to the popular struggle, or who did not understand its meanings and were afraid of its forms, everything seemed to have perished in a maelstrom from which there could be no escape.

The man standing at the edge of a grave, studying the gaping holes that are the eye-sockets of a skull, overshadowed the content of the tragedy. *Hamlet* is a poem of death, wrote Théophile Gautier; it is a drama of existence in a real world.

In the words of the drama critic Lunacharski, Gustave Salvini (the son of Tomaso) was "a monumental mourner for the destiny of man. The gigantic black shadow of the Danish Prince, tear-stained and stooped over Yorick's skull, melted the whole hall and projected himself through a megaphone of melancholy out into the space of worlds. Words, like the strokes of a funeral bell, like a requiem hymn for all hope. . . ."

Hamletism came into fashion. Mystic clarity became boulevardier banality. In the tourist bars in Montmartre, they sat on coffins to drink and threw their cigarette butts into a skull. New words were formed, and appeared in the jargon of the bohemian quarters: "hamletomania," "hamletomaniac," "to hamletize." One scholar has listed several dozens of these little words.

The word "crisis" adhered to the tragedy. Most studies maintained that *Hamlet* is the crisis of reason, of faith, of knowledge, of hope. Some sort of universal crisis.

The "to be" was small and barely pronounced; the "not to be" grew vast and contentious. The play became a symbol of the ruin of European culture. Everything became a hieroglyph: the book was the futility of knowledge, Yorick's skull was the sum total of hopes, and the ghost was the abyss into which humanity was falling. These associations grew so complex that they could in no way have originated from Shakespeare's text. This troubled no one. The word was seen as a cipher which concealed an idea having little to do with what was directly perceived on the page. There began a period of search for the secret meaning of every phrase. Everything seemed vague, insecure. The ordinary theses obtained by reason no longer existed. In the opinion of the scholars and artists of the modernist trend, Shakespeare did not write in images, but in code.

Hamletism became hyperbole. Shaken by life's contradictions

and unable to see any escape from them, poets, philosophers, and scholars used Hamlet as a symbol of European culture as a whole, and, with his help, they mourned its demise.

"Today, from an immense platform that stretches from Basel to Cologne and that reaches the sands of Nieuport, the marshes of the Somme, the hilltops of Champagne and the granites of Alsace, our European Hamlet contemplates millions of spectres," wrote Paul Valéry after the First World War.

Psychoanalysis added the oedipus complex to hamletism. They discovered a real psychological illness in the hero: the shock had been caused by news of the incestuous love of his mother and uncle. Pessimism was given its most extreme expression: it was not the time that was sick, as Shakespeare had conceived it, but the human soul, mutilated by a pathological subconscious. The ailment was diagnosed as resulting not from the infamy of Claudius's reign, but from displaced desire, whose dark processes had oppressed the man since the dreams of childhood.

In 1942, the Sadler's Wells ballet troupe performed *Hamlet* in London, using Tchaikovsky's music. They began with the funeral: like delirious ravings, the action swept past in Hamlet's subconscious at the moment of death. The set was constructed of deformed fragments of real figures. A huge warped hand was transfixed by a dagger that grew out of the columns. A devil, running and holding a sword in its hand, covered the backdrop. A perspective of doors withdrew strangely into infinity. Wispy clouds scudded over staircases that led off into regions unknown. In black tights, silver-buckled, with a paw piercing a heart, wearing a large cross on his chest, and with a whitened emaciated face and gaping eyes, the Prince himself was an apparition from a surrealistic nightmare.

The performance summed up all previous productions, incorporating their contributions to the development of hamletism. It was not by chance that the last phantom of hamletism appeared in Europe, where the ruins of bombed buildings were still growing blacker and air alerts still screamed in the night. Never did the possibility of the destruction of European civilization seem so real. One who saw only this infinity of ruin would not wish to turn to Shakespeare's Hamlet, but rather to the specter that symbolizes his feeling of endlessness, horror, and despair.

This was the end of the fixed tradition. It had been so distinct a phenomenon that, in an article on *Hamlet,* one of the English encyclopedias wrote:

As a result of the literary criticism of the Romantic period, Hamlet came to be regarded as the prototype of the modern introspective man, the first outstanding representative of this psychological phenomenon in a development which culminated in the 19th-century decadents.[14]

. . . The nickname had gone its way after separating from the proper noun. Now it even began to express phenomena which were totally opposed to the thinking of the author of the original.

This was one of the developments of hamletism. Of course, I just speak of hamletism: contemporary English theatre is far from being defined by the ballet production. John Gielgud, Laurence Olivier, and Paul Scofield (whom we saw recently when his tour brought him to Moscow in Peter Brook's brilliant production) found entirely different qualities in Hamlet. Characteristics varied; time changed concepts; and with the years one actor will change his understanding of the role.

In our country, the play—once written for the popular stage—returned to the popular stage. The theatre now had an unlimited house; millions of people saw the tragedy. The profundity of the play could be appreciated by more than the chosen few, for culture had come to belong to all of the people.

Nevertheless, Shakespeare as read by Pushkin, Goethe, Edmund Kean, Mochalov, Stendhal, and Belinski has not been forgotten. But human knowledge does not come about by a process like laying bricks on top of one another, nor is the study of Shakespeare like the gradual erection of a brick wall. We achieve knowledge in conflict and struggle. Culture was battled for. The fight for Shakespeare always seemed to be a skirmish of the progressive with the backward. With Hamlet's help, there were calls to revolt; but others tried to turn the same play into reactionary propaganda. Hamletism was one of the forms taken by these melees, one of the costumes worn in the masquerade of ideas, of which Marx wrote. History records that Luther disguised himself as the apostle Paul, that Cromwell spoke in Old Testament language, and that the French Revolution draped itself in a Roman

[14] *The Reader's Encyclopedia,* William Rose Benét, ed. (London, 1948), p. 476.

toga. Thus, in the words of Marx, originated ideals and artistic forms, and illusions that concealed how limited was the goal of the struggle.

When illusions faced bankruptcy, Hamlet's mourning sometimes came into fashion. He costumed himself in feudal Danish, either as a challenge to the full dress of triumphant reaction or as a lament for humanity. Herzen wrote that there were donquixotes of revolution and of reaction; he was not discussing the Cervantes character, but the concept of donquixotism. It was the same with hamletism.

Now the black cloak is rotted and its threads unravelled. Ideas no longer needed this masquerade, or any masquerade. There was a definitive goal, whose strength was not in illusion but in truth. The time for costuming ideas had come to a close.

Hamlet lives on as a great artistic work. Art and scholarship not only do not limit themselves to defining the tragedy in terms of a single theme, but, to the contrary, work to expose the depth and diversity of its vital content. Among Hamlet's traits are included a complex attitude in relation to the reality of his time, and sorrow at not finding reasonable attitudes in life and at knowing that he could not. His feelings are noble; his thoughts soar. But his grief also entails discrepancy of action. Every era interprets the discrepancies in its own way.

Recently discovered was the diary of Ula Gromova, a young Communist executed by the Nazis. There is an entry on one page which reads: "I must be cruel only to be kind (Shakespeare, *Hamlet*)."

The heroine of Fadeev's novel *Young Guard* reaffirmed the conceptual depth of Shakespeare's thought by her own life.

This is a new chapter of man's reading of the Shakespearean tragedy.

The man who gave too large a swinge
to his owne wit

DAGGER-WORDS

Before the closet scene, Hamlet states that no matter how great his anger, he will not use a dagger against his mother but will use them in the words he speaks to her.

The Queen of Denmark, whom rebellion could not frighten, drops to her knees before her son and begs him to be silent. She has not the courage to hear him out or to bear those words.

Shakespeare looks for a comparison that will give a precise rendering of the force of Hamlet's words. He likens them to a mirror capable of reflecting the invisible. The simile applies: Gertrude beholds an accurate reflection of her soul's innermost part. She is not only aware of her crime, but her concept of it is so distinct that she can even discern the color of her shame. The notion of conscience is condensed to a material phenomenon, and can be looked at like an object.

The words compel eyes to turn in their sockets and look at conscience; the clarity of sight is an agony worse than the most excruciating pain. The mother asks but one thing of her son: not to speak.

> O Hamlet, speak no more.
> Thou turn'st mine eyes into my very soul,
> And there I see such black and grainèd spots
> As will not leave their tinct.

In the original, real spots appear to Gertrude's spiritual vision; black, deeply embedded, colorfast.

The words have cleft Gertrude's heart "in twain."

One does not have to say that these words are heard, apprehended, and taken into the consciousness. All this fails to express the character of their action precisely. The verbal weapons pierce the flesh, stabbing and slicing. Physical pain compels Gertrude to see the same thing her son had seen. Wounded by his words, she entreats,

> Oh, speak to me no more,
> These words like daggers enter in my ears.
> No more, sweet Hamlet!

The image of verbal daggers is like a clot of the essence of Hamlet's poetry, of a poetry at once amazingly complex and utterly simple. It is complex because Shakespeare strives to penetrate the unseen processes of history and the invisible movement of the human spirit. Its simplicity lies in the conversion of invisible into visible.

Scholars have for a long time noticed the concreteness of

Shakespeare's imagination. As early as the eighteenth century, Thomas Gray wrote, "Every word in him is a picture." The pictures are bound up with the phenomena of everyday life.

> I grant I never saw a goddess go,
> My mistress, when she walks, treads on the ground.[15]

Hamlet walks on the ground; he has keen sight and sharp hearing. Before his eyes is life. To whatever unknown distances thought may strive, it is limited by the real. The ideas that seem most abstract arise from simple life situations, and are expressed in an imagery of the commonplace. The simple is made complex, but the complex is revealed through the simple.

The meaning of the "To be or not to be" monologue has been a topic for debate for generations. The passage was frequently considered an example of abstract thought. Scholars sought its philosophic subtext with so much diligence that they sometimes forgot the text itself. Later, the nature of the thinking was inferred from rhetoric. Hamlet's discourses on life and death were attributed to the pedagogic achievements of the Stratford school, where Shakespeare studied his rhetoric: six hours a week of Greek rhetoric, and eight hours of Roman.

Professor Donald Clark of Columbia University wrote that this monologue is an example of formal thought and that the very question "Which is higher, to be or not to be?" is merely an exercise on a set theme, which was not unusual for lessons in rhetoric. He concludes that only an understanding of the total abstractness of the topic—formal thesis, antithesis, and arguments—makes it possible to determine the meaning and place of the monologue.

I find it hard to agree with this.

Of course, the tradition of Seneca, court speeches, church sermons, and rules of Cicero are all important for an understanding of the literary soil of the Elizabethan period, but the whole point is that Shakespeare's art was not restricted to this, but rose high above it. Hamlet's words resound not with conventional rhetorics, but with the intonation of life itself. The ancient "slings and arrows of outrageous fortune" of the first lines of the monologue are explained by pictures of the rule of the unworthy over

[15] Sonnet 130.

the worthy, the oppressor's wrong, the proud man's scorn, the pangs of rejected love. These are not the figures of eloquence for Hamlet, but that which he experiences himself. And Shakespeare specified it all, down to the daily "law's delay" and "insolence of office." Only the uncertainty of the existence after death compels man to "fardels bear,/ To grunt and sweat under a weary life."

A court of law, officials, heavy burden, sweat . . . Dull and cheerless days go by in Shakespeare's poetry. The shadow of prison bars had fallen over life. The world is like that prison: it has a number of confines, wards, and dungeons; it is a model penal institution. Denmark is the worst of them all; jail breaks are impossible here. Death does not come like the legendary skeleton with his scythe; it resembles, rather, an employee of the Commission of Corrections. "This fell sergeant, death, is strict in his arrest."

Artists who illustrate the play display particular enthusiasm in portraying Hamlet with a skull in his hand. The symbol is suggestive in itself: the man seems to be gazing into the limitless depth of nonexistence. However, everything that happens in the graveyard is at variance with the symbol. Even the skull in Hamlet's hands is not a vague symbol of death, nor simply nondescript "remains," but the skull of the jester who used to live in the castle of the dead King.

When he was a child, the Prince used to play with this fool. The fool gave the little boy piggyback rides, and the child kissed him. We know his name: Yorick. He sang couplets, tumbled, made puns. Once he played a spiteful trick on the gravedigger, doused him with wine—more specifically, he emptied a flagon of Rhenish over the man's head. His corpse had lain in the ground for twenty-three years and had rotted, leaving only the skull. They had just tossed it out of the grave; it was packed with clay and smelled foul.

And that's all. There was nothing more to say about him. The human substance had disappeared. Only the attributes of a skull remained.

This is developed by the poetry. The gravedigger throws other skulls up from out of the earth too, and they look like the remains of Yorick. There is no difference among them, but how very different is all that has disappeared.

Hamlet tries to describe the qualities that have vanished. He gazes at a skull, or, more accurately, listens closely. The portrait of the dead man arises in the sound of a voice, in its intonation. The death's head seems to begin a worldly conversation. Hamlet hears the streamlined trifles distinctly: "Good morrow, sweet lord! How dost thou, good lord?" The courtier-skull praises the horse of another amiable courtier, counting on being made a present of it.

And here is another. His portrait is evoked by a different poetry. Hamlet suggests that this dead one might have been a lawyer. The rasping voice of a pettifogger is heard. Subterfuge, casuistry.

There is still another skull in front of Hamlet. Terminology alone sketches this third portrait. The poetry includes specialized expressions in its vocabulary: "his statutes, his recognizances, his fines, his double vouchers, his recoveries." This is the skull of a land speculator.

The portraits are drawn by vitality of intonation and an air of the professional lexicon. Shakespeare's subtext is one with his text. His images are not costumes for ideas, but are their very flesh; they are always solid.

"We all live in the universe—this we should not forget," wrote the poet Marshak, "but aside from that, we each have a simpler and more definite address: a country, a province, a city, a street, a building, an apartment. The presence of so precise an address may serve as a criterion by which original poetry is distinguished from the pretentious and artificial."

The poetry of Shakespeare always has an address. Students of the Shakespearean lexicon long ago turned their attention to the poet's weakness for the unpoetic phrase. The eighteenth century crossed them out; they were too low, too obscene for the sublimity of tragedy.

Caroline Spurgeon grouped the metaphors most frequently met in Hamlet's speeches. They refer to gardening and truck-farming, food and drink, disease and medicine, the hunt, sports, jurisprudence, fortifications, and the ordinary affairs of soldiers, prisoners, vagabonds, actors, carpenters, and gravediggers. Hamlet knows how they till the soil, build cities, make war on land and sea. He expresses the most complicated ideas in the imagery of everyday existence.

Daily life had broken its normal stride. A distortion of social and personal relations revealed itself to Hamlet. He sees a world that is reminiscent of a neglected kitchen garden where everything that was living and fruitful has been destroyed. It is ruled by the lewd, deceitful, and base. It is a world of dissonance.

The theme of death, basic in the tragedy, begins well before the graveyard scene. The smell of corruption emanates from more than Yorick's skull. Marcellus's words, "Something is rotten in the state of Denmark," have been justly cited many times; the words are important. The state-prison is decaying.

Metaphors concerning gangrene, putrefaction, and decomposition fill the tragedy. Students of poetic imagery point out that the notion of sickness as leading to death and decay is dominant in *Hamlet*. The disease is not visible. A number of similes contrast events with an internal tumor that is growing and is killing the organism, but that does not yet show.

"The fatness of these pursy times" proves the time to be an adipose loafer. It is an unhealthy obesity; it is already hard to breathe, and the heart does not beat easily or steadily.

Time is not an abstract idea in Shakespeare; it is, rather, an aggregate of circumstances.

Everything has fallen off its track, moral bonds and political attitudes. All the circumstances of life have been turned inside out. The era has abruptly swung off the road. Things have become unhealthy and unnatural—like a dislocation.

The damage hit everything.

People were possessed by base carnal principles. Infamy of action hid under lying words that Shakespeare calls painted. Claudius says, "The harlot's cheek, beautied with plastering art,/ Is not more ugly to the thing that helps it/ Than is my deed to my most painted word." Genuine life is concealed by the plastering art. If the retouching is removed, it becomes evident that the heart of events is surprisingly uncomplicated and ordinary. Spirituality and sincerity are only painted words, but in reality everything is simple, simpler than with animals.

Gertrude forgot her first husband two months after his death: "A beast that wants discourse of reason/ Would have mourned longer. . . ." But even this simile strikes Hamlet as complicated and high-sounding, so he seeks one more graphic and usual: The

Queen remarried ". . . ere those shoes were old/ With which she followed my poor father's body,/ Like Niobe all tears." Niobe's grief was conveyed by make-up, but feminine loyalty had, in fact, less durability than the soles of feminine shoes.

The new marriage followed so swiftly, because of "Thrift, thrift. . . . The funeral baked meats/ Did coldly furnish forth the marriage tables." The haste was occasioned by economic considerations merely: the food would go bad, so they sped up the wedding feast. The desire to provide refreshments more cheaply was stronger than conscience.

Comparisons are influential in their contrast. The confronting of Niobe's picturesque tears with the soles that haven't worn through yet destroys the polar opposition of high and low style. Falsehood is manifest in apparently lofty forms, and a true situation is particularly prosaic. In this lies the artistic significance of a number of the metaphors that express Hamlet's ideas. Everything in the kingdom, from the concept of power to that of morals, is reduced in these comparisons to the physiological simplicity of animal instincts or street ribaldry.

The overthrow of government effected by Claudius is an ordinary criminal act; it is not even a seizure of power, but petty larceny. The crown of Denmark, the symbol of supreme power, is only a valuable object for a king like Claudius, something which can be stolen like any other thing if it lies within reach. Filch it, see if you can't scalp someone for it later. Hamlet tries to express this as clearly as he can, delineating Claudius's idea of the nature of power. Gertrude's second husband is "A cutpurse of the empire and the rule,/ That from a shelf the precious diadem stole/ And put it in his pocket!"

At one time, clergymen placed the crown on a ruler's head, and his person became inviolable. Now a thief pinches the crown, and pops it into his pocket, where it sits with tobacco, a well-made knife, and an unpaid tavern bill. What had occurred was not a coup d'état, but a rub-out.

The poetry reduces the prosy metaphor to parody—but a tragic parody, since its subject consists in the vital relationships so important to Hamlet.

"What have I done that thou darest wag thy tongue/ In noise so rude against me?" asks Gertrude. Hamlet answers that her deed

". . . from the body of contraction plucks/ The very soul, and sweet religion makes/ A rhapsody of words."

Human relations have become soulless. In *King Lear,* the Duke of Albany says life is moving toward such a pass that "humanity will perforce prey on itself, like monsters of the deep." The society portrayed in *Hamlet* is frightening neither by its resemblance to the savage existence of beasts of prey nor by the particular cruelty of bloodthirsty fiends, but by its callous emptiness. The noble and the spiritual have vanished from life. It is not bestial crimes that arouse horror; it is normal human relations which have lost their humanity.

Painted words create no more than a semblance of humanity and nobility; it is all a lie. In order to expose it, Hamlet fights the make-up with boundless physiological coarseness. He tells the Queen that her marriage is lechery in a nasty sty. The son yells at his mother that she is living in the rank sweat of a sold bed, greasy with debauchery. A gentleman converses with the maiden he loves as though she were a slut from a cheap joint.

Hamlet wants to make people stop lying. He proves the lie in all human relations, and shows people the abomination of life deprived of soul. He is convinced that this kind of existence continues only because the habit of lying entails the loss of natural feelings. It is as though people have lost their sense of touch.

If Gertrude had retained a single human emotion, then it could not have sanctioned the exchange of past love for present. No one sense could prefer Claudius:

> Eyes without feeling, feeling without sight,
> Ears without hands or eyes, smelling sans all,
> Or but a sickly part of one true sense
> Could not so mope.

Hamlet's purpose is to awaken those feelings that have fallen asleep, to melt his mother's heart by the ardor of his image: "If damnèd custom have not brassed it so/ That it be proof and bulwark against sense." He forces her to see and hear; he revives her conscience and kindles her imagination.

He introduces into his hyperbole the trite, the bestial, and the disreputable.

Neither his words nor his appearance indulge in pointless

poetic adornments. Until the start of the events dramatized in the play, he was "the glass of fashion." Now, as Ophelia puts it, he goes about in an unbraced doublet, without a hat, fouled stockings and those "ungartered and down-gyved to his ankle." Claudius tells Rosencrantz and Guildenstern that Hamlet has changed so that ". . . nor the exterior nor the inward man/ Resembles that it was." Gertrude speaks of "my too-much-changèd son." Hamlet feigns a gloomy sort of madness: "Grating so harshly all his days of quiet/ With turbulent and dangerous lunacy." His conduct not only lacks graceful manners, but is characterized by their contrary, a desire to annihilate etiquette and to insult the court by acerbity of thought and tone.

The figure fascinates despite notions of its youthful grace and attractive appearance. It is possible not to credit too much significance to mentions of his thirty years, his corpulence, and his short wind. These are mere phrases occurring separately, but to consider them nonexistent and irrelevant to the author's conception of Hamlet is hardly reasonable.

In Hamlet's grief, there is nothing to please the eyes or ears. He despises the ostentation of "the trappings and the suits of woe"; it is all simply fraud, "show." His notorious mourning black pertains little to his unchanging sorrow. It would be possible to risk an unexpected comparison here: the "inky cloak" is somehow reminiscent of the woman's yellow jacket affected by the young Mayakovsky. Hamlet offends court custom: he infuriates his associates by appearing at court receptions inappropriately attired. His mourning was never external and graphic. The mourner uses his black, rather, to raise cain in the chambers of Elsinore and to be rude to the King.

He curses himself as a rogue and slave, a scullion.

Once he gave Ophelia not only gifts but ". . . words of so sweet breath composed/ As made the things more rich." Now he despises these words. As his situation grows more tragic, his speeches become more cutting.

"The whole ghost scene in *Hamlet* is written with humor, even in an ignoble style, but Hamlet's jokes make your hair stand on end," said Pushkin. In many passages, the poetry of Hamlet's part is not separable from the low, popular style that nonetheless expresses the weightiest thought and the very sense of tragedy. Despising make-up and painted words, Hamlet resembled nothing so little as a magnificent prince in elegant dress.

Both Edmund Kean and Pavel Mochalov sensed this. The several contemporary critical reproaches regarding "ignoble manner" and "the absense of greatness" did not concern the natural qualities of the actors at all, but their interpretation of the role. These artists sought strength, acuity, and a rebellious spirit in their hero. Both Kemble, the celebrated performer of "noble Romans," and Karatygin, the tragedian of the palace guard, played with a full measure of beautiful manners and courtly elegance. Theirs was not the victory.

The role of Hamlet was first created under an open sky on the sideshow stage of an era still quite crude. London apprentices, draymen, sailors on leave, and farmers in the big city all laughed at Hamlet's jokes and sympathized with his feelings. This was a character who was understood and appreciated not only by the connoisseurs but by all those who stood on the three sides of the Globe stage.

In the very beginning of the seventeenth century, Anthony Scoloker wrote of the two paths of art: "It should be like the *Never-too-well read Arcadia,* where the *Prose* and *Verse* (*Matter* and *Words*) are like his *Mistresses* eyes, one still excelling another and without Corivall: or to come home to the vulgars *Element,* like *Friendly Shakespeare's Tragedies.*"

The refined charm of Sir Philip Sidney's poetry was opposed to the art of Shakespeare, which pleased "all, like Prince Hamlet."

The word "poetry" has a number of meanings. One dictionary defines it as "the gift of renouncing the basics of life to create prototypes of beauty." Shakespeare did not have this gift. He never rejected the vital; in this consisted one of the characteristics of his genius. The poetry of Hamlet grew out of everyday prose, stripped of ornament, often coarse and cruel as well as merely severe. Hamlet is a popular figure of a man who speaks truth in "words like daggers."

THE SHADE OF HIS FATHER

Hamlet's character is revealed not only in the tension of tragic conflict, but in usual daily relations with people.

Until the reason for the arrival of Rosencrantz and Guildenstern becomes obvious to him, Hamlet is affable and benevolent, and sincerely pleased to see his childhood friends.

Greeting the actors, he is a kind and hospitable host, a princely patron fascinated by the theatre. An amateur actor himself, he readily declaims a monologue from "Priam's slaughter." These pompous speeches from a play in the classical spirit are precisely what pleases him; they flop with the public at large, but are valued by connoisseurs.

To Ophelia he dedicated mediocre verse, verse written by one who has "not the art to reckon my groans."

He laughs, besides going through suffering and anger. Childish games are still remembered, and the rules of sport are familiar: he practices his fencing tirelessly. Proverbs and popular riddles populate his speeches. He is absorbed by the wisecracks of a slightly tipsy gravedigger and, forgetting worldly concerns, he willingly listens to the clown's jokes about how a prince was sent to England because of his madness.

At a frightening moment, he remembers his notebook—from his student's custom of writing down observations, impressions, and sayings from books.

He loves his father, is capable of friendship. He is a man, a man without any mysterious capital letters, just a man with a clear biography, human habits, a human tenor of life. His thoughts are concerned with news of the theatres of the capital, as well as with questions of good and evil. The role includes a number of quite ordinary characteristics. There are sufficient grounds for considering the hero's character realistically conceived. But could one contend that Hamlet is "a typical character in typical circumstances," following Engels' definition?

It is not easy to apply this kind of criterion to the tragedy; difficulties arise at once. To what degree is Hamlet typical of Denmark, a country about which Shakespeare had only the roughest notion? And how can one consider typical of the twelfth century (the time of the action, judging by the sources) the student of a university not founded until three centuries later? It is easier, of course, to imagine Hamlet in Elizabethan England. But then the circumstances do not seem typical. To begin at the beginning: How can the appearance of a ghost be considered typical? Can the tale of the specter be attributed to a world of typical circumstances, this story of his murder by a brother who poured poison into "the porches of my ears"? Does this really sound like normal events? Could it be taken as a reflection of reality?

The Ghost thrust a mote into "the mind's eye" of Horatio—and of everyone who tries to measure the play with the help of the usual yardsticks of realism. They have tried to remove the mote in the widest variety of ways. They excused the author by reason of the barbarism of old tastes and by the rules of the genre. Later, in our century, they proved that the Ghost was not a ghost at all, but something else. Scholars and artists of various tendencies sought the possibility of a modern treatment of this figure. By "modern" was understood the ideas of the new era, in which people not only do not believe in ghosts but consider this kind of belief naïvely archaic.

The ghost of Hamlet's father became like a puzzle rebus in which something is drawn which, at first glance, looks like a ghost though it is really something completely different. This other thing is not hard to find; you only have to turn the picture upside down or stare fixedly at some apparently nonexistent part of it. Just do that, and the contours will change: the form of a hunter will emerge from the leaves, and the house turns out not to have been a house at all, but a doe. The transformation of a ghost into an analogy of this kind of picture probably began from the notion that a genius could not have seriously believed in ghosts, so that everything in the scene where the dead King appears evidently has a special meaning.

Gervinus had already noted that only one man in the play sees ghosts; this is true of *Julius Caesar* and *Macbeth* as well as of *Hamlet*. Only the hero associated with phantoms, and he is about to start having hallucinations anyway. The even-tempered Gertrude sees no dead husbands, and Lady Macbeth does not notice Banquo's ghost. According to the theory of Gervinus, the ghosts are not characters, but the result of delirium; they are only seen by someone who is predisposed to extreme forms of ecstasy.

Different parts of the puzzle picture are subjected to intent scrutiny.

Dover Wilson, a most formidable modern Shakespearologist, acknowledged his debt to Walter Greg's article "Hamlet's Hallucinations" for much of his own book on *Hamlet*. Dr. Greg, whose

article was the first attack on the usual explanations of the story of
the Danish Prince, was particularly interested in the pantomime
that begins the performance of the wandering players: Having seen
all the details of the poisoning in the garden as portrayed by the
dumb show, Claudius remained completely calm, his conscience in
no way troubled. Everything that made him leap from his chair
later and run out of the hall, produced no impression on him.
What is the solution? Greg simply proposes that Claudius did not
commit the crime. The King's embarrassment during the performance was not caused by his memories but by the unseemly
behavior of the heir to the throne. The Prince, psychologically ill,
had once seen *The Murder of Gonzago*. The scene of the poisoning of a sleeping man had remained in his subconscious, so
that Hamlet imagined that something along those lines had been
committed by his incestuous uncle. The picture was turned upside
down, and they discovered that the tragedy was grounded not on
events in the kingdom of Denmark but on incest.

Nevertheless, the ghost did appear on the stage, and Claudius
himself admitted his guilt. Considering this admission, the plot
became inconsistent. The ends do not meet in any way. But this,
too, was explained. Shakespeare wrote both for connoisseurs and
for the crowd, but—in Greg's opinion—since the apprentices and
sailors only paid their money for ghosts and melodrama, a performance without the participation of a ghost would not have been
good box office. Shakespeare tipped off the connoisseurs that the
ghost was a hallucination, but the London rabble was entertained
by these coarse effects.

A similar treatment was given *Hamlet* in the theatre. On the
stage of the Second Moscow Art Theatre stood Mikhail Chekhov's
unsteady Hamlet. The spotlight illumined his pale face and closed
eyes as he spoke the lines, both his and the ghost's, in delirium. All
this could not agree with what Hamlet says to Gertrude:

> My pulse, as yours, doth temperately keep time,
> And makes as healthful music. It is not madness
> That I have uttered. Bring me to the test
> And I the matter will reword, which madness
> Would gambol from. Mother, for love of grace,
> Lay not that flattering unction to your soul,
> That not your trespass but my madness speaks.

Such treatments sprang from a desire to play with the idea, as though life's misfortunes were hidden and still hide in the cache of a single soul, and not in the conditions of social existence. In this kind of interpretation, not only does the ghost disappear from the tragedy, but Denmark ceases to resemble a prison.

The ghost has been frequently subjected to symbolic deciphering. In him is expressed an abyss, fate, the elicited secret of being. In such conjectures, there are not so many real achievements as there are curiosities, later to be gaily quoted by serious students who wished to enliven dry scholarly material.

During the 1930's, books and articles appeared with the announcement that the quest for depth of content was antiquated. They found nothing in the play save an effective plot, which revolved around a struggle for power. In all this, Shakespeare was included in the role of an Elizabethan play-scribbler who wrote plays, using the clichés then current, for a few pounds. Often enough, one was able to read that nineteenth-century philosophers and poets invented all those things of which the actor from Stratford had never thought.

Now an explanation revealed itself without any difficulty.

In an old performance at the Vakhtangov Theatre, the ghost was replaced by Horatio, who shouted into an earthenware pot (for an ominous sound-effect) words that Hamlet had written himself; rumors of ghosts should frighten Claudius and his supporters.

All this is worth recalling not in order to pick an argument with works written many years ago (their authors probably have different ideas now), but rather as hypotheses examined by time. It all points out that Shakespeare's art is not a puzzle picture, and if his play is turned upside down (the way one does with a rebus), the result is not a new picture but chaos of line and confusion of form.

The discovery of a new meaning was not aided by the careful study of separate, albeit definitive, sentences, or situations. A number of such definitive passages have come up, but when taken separately, they contradict one another.

Supporters of the "box office" theory have not yet managed to count up the profits of Burbage's company or to establish that plays without ghosts (*Romeo and Juliet, Othello*) brought less income than performances with ghosts. As regards the appearances of ghosts only in the minds of mentally ill protagonists, other scholars have stated quite reasonably that even experienced psychiatrists do not specify what complex afflicted Marcellus, who saw the ghost just as distinctly as Hamlet.

It must be said that, if one analyzes the play rationalistically, it is not difficult to arrive at the conclusion that the role of the ghost is not so very significant. It would seem, moreover, that the role could simply be cut. However blasphemous the proposal might seem, it is entirely possible to imagine all the events in the tragedy without any participation of a ghost.

At first glance, nothing substantial would be lost by cutting the part. Hamlet's spiritual tragedy is prepared in the first scene; two blows have already hit him—the death of his father and the hasty marriage of his mother. Reality itself has opened the young Prince's eyes to life. His image of the world (" 'Tis an unweeded garden,/ That grows to seed. . . .") appears in his first monologue. The abominations of his surroundings are unbearable, and suicide is the best way out for a man doomed to live in this world. Hamlet already suspects that there is some secret connected with the death of his father. When the ghost discloses the name of the murderer to him, he exclaims:

> Oh, my prophetic soul!
> My uncle!

Only some corroboration is necessary for the dramatic development—some evidence, like Desdemona's handkerchief. Could the tale of the ghost be replaced by some normal circumstance, to give a realistic explanation for the action? Of course it could. It is not hard to imagine Hamlet receiving a letter, and the sudden appearance of a witness to the murder who now repents of his silence. One has only to remember the last acts of Shakespeare's plays to understand that he did not strive for complexity in disclosing secrets. Marcellus or Bernardo could have told Hamlet the story of the poisoning in the garden without any dramatic embarrassments.

Hamlet's desire to verify the truth of the intelligence he has received by means of the performance would have become even more natural. There would have been no alteration in the flow of events, and the character of the Prince could have been preserved without change. It could be suggested, moreover, that the logical justification for Hamlet's deeds would have been strengthened and that the plot would have acquired more harmony. All this with the loss of one quality of Shakespeare's art—but it would have been a great loss. This detriment would have depreciated the whole tragedy. The abridged *Hamlet* would lose not only the supernatural element but also the poetry.

The whole poetic conception of the tragedy would have been annihilated: its scale and expression would have disappeared. They are part and parcel of the image of the ghost.

The presence of a ghost makes talk about realism meaningless. But if the appearance of a ghost is not customary in a realistic work, then this kind of ghost is even more unusual for a mystic apparition. One could say that the ghost in *Hamlet* is a completely atypical ghost.

One would think that the figure, by its very nature, would be deprived of solidity, but it is shown quite substantially. The incorporeal spirit appears in the flesh. The mummified head of Olivier's movie does not resemble Shakespeare's description. The spirit has a human face: the visor of his helmet is worn up, and Horatio sees the face of the King of Denmark as it had been in life, not a skeleton or the rotted look of a corpse. The description is clear and specific. Even the color of his beard is precisely indicated: not gray, but graying. The expression of his face is more sad than angry.

Sad too are the words addressed to Hamlet—not conjuring, but compliant. The father tells his son of his love for his wife and of the injustice of her betrayal. He asks his son not to remain indifferent to what has happened. The words of the ghost are filled not so much with the poetry of the horrors beyond the grave as with real emotions. He perceives all the events just as the other characters do. He feels the cool of the morning breeze, and sees how the firefly begins to dim his lamp, indicating the approach of morning.

Dover Wilson writes that, in comparison with the other specters of Elizabethan dramaturgy, Shakespeare's ghost is an achievement in realism. The idea is creditable. The ghost is not a mystic apparition, but a character, endowed with human thoughts and emotions. Perhaps this makes it possible to think that the importance of the father's ghost lies not in the fact that he is a ghost but in that he is a father.

This kind of idea was expressed in Y. Yuzovski's interesting study *Image and Epoch*. In a chapter on an Armenian Shakespeare festival, Yuzovski talks about the staging of the ghost scene in one of the theatres of Yerevan. Judging from his description, the director tried to frighten the audience by flickering mysterious spots of light and by projecting declamations through a megaphone (reminiscent, in the words of a critic, of poor radio broadcasting). Ridiculing these devices, Yuzovski suggests his own staging of the scene.

"We would want the conversation with the ghost to be more human, and even sincere, perhaps intimate, so that it corresponds more to 'this' world rather than to the 'other' one. We imagine that the son went right up to the father, or the father to the son, that they sat down almost cosily, and that the father would have told his son all that had happened with a minimum of affectation and other-worldly pretentiousness but with profound agitation and humanity."

Before imagining this conversation, let us go back to what was said in the play about the appearance of the ghost.

When the star that lies west of the North Star had moved in its course and the tower clock had struck the hour, there appeared before Horatio, Marcellus, and Bernardo something that assumed, as Horatio put it, ". . . that fair and warlike form/ In which the majesty of buried Denmark/ Did sometimes march." The ghost was arrayed in armor. His step was not only majestic but "warlike."

"Armed, say you?" Hamlet asks them to reiterate.

"Armed, my lord."

"From top to toe?"

"My lord, from head to foot."

Not only the appearance of the dead man is ominous, but his very aspect has some kind of special, evil significance. "My father's spirit in arms! All is not well," Hamlet exclaims.

Seeing his dead father, he turns to him and again enumerates the distinctive features of his outer aspect as though he is seeking a secret meaning in it.

> . . . What may this mean,
> That thou, dead corse, again, in complete steel,
> Revisit'st thus the glimpses of the moon,

There is something in the cold luster of the arms which is essential, which is bound up with the poetry of the figure. The particular structure of the poetry appeared immediately, in the first verses of the tragedy. The guard's password begins the action. The guard is changed at night, on a deserted platform. The scene is military. And the whole imagic structure of the slain King's appearance is grim and menacing. The dead warrior, armed for battle, with a heavy military tread, passes by the guard.

This is a special night. Marcellus says, ". . . this sweaty haste/ Doth make the night joint laborer with the day." In Denmark, they were casting cannon, importing equipment from abroad, and impressing shipwrights into service. Military disturbances were approaching the borders. In this threatening hour, the dead warrior King returns to his country.

He does not arrive solely to complain to his son, but also to demand of him fulfillment of duty. "Pity me not, but lend thy serious hearing/ To what I shall unfold." By spreading lies about a natural death, Claudius deceived not only Hamlet but also the people of Denmark. The heir to the throne must know, "The serpent that did sting thy father's life/ Now wears his crown." The scene ends with lines that little resemble a heart-to-heart talk: "If thou hast nature in thee, bear it not./ Let not the royal bed of Denmark be/ A couch for luxury and damned incest."

Scholars who try to psychoanalyze Hamlet have paid special attention to "bed" and "incest," but they have forgotten that it was not just any bed that was under discussion, but the *royal* bed—the symbol of the continuation of the royal line. The ghost is not talking about a sexual crime, but about the defamation of the throne.

The poetry gives voice to the noble theme of social duty. In the scene with the royal ghost, the heir to the throne is shown not only the outrage to the bonds of family but also a picture of the destruction of the state, now ruled by an incestuous murderer.

In the literary sources for *Hamlet,* there was no ghost. The legend of Saxo Grammaticus and that of Amleth both managed without one. Scholars usually relate the ghost to tragedy of revenge, and his appearance in Shakespeare's play is attributed to tradition. Actually, works of this kind rarely managed without apparitions that howled "Revenge!"—like an oystermonger, to use the expression of a contemporary.

Shakespeare was not only influenced by the tradition of a dramatic genre, however. Ghosts also existed in works of another kind and scope. Horatio compared the appearance of the ghost with the signs of another era:

> In the most high and palmy state of Rome,
> A little ere the mightiest Julius fell,
> The graves stood tenantless, and the sheeted dead
> Did squeak and gibber in the Roman streets.
> As stars with trains of fire and dews of blood,
> Disasters in the sun, and the moist star
> Upon whose influence Neptune's empire stands
> Was sick almost to doomsday with eclipse.

The tale is borrowed from Plutarch's *Parallel Lives,* a book perfectly familiar to Shakespeare; in it, there is frequent mention of ghosts. And they are not literary digressions or fantastic inserts, but essential facts of the story itself. Supernatural phenomena were described on the same level and in the same tone as battles, conspiracies, coups d'état. They were an indispensable part of particularly calamitous events, not ordinary human disasters and misfortunes, but catastrophes of universal and historical significance. According to the accounts of historians, ghosts manifested themselves to people during the days that preceded popular calamities.

Things that seemed unnatural in historical development were anticipated by the unnatural in nature. The order of peaceful life was destroyed, and then things that had never happened and that apparently could never happen by the laws of reason—happened. Plutarch described how the earth shook, and unknown birds flew towards the Forum, and the sky was intersected with fiery people.

Shakespeare borrowed both the witches and the visions of the night of Duncan's murder not from fairytales, but from an episode in Holinshed's chronicle about the murder of King Duffe by the thane Donwald. The chronicle tells of the unnatural phenomena at the same time that it indicates the date 972.

History was still full of superstition. The language of science was quickly transformed into poetic speech. Historians composed lengthy monologues for statesmen long dead and gave businesslike descriptions of wonders.

It is a substantial point that no benighted warrior told of the signs given to the Romans on the ides of March; it was related by the philosopher and bibliophile Horace. Plutarch helped Shakespeare understand the significance of the ghost's coming. It is the same as in the other cases known from history.

> And even the like precurse of fierce events,
> As harbingers preceding still the fates
> And prologue to the omen coming on,
> Have Heaven and earth together demonstrated
> Unto our climatures and countrymen.

The ghost is the herald of national disasters. In accord with the notions of that time concerning history, he is a typical figure that gives forewarning of events. Everything in Denmark is going to ruin; everything is repulsive to the nature of human relations.

Natural laws are destroyed to such a degree that the image summarizing the epoch springs from a comparison of the time to a painful mutilation. The heir to the throne must not only revenge the murder of the lawful King but also return the time to its natural course. The Prince could learn of his father's poisoning from a letter or from a witness to the murder, but to learn that the time was out of joint, he had to gaze into the depths of social relations, depths more frightening than that of a bottomless abyss.

Hamlet had suspected, and now knows, that a murderer sits on the throne of Denmark, that both the sanctity of the throne and the solidity of the family have been destroyed. The human concepts of truth, duty, and conscience are no more. He has looked into an abyss whose bottom was not to be seen with impunity. Poetry creates an image of this fatal view. Hamlet looks into the eyes of his dead father.

The dead warrior, chained from head to toe in fighting steel, appears in the poetry not as a mark of the tragedy of revenge but as the image of a work portraying events on a universal and historical scale. It made no difference where the Prince went, the voice of the ghost sounded from beneath the ground at every point.

GRIGORI KOZINTSEV

On March 14, 1966, Grigori Kozintsev's *Hamlet* had its American *première* in New York City. The Russian translation used in the picture is by Boris Pasternak, the musical score by Dmitri Shostakovich. Mr. Kozintsev directed and wrote the screenplay. The cast is listed below.

Stills from the film appear on the following pages. They are printed here through the courtesy of United Artists.

Hamlet	Innokenti Smakhtunovski
Claudius	Mikhail Nazvanov
Gertrude	Elsa Radzin
Polonius	Yuri Tolubeev
Ophelia	Anastasia Vertinskaya
Horatio	V. Erenberg
Laertes	C. Olesenko
Guildenstern	V. Medvedev
Rosencrantz	I. Dmitriev
Fortinbras	A. Krevalid
Gravedigger	V. Chekoerski

Gertrude and Claudius shortly after their wedding.

Ophelia kissing the hand of Polonius.

Ophelia

Hamlet and Ophelia

Hamlet, with Rosencrantz (left) and Guildenstern, who have just arrived at Elsinore.

Hamlet

The bedroom scene: Queen Gertrude and Hamlet

Horatio (in cape and black hat) and Hamlet at Ophelia's burial. Laertes (at right) is being restrained as Hamlet speaks.

Fortinbras (holding headpiece) leading his army to Elsinore.

Horatio and Hamlet
as they spy
Ophelia's funeral
procession.

Hamlet with the
skull of Yorick.

Ophelia

"Well said, old mole! Canst work i' the earth so fast?" Hamlet exclaims. Marx recalled this phrase, and purposely made it an image of the continual subterranean work of history.

Did Shakespeare believe in the existence of a supernatural world? Did he think the appearance of ghosts possible? The questions are idle, and no sure answer can be given to them. It is another thing to ask whether Shakespeare believed in the poetic force of this kind of imagery. This is easily answered in the affirmative. Not only did he believe in it, but he created the ghost of Hamlet's father.

In his debate with Voltaire concerning the role of phantoms in the theatre, Lessing noted that, when the ghost appears in *Hamlet,* "the hair stands on end, whether it cover a believing or an unbelieving brain."

It is not enough, however, to say that a ghost is a ghost and that the poetry here not only concerns chimeras but also involves superstitions already adopted by the historical science of the time. It is a feature of Shakespeare's art that he transforms an unnatural phenomenon into a practicable image. Yuzovski is absolutely right not to agree with a mystical treatment of the scene, and to write that the ghost is, above all, a father. But he errs in forgetting that the father is the dead King of Denmark.

This does not, however, exhaust the ghost's imagic content; it is complex, with many meanings. The image appears in the tragedy at the intersection of a number of lines. The scene of Hamlet and his dead father delves into the heart of the theme and lends special meaning to the action.

The ghost is not only the shade of a dead man but also the shade of an era. The lifeless brilliance of his armor makes the soldiers remember the armor in which the King battled the ambitious King of Norway. It was a time of honesty, and the elder Hamlet had triumphed in honest single combat. He had acquired Norwegian possessions by right. All that is forgotten now; the new era decides matters differently. Young Fortinbras has recruited hungry cutthroats, and wants to steal that which belongs to Denmark by the noble code of honor. Claudius, a ruler difficult to picture in armor and wielding a weapon, sends ambassadors and plays the complicated game of diplomacy.

The dead King comes into the tragedy from the stern sagas of the past. He is foreign to the new epoch and its morals. He seems to be a reminder of what had once been knightly valor, honorable relations among sovereigns, the sanctity of throne and family.

The quality of this character may be ascertained from his own speeches and from those of others. Each who speaks of the King remembers him in his own way.

For Marcellus, he's a warrior, a strong and courageous man. His characteristics are more accurately expressed by a brief tale: having become angry with an envoy from Poland, the King dragged him from his sled and flung him onto the snow. Since it is in no way connected with the events of the tragedy nor with the King's relationship with Hamlet, the detail would appear totally extraneous, save that the memory of this rough brawl is both characteristic for Marcellus and important for the thinking of the author. Shakespeare could not forget reality even while composing legend, and this sort of detail places the legendary hero on the wild ground of the Middle Ages.

For Horatio, he is a goodly king. As though raising an objection to his friend's opinion, Hamlet says, "He was a man."

But Hamlet gives a totally unnatural description of this man. The image of his father which the Prince creates for the "mind's eye" is distinguished both by unusual beauty and, at the same time, by utter lifelessness. The description consists in mere references to the qualities of Mars, Jupiter, and Apollo. Bradley claimed that when the Prince begins to speak of the dead King, his words melt into music.

Hamlet views his father as the only goodly man that ever lived, a man endowed with all the charm of the qualities of man. This unique and really worthy person exists no longer; he is dead. Slain. Only his shade has come to Elsinore.

Beside this ideal, people seem particularly loathsome. They are slaves to egoistic passion, citizens of the pursy times.

The towering poetic structure brings out yet another theme: the contrast of ideal love with bestial fornication. A repulsive picture of adultery and incest is compared with the genuine feeling that went ". . . hand in hand even with the vow/ I made to her in marriage."

Hamlet's father so loved his wife "That he might not beteem the winds of heaven/ Visit her face too roughly"; so tender and jealous was this love that it seemed to live on the heights of mountain pastures. This kind of love does not die even with the lover. Despite his wife's betrayal, he—killed by her paramour—continues to protect her, now from the just anger of her son.

This line of the image begins in Act I. It finds its completion in the closet scene.

In the edition of 1603 the appearance of the ghost in the closet scene is preceded by the remark, "Enter the ghost in his night gowne." These words seem strange today, but there is sense in them. It is not a question of the necessity of this exact costume, of course, but of the indication of a change in the guise of the apparition. The relations of the protagonists to the ghost are also different. Hamlet sees his father just as clearly as he did in earlier scenes, but Gertrude does not see her husband at all. It is strange that on the platform the ghost appears not to Hamlet alone, but to Horatio, Marcellus, and Bernardo as well. All those whom he passed could clearly discern his form, and even his facial features. Now, in the Queen's closet, one character sees the ghost as though he were a living man, and the other simply does not see him. Gertrude interprets as delirium Hamlet's lines about the presence of his father.

What is the meaning of the author's change of attitude toward the properties of the ghost?

Remembering his dead father, Hamlet tells Horatio that he recalls the King as distinctly as if he then stood before him. The father has departed this life, but even now he is beside his son

"Oh, where, my lord?" asks Horatio.

"In my mind's eye, Horatio," answers the Prince.

Hamlet is faithful to the memory of his father. Neither Horatio, nor Marcellus, nor Bernardo has forgotten the King. And they, too, see him. Gertrude has lost memory of him; she forgot her dead husband shamefully soon. The poetry creates an image of memory and an image of oblivion. The metaphor is literal: Hamlet sees his father because he remembers him; Gertrude does not see her husband because he has disappeared from her memory. Her mind's eyes are closed, leaving her spiritually blind.

The ghost is not in armor now. In this scene, he is not a sign of national disaster. Husband, wife, and son have gathered by the bed of the kings of Denmark, where Hamlet was conceived and born. The husband protects his wife from the anger of their son, for such is his love for her. But it is not given to the faithless wife to see him.

Using just this example of the ghost, it is clear how limited is a one-sided interpretation of Shakespearean poetry. The complex unity of an image is revealed only in the clash of its various features. The ghost is both fantastic and real, but the fantasy bears no resemblance to the mystic, nor is his reality similar to the commonplace. It is an image of poetic reality. Portrayed forms are sometimes lifelike, and sometimes the proportions are displaced. Its essence is shown in a clotting of definitive qualities. Its generalization then acquired such scope that place and time are lost, and history and the universe appear in all their awesome power.

Realism becomes winged.

Then the commonplace takes on such force that the spirit grasps, but cannot see, how an artlessly ramshackle carriage, to which they have harnessed a dappled horse, and a bay, and also a chestnut steed called Assessor, will suddenly become an enigmatic bird-troika, will tear itself from the dusty earth and fly to all four corners of the world.[16]

Then streets and squares tremble, and a diminutive figure of a Petersburg functionary, his happiness lost, is pursued by a rushing bronze monstrosity, an immovable horseman on a permanently rearing charger.[17]

Then a dead king returns to his country at a threatening hour in its history.

And it is not easy to notice by what artistic means the real figure of an aging and sorrowful warrior is transformed into an ironclad herald of history.

[16] From the conclusion of Book I of Gogol's *Dead Souls* [trans.].
[17] From Pushkin's narrative poem *The Bronze Horseman* [trans.].

WITTENBERG AND ELSINORE

Nineteenth-century German writers paid particular attention to Hamlet's past. As is known, the Prince had been instructed at the university, and after his father's death he sought to return to his studies.

And just what sort of studies were these? Boerne wrote that "the king's son, educated for war and the hunt, learned in Wittenberg to conquer strange theses and to track cowardly sophisms."[18]

In an attempt to turn Hamlet into a convenient symbol for polemics on topical themes, Boerne sat the Shakespearean hero down at the desk of a completely different school and assigned him teachers who were born many years after the death of *Hamlet*'s creator. The theses and sophisms of Boerne's discussion belonged neither to the times of Saxo Grammaticus nor to the epoch of Elizabeth I.

"As a Fichtean he only knew one thing," noted Boerne, "that I am I, and he was occupied only with defining his 'I.'" Heine added that heavy German philosophy had formed Hamlet's character. Of course, all this bore on the German character, not on the English hero. Yet the very heat of the argument and the degree of exaggeration help one to see the subject, by contrast, in its true light.

The verbal style of the two periods is worth comparing.

Heine composed an imaginary conversation with Hegel in which one of the topics was poetry. The philosopher appeared to the poet in a dream and maintained that the time of poetry had drawn to a close. Heine understood; soon the grocer would tear pages from books of verse to wrap his merchandise.

The conversation turned to stars, the invariable companion of poets. "Stars?" the author of *Phenomenology of Spirit* asked the dreaming poet, "Mere spit in the sky."

Hamlet once saw the sky as "this most excellent canopy, the air, . . . this majestical roof fretted with golden fire."

In order to understand the significance of daydreams about the sky, it is first necessary to see the earth on which the dreamer walks. The Prince came to Elsinore not from nineteenth-century

---

[18] Boerne, *Of Shakespeare's Hamlet* (St. Petersburg, 1886), p. 130.

Bonn, having just left Fichte's lectures, but from Wittenberg, the "Athens of Germany," as Giordano Bruno called it. Wittenberg was a city of students and professors. Founded in the beginning of the sixteenth century, the university soon overshadowed Erfurt and Leipzig. It was here that Luther nailed his theses to the door of the cathedral. In the auditoriums of this university, passions raged about the discoveries of Copernicus. Giordano Bruno was raised to its faculty.

Today, if you were to pass through the quiet side streets of Wittenberg, looking about and trying to find something related to Hamlet's life, I doubt whether your stroll would be at all satisfactory. Many of the houses have been reconstructed—old walls and tiled roofs are not necessary for a sense of Hamlet's Wittenberg. One tries to feel the spirit of Renaissance learning.

The spiritual milieu in which the princely student grew up was distinguished by unique traits. Both the discrepancies in Hamlet's relations to reality and the oddity of his behavior look different if one sees the Wittenberg student in definite conditions of life, rather than in a vacuum. Once more, the prehistory of a hero was never incidental to Shakespeare.

The spirit of Wittenberg was distinguished not only by heavy abstractions but also by an atmosphere of unique intellectual activity which was opposed both to weightiness and to suspension from reality. Scholars roamed between Venice and London, Leipzig and Paris. The itinerant preachers of truth were shown much kindness by noble patrons. One day they would introduce a free discussion of the infinite possibilities of human cognition into a circle of connoisseurs of learning and art, but the next day's dawn might see them receiving a note from a friend and surreptitiously saddling a horse so that they could make their way through the gates in time to avoid landing in a dungeon. During violent debates, which went on for weeks, principles of theology were smashed under a screen of tangled allegory and rhetorical beauty. But the decisive word was often pronounced by a tribunal of the Inquisition.

Words led to the stake, for it was with words that they fought.

These were strange words. It is not easy now to find the seditious meaning of many of the passages, or to subdue the very form in which statements were made. Giordano Bruno taught science in verse; Erasmus preached in grotesque.

All this was covered with poetry, filled with passion, moved by the "adventurous spirit" of the age.

There is no reason to be surprised by the fact that the Wittenberg student pondered the essence of life and death, and also mastered the rapier. The confusion, buffoonery, and the rhetorical whimsicality of many of Hamlet's speeches were characteristic of Humanists from Oxford and Cambridge, as well as of the Danish Prince.

But Hamlet studied in Wittenberg at the university, which was, to some extent, even legendary for Shakespeare's contemporaries; it was like a symbol of the learning of the Renaissance. According to legend, it was here that Doctor Faustus studied all the secrets of heaven and earth, after having sold his soul to the devil.

In Giordano Bruno's description, Wittenberg is not presented as a real city, but as the capital of Utopia:

"Here, wisdom raised a temple to itself. Here she placed seven columns. Here she blended the wine of most excellent sacrifice. . . . Hence she summoned the unbidden, and they came. They came from all peoples and tribes, from all the educated nations of Europe: Frenchmen, Spaniards, Swiss, inhabitants of the arctic islands, Sarmations, Huns, Illyrians, Scythians; they came from east and south, west and north."

Shakespeare frequently painted the past of a hero in half-real, half-fantastic surroundings. Othello was a wanderer and warrior from childhood. This sort of biography was natural for a black general. However, during his travels, the Moor even discovered lands inhabited by people whose heads grew beneath their shoulders. Only the elect of Desdemona could have reached such places.

Whatever else the protagonist of a tragedy might be—warrior, merchant, king—he was also more or less a poet at the same time. It is not simply that his lines are in verse; the important thing is that his perception of the world was poetic. Both Cassio and Brabantio spoke in iambs, but they could not see the things that appeared before the eyes of Othello; their horizon was limited by the bounds of reality.

Hamlet was familiar with university lecture halls, but he had looked into the depths of the eyes of the dead King of Denmark.

In the university of those times, whose actual features are not hard to imagine, Horatio mastered the philosophy of the Stoics; he could have been taught this during his years at Wittenberg. The heir to the Danish throne sat beside Horatio on an oak bench in a room with whitewashed walls or oaken panelling. All this is important for the vitality of the story. The moods of this character are reminiscent of the moods of many English university gentlemen during the years of reaction after the 1580's. He was not simply transported out of life and onto the stage; he had been poetically recreated. Hamlet knew of what Horatio's philosophy had dreamt, and of what it had not.

The debate has gone on a long time: Can one discover the essence of Shakespeare's characters seen as real figures, or are they no more than inhabitants of conventional space, limited by the dimensions of the stage?

Many scholars of the past few decades, particularly Americans, have rejected the possibility of a psychological evaluation of Shakespeare's tragedies. We do not know how many children Lady Macbeth had, they have said, and calculating Hamlet's age is an unproductive effort. Like every brief and overly definitive statement regarding Shakespeare's work, this is only partially true. Some motivations and details, archeological and geographic, are really difficult to grasp, but it is sometimes pointless to reestablish them with the reader who is accustomed to contemporary erudition. However, the director or actor working on *Macbeth* or *King Lear* knows from experience that the feelings of the protagonists are invariably genuine and their logic of behavior irrefutable. Chekhov reflected reality in one way, Shakespeare in another; as far as this is concerned, scholars of the "historical school" are right. But John Gielgud and Yuri Tolubeev sometimes play Chekhov on Friday and Shakespeare on Saturday. Actors trained in realism will hardly change the principles of their art from one performance to the next. To me, this seems just as incontestable as the fact that *The Seagull* and *Timon of Athens* are not to be performed in one and the same way.

Of course, Shakespeare's theatre is poetic, but it is poetic realism.

Not one of the characters in *Hamlet* slips out "from behind the wings," as we say in the theatre. The prehistory of a character, even one who makes a brief appearance on the stage, can be reconstructed. It is a vital story.

Hamlet's prehistory does not have to be supplied for the author, or sought out from between the lines; it exists in the text itself. The thought and feelings of Wittenberg were not like Boerne's "strange theses" and "cowardly sophisms." Hamlet left the university full of pure and fervent faith. He himself speaks of faith, but in Elsinore the Wittenberg ideals are dismissed as a form of negation. This negation is complex, however; the Prince did not betray his faith, nor did he desert to another camp.

A whole library has been written about the "to be or not to be" passage, but the monologue about "man" has been given less attention. In Olivier's film, these lines were frankly cut.

"I have of late—but wherefore I know not—lost all my mirth," the Prince says to Rosencrantz and Guildenstern, "forgone all custom of exercises, and indeed it goes so heavily with my disposition that this goodly frame the earth seems to me a sterile promontory. This most excellent canopy, the air, look you, this brave o'erhanging firmament, this majestical roof fretted with golden fire—why, it appears no other thing to me than a foul and pestilent congregation of vapors."

How many times has it been said of Hamlet's character that he was changeless from birth, unsociable, plunged into inconsolable grief. . . . Are not the words quite clear, "of late," "mirth"? Is there some ambiguity in their combination? The youth who wrote verses to Polonius's daughter, "the glass of fashion," the theatre buff, was both gay and industrious. There are no doubts as to the nature of his occupations. What would permit him to see the earth as "this goodly frame," to compare the sky with a "majestical roof fretted with golden fire"? . . . Confidence that the creature which treads the earth, desirous of discovering her riches, fixing his gaze on the movement of distant luminaries, was an excellent creature, infinite in his possibilities, and created for happiness on a fecund earth under a beautiful blue sky. This was a faith in the lofty destiny of man freed from all restrictions and dogmas—a godlike creature, to whom the world and all its wonders belong.

"What a piece of work is a man!" Hamlet seems to repeat words that he had often exclaimed at one time. "How noble in reason! How infinite in faculty! In form and moving how express and admirable! In action how like an angel! In apprehension how like a god! The beauty of the world! The paragon of animals!"

But the Prince speaks these words within the walls of Elsinore. Before him stand the friends of his childhood, informers for the murderer King; the walls have ears.

"And yet, to me, what is this quintessence of dust?" The Wittenberg speech nears its end with an Elsinore touch.

In analyzing a Shakespearean situation, however, one never has to confine oneself to black and white. Rosencrantz and Guildenstern not only are success-seekers in court reception chambers, but they are also students of Wittenberg. A small but substantial feature serves to create lifelike complexity: Various people studied in the temple of Renaissance learning, where the greatness of man was glorified; there was the very honest Horatio, the heir to the throne of Denmark, and there were future informers. . . .

Probably little time elapsed between the Prince's university days and his stay at the court of Claudius. But between the prehistory and the events of Elsinore a century had passed. In a generalized system of ideas, this was a sort of collision between the ideas of the flowering of the Renaissance, and a picture of the decline of a movement.

The discussion here concerns the separate conditions of the tragic theme which develops. It is hardly possible to attribute the action of the play itself to one period or the other, especially as all works of genius invariably outgrow their historical frames. The imagic world of Hamlet recalls neither the sage peace of Giotto nor the frenzied contortion of El Greco. There is probably not even another Shakespearean play in which the preachings of Humanism, and the negation of it, are pronounced with such passion.

Just what is man, an angel or the quintessence of dust? With this question, another is inseparably bound; the second question is more famous: To be or not to be?

Is the victory of "some craven scruple" final, so that it is senseless "to take arms against a sea of troubles," or can the social relations that reduce the person to "dust" be destroyed?

It is impossible to combine human worth with existence in a

society based on contempt for man. To reconcile oneself, to swim with the current, is ignominy. It is better "not to be."

This tragedy portrays a man who does not find himself between life and death, but between one era and another. In the prologue to his novel *The Death of Vazir-Mukhtar,* Yuri Tynyanov wrote, "The time was suddenly broken"; he had probably once pondered Hamlet's words, "The time is out of joint."

As always in Shakespeare, "the times" are expressed both in accurate pictures of the life contemporary to them, and in generalizations that penetrate the depths of an historic contradiction developing in different forms and in a more distant epoch.

There is hardly one of our articles on Shakespeare which does not cite Engel's words about the "titans of the Renaissance." But the implication of Shakespeare's tragedies is that the poet saw a time which no longer needed titans.

When Christopher Marlowe was killed by an agent provocateur, who plunged a dagger into his eye during a tavern skirmish arranged by the police, the puritan Thomas Beard wrote that Marlowe was a man who gave "too large a swinge to his owne wit. . . . But see what a hooke the Lord put in the nosthrils of this barking dogge."

The era of those who gave "too large a swinge" to their "owne wit" had come to an end. While the hot-heads within the walls of universities celebrated the greatness of man, there came into power a social structure that abased man and paralyzed his finest aspirations. "The wine of most excellent sacrifice" imbibed in the temple of wisdom had no effect on the gods. The spiritual liquor only intoxicated the dreamers themselves, and their drunkenness did not last long. A picture of real life was unveiled; it did not resemble "this goodly frame the earth." Under the leaden skies of many Elsinores, they harnessed "the beauty of the world" to their yokes, and freighted him with a burden heavier than that of the feudal epoch.

Freedom of thought began to lead to executions. Church synods and councils of state regulated incentive and lay in wait for desire. Twisting arms, they filched professions of the truth of dogmas. With the support of the rack, they demanded voluntary confessions of heresy.

Europe ran with blood—of the Moors and Jews in Spain, of the Waldenses in the Alps and Calabria, and of the Calvinists in the Netherlands. At night, pogromists howled, and women and children wept. . . . And where was the place without its Bartholomew's eve?

Candles guttered on the tables before the tribunals of the Inquisition; they had interrogations round the clock. Jesuit psychologists specified exercises and worked out scientific systems for the suppression of everything human.

"Better to be a wild chamois than a man," wrote Geronimo Cardano. "Both the one and the other are in constant danger. Both always risk being killed. But man lives in far the worse condition, for he may be easily caught, and undergoes a more prolonged torment and a crueller anguish. . . .

"It would be a greater blessing not to live at all, than to be born to live thus, and thus to perish. . . .

"And is there any corner of earth where they would not have to do evil and where safety could rule?" (*Of His Books*)

Thoughts and images reminiscent of Hamlet's can be found in the works of many writers of the period. The reason for this does not lie in that in such-and-such a year Giordano Bruno was in London and Shakespeare could have met him through lord so-and-so, nor in that the playwright used the ideas of Francis Bacon or Montaigne (quotes are compared in some interesting studies). There is another, more substantial reason: these people beheld similar events in life. If, as Pushkin once wrote, the devil had told these people to be born with "wit and heart," then they all interpreted events with identical feelings. Every country had its chronology of the crimes of reaction, but from the middle of the sixteenth century, reaction gradually became triumphant everywhere. Old forms of oppression were replaced not by free associations of wise citizens but by an even crueller slavery. Many titans of the Renaissance had come to learn how "Wittenberg" yielded to "Elsinore."

Hamlet was the expression of more than the personal tragedy of the princely student; it was also the historied tragedy of humanism, the tragedy of those who gave too much swing to their wit. The time came when thought led to suffering.

Two centuries later, there appeared a definition: woe from wit.[19]

The tableaux of Sonnet 66 serve as a kind of panorama of the times. It is better to sleep than to see all this:

> . . . to behold desert a beggar born,
> And needy nothing trimmed in jollity,
> And purest faith unhappily forsworn,
> And gilded honor shamefully misplaced,
> And maiden virtue rudely strumpeted,
> And right perfection wrongfully disgraced,
> And strength by limping sway disabled,
> And art made tongue-tied by authority,
> And folly, doctorlike, controlling skill,
> And simple truth miscalled simplicity,
> And captive good attending captain ill.

All this was before Shakespeare's eyes.

But such images may be found in works written centuries before Shakespeare's birth:

"Then was virtue suspect, depravity esteemed by all. . . . Everything human was profaned, and one only desired to forget all that one saw as quickly as possible. And we saw a Senate timid and mute; to speak in it was dangerous, to be silent shameful. . . . From that time and for all our lives, our hearts became hardened, exhausted, and defeated." Thus Pliny described the time of the Emperor Domitian.

"Sweet it is to sleep, but even sweeter to harden into stone so long as infamy and disaster reign," says the inscription which Michelangelo composed and carved on the sarcophagus in the Medici chapel, "to see nothing, to feel nothing—this is my happiness . . . but softly . . . do not wake me. . . ."

The destruction of the humanistic illusions of their time and the ascendancy of reaction evoked similar sentiments from people with thin skins.

"Who more than our generation has primarily celebrated the eighteenth century, the light of philosophy, the mitigation of custom, the general spread of the spirit of community, the most intimate and amicable bond of peoples, the mildness of the

[19] Title of a play written by A. S. Griboyedov in 1825 [trans.].

government?" wrote the littérateur N. M. Karamzin at the end of the 1790's. "Where is this consoling system now? It has been destroyed in its foundaton; the eighteenth century is dying, and the unhappy philanthropist takes two paces to measure his grave, in order to lie in it with his deceived and shredded heart and close his eyes forever."

Hamlet's words could continue those of Pliny or Karamzin; one senses no transtion in thought or feeling, although there are centuries between these men.

> . . . To die, to sleep—
> No more, and by a sleep to say we end
> The heartache and the thousand natural shocks
> That flesh is heir to. 'Tis a consummation
> Devoutly to be wished. To die, to sleep,
> To sleep . . .

"Who could have thought, expected, foreseen?" In agony, Karamzin sought an answer. "Where are the people whom we loved? Where is the fruit of science and wisdom? Age of enlightenment, I do not recognize thee; in blood and flame, amidst murder and destruction, I do not recognize thee."

In many eras, the finest men knew despair; lofty dreams proved so obviously futile. The time came when the heavy cannon of the "Elsinore" of the times dispersed the ideas of the "Wittenberg."

One could swim with the current, live thoughtlessly and even comfortably. To consider that whatever exists is right is not to think. Not to seek out the crux of anything which cannot be changed by one man is to be concerned only with oneself, or, at best, with those close to oneself. But then, in this diminutive worldlet, it would be possible to find peace. There were people, however, who were affected by the movement of the whole course of history; they could not live with the feeling of general injustice.

If the conscience of man did not grow deaf, he cursed the brutality with all the force he could muster. And he cursed himself if he was unable to fight it.

Personal misfortune and individual injustice were not discussed; Shakespeare was involved with all the enormity of historical injustice. His tragedy was infused with a particular depth of feeling. The sense of catastrophe, on the great scale of all time and all place, fermented in his poetry.

The echo of a like feeling across the centuries was to affect the souls of many.

"I think a relentless feeling of catastrophe was deposited in the hearts of people of the past generations." This was written during a reactionary period by Aleksandr Blok, a poet bound to Hamletian motifs in many ways.

Characters and milieus vary in Shakespeare's tragedies, but a sense of catastrophe is alloyed in all of them—in the love of Romeo and Juliet, in the family matters of Lear, and in Macbeth's affairs of state, even in Falstaff's desire to drink and be merry for free. The world is overcast by the shadow of a huge black roof, which is the approach of disaster. "Kind and credulous philanthropists had success upon success," Karamzin wrote. "They saw their goal of perfection near, and they cried in happy rapture, 'shore!' " But suddenly the sky clouded and the fate of mankind was hidden in threatening thunderheads! Oh, posterity! What lot awaits you?

"Sometimes an unbearable melancholy constricts my heart; sometimes I fall to my knees and stretch my arms out to the unseen. . . ."

Herzen called this passage "fiery and full of tears." It comes to mind when you reread descriptions of the "Mochalov moments"; as his contemporaries told of them, it was at precisely these moments that the real Shakespeare came to life on the stage. Mochalov, whose performance could be disappointing for whole acts at a time, would suddenly become somehow transfigured, as only Mochalov could. The "volcanic moments" (*Apollon Grigoriev*) ensued; the house died down and held its breath. Hamlet was on the stage.

Evidently, the actor found a deep unity with the author during these instants. It was then, to go by the descriptions, that the tears and fire appeared. And at these times, the actor possessed—and conveyed to the audience—the tragic sense of an imminent catastrophe that threatened mankind.

Elizabethan Humanism and the humanism of today have little in common, since humanity today asserts itself by the very system of social relations which exists in a significant part of the world. Yet

Hamlet's words do not leave modern audiences cold. Our memories retain the fire and tears paid for the numbing of the soul of human bonds, for power rooted in inhumanity. Its atoms are retained in nations and in souls. A modern Elsinore would have no objection to closing the barbed wire of concentration camps around humanity like a crown of thorns.

For this reason, when the man in black stretches his arms to the unseen and says that love, loyalty, friendship, and humanity are not more empty noises, we regard his words as more than the beautiful sounds of ancient poetry.

POISON

When Rosencrantz and Guildenstern try to elicit his secret by remarks about ambition, Hamlet replies that he does not dream of power but the contrary. He desires an existence in the smallest of worlds, shut off from reality.

"I could be bounded in a nutshell," he says, "and count myself a king of infinite space were it not that I have bad dreams."

Wittenberg was happiness in a nutshell. The shell has cracked and broken, and a door has opened in the blank wall of the university. The student comes out into life. The youth had spent his days behind this wall, like those others: a ruler protected from the world by castle fortifications—King Lear; a dark-skinned wanderer through far-off lands—Othello. The same wall separated them from reality. And so, in most of Shakespeare's tragedies, there are other heroes who are foreign to the contemporary order of things by reason of the same biographical constitution, the same character traits.

Hamlet travels real life in the same way that Lear roamed feudal castles. But the Dane completes his journey without leaving the palace at Elsinore. Here, the Wittenberg student discovers a new and unfamiliar world, types of people which had been unknown to him, social relations and moral norms of which he had not learned. Here, in Elsinore, the life of the times moves before Hamlet's eyes. He passes through the range of this life: through the state structure and family relations. The ages of man stand before him: youth, maturity, old age. Before him are the feelings and thoughts of his era.

Hamlet discovers the world in which he lives. He discovers the souls of his mother and his beloved, the consciences of his friends, the moral philosophy of the courtiers. He discovers himself. And then he dies, because one cannot live on, having learned all that he has.

He dies from poison.

The tragedies end with the death of their protagonists, but each of them perishes in his own way. Othello and Juliet choose the dagger. Cleopatra presses the asp to her breast. Lear's heart fails. Hamlet is not the only hero to die of poisoning, but in *Hamlet* there is a circumstance that lends special significance to this kind of death: poison also undoes Claudius, Gertrude, and Laertes.

Poison, which squares accounts with life, is specially described. It is characterized by strong action should even the smallest drop penetrate the organism. Laertes says that the finger need only be scratched with the envenomed blade, and death will be inevitable. The poison that Claudius had poured into the wine is so lethal that only a sip need be drunk from the goblet.

However, the motif is not limited to its literal meaning. In the poetic fabric of Shakespeare, theme and situations are tightly interwoven, so that *Hamlet*'s structure recalls the "labyrinth of cohesions" of which Lev Tolstoy wrote.

Hamlet says before his meeting with the ghost, "The dram of eale/ Doth all the noble substance of a doubt/ To his own scandal." The Cambridge edition of *Hamlet* cites more than eighty interpretations of this passage. Of course, its complexity consists not so much in the understanding of the individual words as in the echo of their meaning throughout the tragedy. And here, one must return to poison.

The characters of the Elsinore story perish from more than physical causes. They were finished long before the poison had gotten into their blood streams from a scratch or a drink. The action of the drug bought by Laertes from a sorcerer, or of the pearls that the king throws into the wine, only finishes the affair. Other poison, of far greater potency, has long since destroyed the spiritual organism.

A cancer penetrated the soul, and destruction was inevitable. The spark of desire blazed with the fire of lust and incinerated Gertrude's conscience. A bit of ambition corroded the core of

Claudius. Spiritual leprosy was caused by the microbe of career-ism, and Rosencrantz and Guildenstern stumbled onto the execu-tioner's block. The feudal reflex of revenge turned a noble youth into a murderer.

None of the characters is simple: the spiritual mold of the human being is a complex thing. But the beginnings of tragedy form and ripen when one of the characteristics rises as though with yeast. There are no pathological figures or natural villains in *Hamlet*. A drop of evil destroys people who have their own virtues. Gertrude is kind, loves her son, wishes happiness to Ophelia. Claudius is a judicious ruler, prefers peace to war; in the first scenes there is no indication that he hated the Prince.

But the speck of evil corrodes the organism much as a drop of vinegar will curdle milk. What is the nutrient for this sort of development? Time, the historical process, society. In the very atmosphere of a century that has gone off its tracks, each nutrient accelerates with monstrous power the growth of even the smallest malignancy.

Hamlet not only stabs the King and makes him drink the poison; he also dissects the corpse of the state, like a surgeon, and points out the reason for its demise.

Poison brings this story to a close. And poison begins it. Claudius poured the juice "of cursèd hebenon" into the ear of the sleeping King; the contamination immediately got into the veins. Shakespeare's description of the agony is frighteningly physiologi-cal: crusty scales covered the skin, the King was covered with scabs, like the biblical Lazarus. The infection was injected not only into the bloodstream of the rightful king of Denmark but also into the circulatory system of society. Everything was infected.

Is there a remedy? It is absurd to think of lotions, ointments, and powders. What iron does not heal, fire will heal—Hippocrates taught—and what fire does not heal, the knife will heal.

Hamlet not only stabs Claudius with an envenomed rapier, he pours a poisoned drink down his throat. Double poisoning should destroy the poisoner.

The heroes die. Theatrical trumpets, a salute, Fortinbras occu-pies the throne. It would seem that this contains a conclusion, that it is an optimistic finale: Denmark will not be ruled by a usurper, but by a just monarch. Prosperity is around the corner for

Denmark. And what else can we predict about the future of the Danish subjects?

Yet there is a figure—who appears only in the last act—who makes it possible to ponder an epilogue. I speak of Osric. Osric has more than a few kinsmen. Through the pages of Shakespeare drifts a round dance of vacuous fools and simpletons: the perfumed lout who appears after the battle and whose appearance makes Hotspur livid with rage; the cavalier Roderigo with his fat purse; that great consumer of beef—Sir Andrew Aguecheek—of whom Sir Toby said that with such a talent for dancing he should go to church doing a galliard and make water doing a sink-a-pace; the curled small fry of Elizabethan times; the lovers of bearbaiting and masquerades and holidays; and all those who scattered themselves on the very boards of the state to show the audience the cut of their cloaks—bullies and cowards.

Each of these appeared as a comic individual, whose preposterous manner accentuated the singularity of the figure. But this time it is put backwards; Osric is one of many. ". . . he—and many more of the same breed that I know the drossy age dotes on," says Hamlet, following Osric with his eyes. The career of his generation is only beginning; Horatio calls him "new-hatched," a "lapwing" that still has "the shell on his head." Hamlet defines his rank: "He hath much land, and fertile. Let a beast be lord of beasts and his crib shall stand at the King's mess."

What distinguishes these obsequious young men on the make? Only one of their qualities is established, and that is thoughtlessness. But it is raised to a fantastically high power. It may be said that this is the pathos of the absence of personal judgment. Osric does not have a private conviction about anything, even whether the temperature is hot or cold, or what a cloud looks like. He is content to be an echo of highly placed opinion. He is a member of a generation which grew up with the notion that it is dangerous to think and pointless to feel.

Dover Wilson discovered the place of this fellow in the action: he not only brought Hamlet the challenge to compete with Laertes, but he was probably one of the seconds—if not the judge of the match. He is an accomplice to the conspiracy; it would have been difficult to switch rapiers without his help.

Yet another matter merits attention: Osric is one more discovery for Hamlet in the world of Elsinore. And it is the last discovery. Before the Wittenberg student who proclaims the greatness of man appears a parody on man. A creature made callous and inane, he proffers the poisoned rapier that will kill the man who gave "too much swinge to his owne wit."

In Mikhail Lermontov's *Masquerade,* the Unknown appeared before Arbenin as a sign of ruin and the approach of the end. The first toll of Hamlet's funeral bell is the arrival of this court minor who sweeps the Elsinore parquetry with the feather on his hat. The sound of the terrible trumpet that summons people to death has been described more than once in literature; Hamlet is called to his death by squeaky, nasal pipes. There is some sort of stupidly comic sound in the prelude to his funeral march. It is produced by an instrument that is far easier to play than a pipe—a semblance of a man, one of the generation brought up by Elsinore.

Sonnet 66 concludes with a thought about a person who was very close to Shakespeare and in whose friendship the poet found the meaning of his own existence.

> Tired with all these, from these would I be gone,
> Save that, to die I leave my love alone.

A number of learned men have tried to discover who this friend was. They have named courtier-patrons, acquaintances of the poet, his beloved. They have tried to smear the author by a certain definition of his inclinations.

It is difficult to evaluate the truth of all these propositions. But, with the exception of the man whose name is mentioned in the dedication (this could only have been a search for a protector in those days), there is invariably another object of the poet's innermost interest. This is a collocutor who is most spiritually close to the poet, who seizes his thought (the way poets dream), and who feels that which the poet himself experiences.

The poet Baratynski (by the way, Pushkin called him "Hamlet") modestly begins an epistle:

> My gift is wretched, and my voice not loud,
> But yet I live—and feel that on this earth
> In my existence someone will find worth.

Who was the person with whom this conversation was conducted? With one whom the author not only did not know but had no hope of ever seeing. And nevertheless, the poet hoped for a special intimacy with this stranger in particular:

> My distant offspring will find him out;
> My verse—how can I know—or then my soul
> Will prove in deep communion with his own.
> And as I found a friend among my peers,
> A reader will I find in future years.

Shakespeare's poetry was not addressed to the mysterious "Mr. W. H." whose intitials are found in the sonnets, to the Earl of Southampton or the Earl of Pembroke, or to any other person, illustrious or unknown, even to the "dark lady" whom the author is supposed to have loved. It is written to those to whom the poet invariably addressed himself, even in his most intimate lines—to all people. Thus the human soul of later centuries "will prove in deep communion" with the spirit of Shakespeare.

Can anyone, in a few sentences or even pages, define the pith and meaning of this intimacy through the centuries?

I am reminded of the well-known description of the ease of creating a sculpture: just take a stone and break off everything extraneous. And how were many of the conceptions about this tragedy created? By taking the work, full of life and movement, and breaking off the important things: the fullness of life and the complexity of movement. A piece of stone was left, engraved with the words: "The theme of this work. . . ."

Of course, the amusing comparison only concerns a few theoretical treatises. At one time, it was customary to curse the commentators, but it is hardly a worthwhile occupation. There are many and various studies; some have grown antiquated, and the others only confused the issue when they appeared. But in the main, the magnificent work of scholarship can hardly be overrated. It is now possible to see *Hamlet* in its ordinary environment, to feel the poetic fabric, and to sense the nature of the images.

Today we know far more than was known in previous centuries about Elizabethan theatre, aesthetics, psychology, demonology, and life in general. And most important, today we know more about the world than our predecessors. I say this not only because we have had the chance to read books unknown to our forefathers, but also because every man of our time has had occasion to know the full measure of fire and tears and happiness. Before our eyes, faith in the greatness of man conquers the forces of reaction and becomes the basis for all vital relations. "Justice" and "humanity" now acquire a special, contemporary meaning.

This is why for us the meaning of Shakespeare's tragedy lies not in the inactivity of its hero but in the tragedy's provocation to action. *Hamlet* is a tocsin that awakens the conscience.

Tavern on the Volcano

> *Great the merit of an artistic work, when it can*
> *slip from the hold of every one-sided view.*
> —A. Herzen, Diary, 1842

An author does not always have complete control over his characters. Sometimes one of them tears himself from his creator's hands, and begins to go his own way; he breaks from the leash, and the man of letters has difficulty keeping up with him. The writer's pen begins to be guided by life itself. It is not easy to trace this struggle of intention with realization. But it is possible to determine influences upon it.

We are speaking here of a figure who is equated with: "A tun," "a huge hill of flesh," a "huge bombard of sack," and "A hulk . . . stuffed in the hold." These are only the main comparisons used. Here are a few of his nicknames: "sweet creature of bombast," "swollen parcel of dropsies," "bolting hutch of beastliness," "reverend vice," "gray iniquity," "vanity in years," and "old white-bearded Satan." And the following may be considered his titles: "bed-presser," "horse-back-breaker," and "globe of sinful continents." Everything swollen, intoxicated, dissolute, obese, and boastful has been his since birth.

I speak of one of the characters of the two-part chronicle *Henry IV*—Sir John Falstaff. And he is, in reality, a coward, a glutton, a liar, and a sot, but it has often been noted that all this is no more evident than the author's love of the personified aggregate of vice he has created. It is not that all this touches on the comic; toward its end, the role is devoid of humor, and the description of Falstaff's death is sad and pathetic.

If we are to investigate the origin and fate of this man who signed himself "Jack Falstaff with my familiars, John with my brothers and sisters, and Sir John with All Europe," we must first turn to the full title of the first part of Shakespeare's chronicle:

> *The History of Henrie the Fourth;*
> *With the battell at Shrewsburie,*
> *betweene the King and Lord Henry Percy,*
> *surnamed Henrie Hotspur of the North.*
>
> > *With the humorous conceits*
> > *of Sir John Falstalffe.*

These elements are also to be found in an old play by an unknown author, *The famous victories of Henry the Fifth,* which included a prototype of Falstaff. This type of dramatic performance could not manage without something of the comic. The clown was to play tricks in the interludes and to amuse the audience between the speeches of the kings and generals, between the swordplay and the solemn processions.

On this occasion, there proved to be an advantageous position for the comedian: the legend about the Crown Prince provided a place for amusing pranks within the plot itself. Tales of the youth of Henry V invariably opened with his dissipation; the Prince whiled away his days with rogues and drunkards, but atoned for the errors of his youth upon ascending the throne.

This sort of comic figure had a long tradition behind him: the lies of a boastful warrier—found in works as far back as that of Plautus—unsuccessful thievery that ends in thrashing and wrangling with procuresses—all this had been portrayed by the comedians of both England and Italy. These scenes could easily have been taken from old plays and legends, and then set into a plot, and this is what Shakespeare did. It was probably thus that Falstaff acquired his first traits.

Shakespearean action usually develops in treatment of characters and simultaneously in a melee of ideas. The secondary characters who surround the primary one take part in the same primary action, and shape its nuances. In unravelling the plot, Shakespeare would make transitions from the elevated dramatic to the vulgar comic, placing the action in two planes at the same time.

It was possible for both perspectives to be present in a chronicle telling of the struggle to unite the England of the king and that of the rebellious feudal lords. This feudal theme is sounded both by grand trumpets, as in the case of the brave Percy, and by nasal bagpipes. Knighthood could find representatives in the legend of Hotspur's indomitable pride and in the farcical escapades of the degenerate mercenary.

An unusual unity is formed. We find in the writings of Marx and Engels: "The *bourgeoisie* revealed that the display of rough force, so admired in the Middle Ages by reactionaries, had its natural corollary in the most idle parasitism."

Hotspur has property: his violent temperament is shown not only in single combat but also during the division of lands. The property gains of the rebels depend upon the success of the rebellion. Sir John's property is an unpaid tavern bill and "one poor pennyworth of sugar candy to make thee long-winded." Castles, lands, and serfs are the real basis of the code of Hotspur's knighthood. The landless knight Falstaff's conversations on the same theme are mere parody. The aim of this mockery is so accurate that Engels bluntly called the period of the decay of feudalism "Falstaffian."

The author's intention seems clear: reprisal by laughter. The work of another writer comes to mind: by the side of the broad shadow of the English knight stretches the long shadow of the Spanish one. The two images were summoned forth to signal the demise of the Middle Ages—Sir John Paunch and Don Quixote de la Mancha. Only a madman could be carried away with the ideals of knighthood, and having once met Falstaff who could believe in feudal valor?

An aspiration to settle accounts with the various remnants of feudalism prompts Shakespeare to conduct the plot on two planes. The lofty thread is Hotspur's rebellion; the adventures of Falstaff provide a parallel comic thread. Both Hotspur and Falstaff fight only to continue their feudal existence. Boundless egoism is fundamental to both figures. Hotspur begins a civil war in the name of pride and its gratification. The egoism of Falstaff lets him forget all laws and precepts if only he can eat and drink to his heart's content. They are both creations of the same social structure. Despite Hotspur being young and Falstaff old, Hotspur is like the elder brother, the heir to the estate, and Falstaff resembles the younger who is left landless, squanders the last of his money, and arrives by stages at complete amorality. Both brothers had to be destroyed by royal power, for it is hampered both by the uproar of feudal violence and by feudal parasitism. Summoned to crush rebellion and to fight a great aggressive war abroad, Henry V is obliged to kill Hotspur and to exile Falstaff. The duel with Percy is the symbol of the might of royal power—its ability to destroy the troops of feudal lords—and the exile of Falstaff is a sign of Henry's subduing of the dissipated habits of youth in the name of the national interest.

These themes, ideas, and attitudes could easily be placed into the dramatic structure of a chronicle play, and that is exactly what Shakespeare did with them.

However, the fate of the glutton from the Boar's Head Tavern and of the skinny hidalgo from la Mancha did not take the shape their authors had intended.

No abstract concept of a theme existed for Shakespeare. The plot development merged with the very life of the protagonists. The theme was brought out by the conflict of the characters' aspirations and ripened with their fates. All this was indivisible from the nature of the emotional impact of the stage situations.

Shakespeare did not resort to false tactics and did not make the audience like, albeit briefly, a villain or ignore nobility. The attitude of the author is clearly seen in the contradictions in his characters, but he was impatient with prolonged clarifications of the qualities of people. His characters often announced the principal traits of their personalities themselves, immediately, in the first monologue. And the clash of characters and ideas began immediately, in the first scenes. The attack was impetus.

In reading the chronicle of Henry IV for the first time, one notices something different. The theme apparently begins to divorce itself from the lives of the characters. Its movement does not coincide with the emotional impact of the scenes. That which the author seems to wish to make persuasive is quite distinct from the nature of the persuasion. In this struggle among contradictory purposes, one still cannot find a main direction.

Rumors of the dissolute adventures of the heir of the house of Lancaster, the son of Henry Bolingbroke, Duke of Hereford, first appear in *Richard II:*

> *Bolingbroke*
> Can no man tell me of my unthrifty son?
> 'Tis full three months since I did see him last.
> If any plague hang over us, 'tis he.
> I would to God, my lords, he might be found.
> Inquire at London, 'mongst the taverns there,
> For there, they say, he daily doth frequent
> With unrestrainèd loose companions,
> Even such, they say, as stand in narrow lanes
> And beat our watch and rob our passengers.
> Which he, young wanton and effeminate boy,
> Takes on the point of honor to support
> So dissolute a crew.

This same motif appears in the beginning of *Henry IV, Part I.* The King envies the exploits of Harry Percy:

> Whilst I, by looking on the praise of him,
> See riot and dishonor stain the brow
> Of my young Harry. . . .

All this disposes the work to a definite harmony. Falstaff is one of those thieves who lie in wait for victims in the darkness of back streets. Holding sway over the will of a boy inexperienced in the ways of the world, the old profligate is the undoing of him who is the heir to the throne. What misfortune is in store for the people from such a friendship!

The fat man's sentence seems to have been passed even before his first entrance. The situation is intensified by a general picture of the life of the state. Civil war threatens the country; sedition has raised its head, and the King, no longer a young man, is in danger. And it is at this time, when every delay threatens death, that the son of the King and the hope of the nation forgets honor and duty and destroys himself in the haunts of Eastcheap.

The story's end is known from the outset; the day comes when the Prince of Wales finds the strength in himself to cast out the crew. Only then, when he has purified himself of the sins of his youth, will he be worthy of the crown. Evidently, this is what the audience is to anticipate with impatience.

For the time being, the audience is making the acquaintance of those of whom we have just spoken. On the stage appears that "young wanton and effeminate boy," Prince Hal, the ringleader of "so dissolute a crew." Yet that of which we spoke is not at all suggested by the action on the stage. The proposed robbery is no more than fun. Hal and Falstaff are not carried away with orgies, but with amusing banter. The wit of both is of high quality. Their only vice is a passion for puns, and it's reminiscent of a tournament of poets. In what way does Falstaff resemble a thief, and in what consists the depraved and ruinous life of the royal youth?

If the scene is put to one side and its events forgotten, it is possible with cold-blooded reason to condemn the pastimes of the Crown Prince as idleness and to blame Falstaff with parasitism. This would probably be logical. But the verdict would not be submitted as a result of the emotional influence of the scene itself. The "riot and dishonor stain the brow/ Of my young Harry" motif is so expressed that it does not evoke dissatisfaction or contempt in the audience.

This is only the beginning. Having made merry to his heart's content, Falstaff leaves the room. Poins and Hall devise a new bit of entertainment. And Poins leaves. The future King remains on the stage.

In Shakespearean dramaturgy, the first monologue of a hero is often of special significance. The hero thinks aloud, as it were. These speeches are somewhat similar to the internal monologue of the modern novel. The thoughts here expressed are crucial for an understanding both of the stamp of the hero's character and of the plot. The hero reveals his intentions and makes his plans.

Hal's first monologue is endowed with the same properties. The thoughts and plans of the Prince of Wales (of which we will speak later) do not seem attractive. Again, there is a contradiction—between the author's original intention to create an image of the ideal king and the content of the first monologue.

Foreign scholars often explain away such difficulties by citing old theatre customs forgotten in our century and by the psychology of the old audiences. As Dover Wilson put it, Elizabethans understood Hal's speech as no more than a reference to the tendency the play was to take. He does not believe that the monologue exposition had any relation to Hal's character, and considers psychological complexities to have been concocted by the nineteenth century, when people were used to realism. Yet Professor Bradbrook begins her book on the conventions of Elizabethan tragedy with the warning that Shakespeare was not the rule for that period but the exception.

Of course, investigations into the aesthetic norms of various periods in the history of theatre are valuable, but a modern audience that is unaware of these norms can comprehend Shakespearean drama perfectly well, and manages without guide books.

Perhaps Hal's monologue does not even need justification by theatrical convention. Let us return to this passage.

The monologue begins with the casting off of a mask, as is usual in Shakespeare. The hero, left alone, makes a pronounced change in his behavior and explains that he had been shamming until this moment.

Hal now expresses his thoughts in poetic images instead of in prose. The change in the style of his speech is important; with the change in intonation, history replaces comedy. The Prince of Wales follows his friends with his eyes.

> I know you all, and will a while uphold
> The unyoked humor of your idleness.
> Yet herein will I imitate the sun,
> Who doth permit the base contagious clouds
> To smother up his beauty from the world,
> That, when he please again to be himself,
> Being wanted, he may be more wondered at
> By breaking through the foul and ugly mists
> Of vapors that did seem to strangle him.
>
> .   .   .   .   .
>
> So, when this loose behavior I throw off
> And pay the debt I never promisèd,
> By how much better than my word I am,
> By so much shall I falsify men's hopes,
> And like bright metal on a sullen ground,
> My reformation, glittering o'er my faults,
> Shall show more goodly and attract more eyes
> Than that which hath no foil to set it off.
> I'll so offend, to make offense a skill,
> Redeeming time when men think least I will.

The meaning of his speech is clear; the Prince's dissipated life is a fable for simpletons. Any comparison of Falstaff's relation to the Crown Prince with the "base contagious clouds" or the "foul and ugly mists" that threaten strangulation is unwarranted. No one makes a drunkard out of Hal or forces him into a slough of vice. His debauchery is a mask. The "young wanton and effeminate boy" is gifted with self-control and a strong will, and is preparing himself to take over the reins of government when the time comes.

The poetic imagery of light after darkness, etc., reveals the essence of his plan: to let the legend of "so dissolute a crew" be painted in new colors and with new details, so that, at the right moment, he can abandon his comrades in "the unyoked humor of your idleness" and appear before the country as a statesman who has rejected everything personal in the name of law and duty.

The popularity of parables about repentant sinners serves to prove the success of the scheme.

What is the right moment for a transformation? This is answered twice. When Hal becomes King, he recalls the days of his youth:

> My father is gone wild into his grave,
> For in his tomb lie my affections.
> And with his spirit sadly I survive,
> To mock the expectation of the world,
> To frustrate prophecies, and to raze out
> Rotten opinion, who hath writ me down
> After my seeming. . . .

In the beginning of *Henry V,* the Archbishop also speaks of this:

> The courses of his youth promised it not.
> The breath no sooner left his father's body
> But that his wildness, mortified in him,
> Seemed to die too. Yea, at that very moment,
> Consideration like an angel came

The regeneration is to occur as soon as the old King lies in his grave. Henry IV dies and a halo begins to shine around the name of the new King. The manufacture of the nimbus is facilitated by the exile of Falstaff, for a start. The fat man is not at all evil, nor is he a hunter of young souls, but a victim, prepared and fattened in advance.

The fatted calf, no less famous in London than St. Paul's Cathedral, makes an especially efficacious sacrifice.

Falstaff responded to the pretended friendship of the Lancastrian youth with sincere love. During the course of the two parts of the chronicle, the Prince played more than one trick on the old man; he costumed himself as a robber and a servant, but the funniest was feigning friendship. The first games ended in scuffling, but the last resulted in death.

English scholars have discovered much of interest in Falstaff's genealogy. The parable of the prodigal son was named as a precursor of the chronicle under discussion, and they have attributed to Falstaff kinship with the Devil of the mystery plays and with Vice and Riot from the morality plays. But it is hard to detect traces of this kinship. If the relationship of Shakespeare's characters were to be that of Virtue and Vice, Vice should appear in a particularly unattractive light in the final scene. The audience should have to banish Falstaff from its heart as does the King of England.

When he finds out about the coronation of his friend, Sir John rushes to London. Exuberant with happiness, he stands beside Westminster Abbey.

"But to stand stained with travel," says Falstaff, gasping with joy, "and sweating with desire to see him, thinking of nothing else, putting all affairs else in oblivion, as if there were nothing else to be done but to see him."

Trumpets sound. The King appears. He draws near, passes by.

"God save thy Grace, King Hal! My royal Hal!" The old man is blessing him. "God save thee, my sweet boy!"

Could Shakespeare really have chosen these words to portray Vice at the moment before his just punishment?

Then the reprisal—arrogant, inexorable. The "sweet boy" bends his eyes towards this old man who loves him.

> I know thee not, old man. Fall to thy prayers.
> How ill white hairs become a fool and jester!
> I have long dreamed of such a kind of man,
> So surfeit-swelled, so old, and so profane,
> But, being awaked, I do despise my dream.

> Make less thy body hence, and more thy grace.
> Leave gormandizing. Know the grave doth gape
> For thee thrice wider than for other men.
> Reply not to me with a fool-born jest.
> Presume not that I am the thing I was,
> For God doth know, so shall the world perceive,
> That I have turned away my former self,
> So will I those that kept me company.
> When thou dost hear that I am as I have been,
> Approach me, and thou shalt be as thou wast,
> The tutor and the feeder of my riots.
> Till then, I banish thee, on pain of death,
>
> . . . . .
>
> Not to come near our person by ten mile.

The card that was not needed for the game was thrown from the table. The moral precepts of the King sound like cruel hypocrisy. But the question of morals was of least importance to the young King's plan. The role of Falstaff in relation to the Crown Prince could hardly be defined as that of the mentor of his riots. Henry V's thoughts are not at all concerned with the salvation of anyone's soul, including Falstaff's. Here was neither a sinner nor a regeneration. Like all miracles, this one was a hoax.

In comparing the first monologue with the last, it is possible to see the complete agreement of the scheme and its execution. Exalted advice should be silent, and those who calculate on the perception of those about them should remember the grave. This is hardly a variant of the parable of Virtue's victory over Vice; here we have Virtue holding Vice up to itself on purpose, so that later it may banish Vice and become even more pure.

Instead of the naïve legend about a princely sinner who repented, Shakespeare developed another motif that is common with him: in order to come into power, one has to be both crafty and treacherous. Yet, in other cases, these character traits did not evoke the sympathy of the author of *Hamlet*. Now the question is seen under a different light: Henry V must become a model, ideal monarch. Nevertheless, when he spoke of the history of a state, Shakespeare did not consider it possible to remain silent in reference to those qualities of beast and serpent which were, evidently, in more minds than Machiavelli's, deemed necessary to rulers—even to the best of them.

In the relationship of Hal and Falstaff appears the motif of friendship deceived; to use it meant to make Falstaff not only funny but also touching in his own way.

The parable of the prodigal son and the theme of the friendship of the old man and the youth are only details in a huge historical picture. Nonetheless, a simple count of the Falstaff scenes shows that they occupy almost half of both chronicles. Why, then, is so much place given to the Falstaffian in a story of the coming to power of an ideal king?

The chronicles form a united whole. The beginning of a motif appearing in one of them must often be sought in the preceding plays. Richard II came to fear Hal's father, Henry Bolingbroke, the Duke of Hereford (and future king of England), when he saw how the latter tried to win the love of the people:

> Ourself and Bushy, Bagot here, and Green
> Observed his courtship to the common people—
> How he did seem to dive into their hearts
> With humble and familiar courtesy,
> What reverence he did throw away on slaves,
> Wooing poor craftsmen with the craft of smiles
> And patient underbearing of his fortune,
> As 'twere to banish their affects with him.
> Off goes his bonnet to an oyster wench.
> A brace of draymen did God speed him well
> And had the tribute of his supple knee,
> With "Thanks, my countrymen, my loving friends,"

The misgiving was warranted. As is related later, the people hailed Bolingbroke's entry into the capital, and threw "dust and rubbish" out their windows at the King.

At the beginning of *Richard II,* Shakespeare described the life of the court, and did not skimp on the dark colors: extravagance, flattery, slander, perfidy.

How did the Lancastrian heir behave himself at this time? In contrast to feudal conspirators and court flatterers, their lives fenced off from those of ordinary Englishmen by stone walls, the young aristocrat appeared unceremoniously among the people. Hal did not forget that his father, at the beginning of his career, counted not only on families of noble blood but also on craftsmen, draymen, and merchants. Shakespeare showed the ideal-king-to-be in the midst of the daily life of the people and in the dirty corners of the capital.

"I have sounded the very base string of humility," boasts Hal. "Sirrah, I am sworn brother to a leash of drawers, and can call them all by their Christen names, as Tom, Dick, and Francis. They take it already upon their salvation that though I be but Prince of Wales, yet I am the king of courtesy; . . . and when I am King of England, I shall command all the good lads in Eastcheap. They call drinking deep, dyeing scarlet, and when you breathe in your watering, they cry 'hem!' and bid you play it off. To conclude, I am so good a proficient in one quarter of an hour that I can drink with any tinker in his own language during my life."[1]

He is not speaking of mischief. The future King fraternizes with drawers, drinks with tinkers, chatters freely in their jargon, and has a reputation as "a lad of mettle." It is not surprising that not only the lads of Eastcheap, but thousands of Englishmen, are willing to give their lives for such a sovereign.

In *Richard II,* there is a tale of how Harry Percy invited the Prince to the tournament at Oxford and how Hal replied:

> . . . he would unto the stews,
> And from the common'st creature pluck a glove
> And wear it as a favor, and with that
> He would unhorse the lustiest challenger.

This, too, is more than a joke. The country has been taxed to exhaustion, and the quitrents go to finance court holidays and tournaments. The Duke's son shuns the costly pleasures of the aristocracy and disdains court entertainment. Along the back streets of London, rumor has it that the heir to the throne prefers carousing with craftsmen to fashionable amusements.

And Falstaff? What is his place in this important political motif? . . . The fat vagabond is a guide showing the future King around his possessions. There is a number of stories in existence telling how the King got to know his people. In order to learn the life of the poor, the King had to disguise himself and wear a false beard, so that the people would not fear him.

Falstaff's friendship opened all the tavern doors to the young Prince, and with Jack he was at home in any company. Despite his

[1] *Henry IV, Part I,* II, iv.

enormous appetite, Falstaff was a welcome guest at every table where primness and flattery were absent. There is gaiety where Falstaff is, and this is dearer than formal entertainment. Jesting is a key to open the heart. There was no better way of earning the friendship of the lads of Eastcheap than to be able to joke with them.

In travelling the distant streets and country roads with Falstaff, Henry V learned popular humor. When Shakespeare comes to the end of his biography of the "king of so much worth," he does not conclude with a pretentious finale, but with gaiety: Henry V jests with Katharine of France much as a soldier with his sweetheart. England does not wish to unite France with itself to the blast of fanfares, but to the sound of puns reminiscent of its taverns.

Everyday life enters the chronicle with Falstaff. Thanks to his participation in the action, the full-dress history of kings and courtiers is jostled by, and gradually begins to yield to, popular history and the scenes of the work-a-day world, in which craftsmen, soldiers, vagabonds, and tavern waiters act out their parts. This history is written in the language of comedy, the language in which realistic art spoke its first words.

The struggle between the sublime and the ordinary, the grandiose and the comic, had already begun in the mystery plays. In order to link heaven and earth in the liturgy being staged in the churches, they had to introduce bits of reality: soldiers playing dice at the feet of the crucified Christ, the repentance of the adultress, market-women. None of these figures were religious in themselves. They were outlined in humor.

Once the mystery play went from the church into the marketplace, the vernacular began to replace Latin. This brought it closer to the popular audience, and the comic elements began to expand. The bells of buffoonery were admixed to prayer. The sacrament came to be destroyed by the comic and realistic.

Bishops and princes excommunicated the comedians from the church and threatened them with the whip. To this they responded with jest, becoming even more daring. It was in this way that the image of the jester was created by many nations. These images also retained the generic traits which had been preserved from antiquity. Various fat men were among these figures; one must go far into the past to begin tracing their history.

The biblical pharoah dreamed a dream:

And, behold, there came up out of the river seven kine, fatfleshed and well favoured, and they fed in a meadow:

And, behold, seven other kine came up after them, poor and very ill favoured and leanfleshed, such as I never saw in all the land of Egypt for badness:

And the lean and ill favoured kine did eat up the first seven fat kine. . . .

Behind the symbolism lay pictures of drought, crop failure, and famine.

If the harvest were good, people gave praise to a god of plenty, of fat flesh.

Included in the constellation of Dionysus were mocking satyrs, among whose number was Silenus. He was the most dissolute of the gods. In those places where Bacchus dwelled, boiling waters turned into wine—Silenus became an inveterate drunkard. He was fat and balding, old and gluttonous, gay and forever drunk.

Horace spoke in support of his divine origin and would not permit him to be placed on the same level as the characters of comedies. Silenus was possessed of the happy mildness of the immortals.

In one legend, the fat dissolute god reared and educated Dionysus, initiated him into all knowledge and art, and taught him how to make wine. In another, King Midas discovered that the fat god was making merry in his kingdom and was mixing wine into the water of his rivers. The god got dead drunk and fell into the hands of the King. He disclosed to his captor his knowledge of the nature of all things and foretold the future.

When the grapes were harvested, and the new wine was first foaming, the vintners of Attica sang praises of Bacchus and his divine suite—in which Silenus staggered along, a merry god of corpulent and sinful human flesh.

The clusters of grapes, the gift of Bacchus, were grown by human labor and made into a beverage that made people merry. When each locale had its own Dionysus, the populace glorified its local god. Songs gave full play to jesting accusation, and everything that hindered the vintner was ridiculed. In Attica, the liquored procession was called *komos,* and it is from the village Komos that scholars begin the chronology of comedy.

During the Middle Ages, the flesh was subdued and mortified. Lent was highly exalted. But even though they buried graven images of the fat god in the ground, he himself did not cease to exist. He could be seen on holidays at fairs, where he joined battle with the god of lean flesh.

In his "Battle between Carnival and Lent," Pieter Breughel depicted the allegorical skirmish. A ruddy, gay man of flesh bestrides a huge cask. He thrusts his feet into stew pots instead of stirrups, and he wields, instead of a sword, a spit with a roast boar's head. A raw-boned and severely dressed figure rides against Carnival. It sits on a narrow church chair; a nun with a withered monk dray in the stage on which Lent is seated. The god of lean flesh aims at the god of corpulence not with a spear but with a long-handled wooden shovel on which are two bony little fish.

All nations loved the fat god. Russia also knew him. In his *Poetic Views of the Slavs on Nature,* A. Afanasiev writes: "In several villages, they still cart about a drunken muzhik who is to represent Shrovetide. They harness about ten horses to a sleigh, with more horses in single file, and they ride each horse with a knout or a broom in their hands. Handbells and rattles are hung wherever possible, and the sleigh or carriage is adorned with besom. They put a cup and more than a liter of vodka into the hands of the peasant Shrovetide, and beyond that, place a keg of beer and bast-box of food beside him."

Amusingly illumined, Merry Shrovetide strode all over Europe to the squeal of tin whistles and the sound of hand bells. One hand held a liter or so of wine, the other a sausage.

The pagan allegory of fertility had withered away, but the rite of popular festival, with the figure of fleshly human merriment, remained.

The name of Silenus appeared in one of the sermons of a new time: "Alcibiades," François Rabelais wrote, "in that dialogue of Plato's which is entitled 'The Banquet,' whilst he was setting forth the praises of his schoolmaster Socrates (without doubt, the prince of philosophers) amongst the discourses to that purpose, said that he resembled the sileni. Sileni of old were little boxes, like those we may now see in the shops of apothecaries, painted on the outside with wanton toyish figures, as harpies, satyrs, bridled geese, horned hares, saddled ducks, flying goats, thiller harts, and other such like counterfeited pictures, at pleasure, to excite people with laughter as Silenus himself, who was the foster father of good Bacchus, was wont to do; but with those capricious caskets called sileni were carefully preserved and kept many rich and fine drugs, such as balm, ambergreese, amamon, musk, civet, with several kinds of precious stones, and other things of great price. . . ."

Silenus here is the image of everything that evokes laughter by reason of its grotesquely comic exterior, but that keeps beautiful things inside itself.

". . . a certain sneaking jobbernol objected that his (Horace's —G. K.) verses savored more of the wine than of the oil," said Rabelais towards the end of his prologue. "A certain addle-headed coxcomb saith the same of my books; but a turd for him. The fragrant odor of wine; oh! how much more sparkling, warming, charming, celestial, and delicious it is, than of oil!"

Freethinking is praised in this book as though it were enjoying a time of feast; the table is set with pitchers, and Bacchus's cluster reigns, heads are turned to merry harmonies. The feast begins with a revelry of images.

The child was born from its mother's ear, and immediately set to draining a jug of wine. The young adult urinated from the bell tower of the cathedral of Notre Dame de Paris: 260,418 Parisians drowned in the flood, "besides the women and little children."

The reader has fallen into a world of the grotesque.

It was mostly things carnal that were subject to this grotesque exaggeration.

However, the pathos of this tale of the functions of the human organism was not evoked by lightheartedness. The roast boar's head on the spit was aimed against the spade with the fish of church fasting. The smell of wine flung back the narcotic of holy oil. Apotheoses of gluttony made them forget to pray before the image of shrivelled martyrs.

If the lives of saints were described as continual fasting and meditation on the vulgar sinfulness of earthly existence, then Rabelais began his description of the morning of Gargantua with the following enumeration: "Then he relieved himself fore and aft, spued, belched, cracked, yawned, spitted, coughed, hawked, sneezed, and blew his nose like an archdeacon; and to fortify against the fog and bad air, went to breakfast, having some good fried tripes, fair rashers on the coals, good gammons of bacon, store of good minced bread, cheese, and chopped parsley strewed together."

Not only is it permissible to speak of all this, but these things should be celebrated, for there is beauty in the manifestations of the human being—even in the lowliest of them.

"Matter, surrounded by a poetically sensual halo, smiles affably at man," wrote Marx about Bacon's works.

New art learned from antiquity and folk art simultaneously. Rabelais's novel grew out of cheap pocket books. The buoyant roughness of folk art was contrasted to refinement. This is not to say that the new art was immediately accepted. Voltaire called Rabelais a "drunken philosopher" and abused Shakespeare as a "savage."

The corpulence of Falstaff made its appearance in an era when the bonfires of the Inquisition still burned and the gray tedium of Puritanism had already descended upon men.

"Allow not nature more than nature needs,/ Man's life's as cheap as a beast's," said Lear. Plenty is one of Shakespeare's favorite images—the flourishing of Nature and of the feeling and thoughts of man.

In the Russian language there is a forgotten word which has fallen out of use: "veselotvornyi"—which means, according to the lexicographer Dal, "that which produces or evokes merriment." Perhaps it is an abundance of just this quality that we find in Falstaff. By the devices of Renaissance ornament, all aspects of humor—from clownery to philosophic satire—eddy in the poetry of his figure, and are transformed into wonders. But the essence of this figure is not easy to understand.

He sleeps, settling with some difficulty into a filthy, broken armchair; he is old and balding, and suffers from gout and short wind. He strikes everyone as a liar, a glutton, and a braggart. The walls of his wretched room have become crooked, the beams in the ceiling blackened with soot. Plates with the remains of a meal, overturned jugs—he has gorged himself for free again.

A beatific smile on his face, he snores. The sack has not yet dried on his lips.

A pitiful picture . . .

But look: the golden rays of a Hellenic sun shine through the window of the Boar's Head Tavern.

The earth witnesses the struggle not only of Shrovetide and Lent, but also of fat and lean words. The miraculous language of the folk is made of words that are able to lighten labors, cure diseases, and put a charm on love, and it was replaced by labels and nicknames for objects and actions. Words were chained to practical purposes. And the colors faded. The syllables lost their ring. The word became a colorless and soundless thing—a lean thing.

Language is a never-ending sport for Falstaff. It is a fascinating game of word-combination, whimsical phrase drawings, streams of metaphor, and a flight of puns that race to overtake one another.

At any given moment, Falstaff is "veselotvornyi," mirthful. It would seem that asking the time of day is a prosaic affair, but the Prince has only to look at Falstaff, and his answer takes on an incredible form. With what sort of watch does Sir John verify the time? The Prince discusses it as follows:

What a devil hast thou to do with the time of the day? Unless hours were cups of sack, and minutes capons, and clocks the tongues of bawds, and dials the signs of leaping houses, and the blessed sun himself a fair hot wench in flame-colored taffeta, I see no reason why thou shouldst be so superfluous to demand the time of the day.

The conversation takes place during Falstaff's first scene. The next Falstaff scene is devoted to "purse-taking." Again, only a game. To suspect Jack of self-interest would be as preposterous as to assume that the fat knight could have any interest in the ciphers and dials on a ticking mechanism. Falstaff is not a swindler; he is one of the "squires of the night's body," "gentlemen of the shade," "minions of the moon," as well as one of "Diana's foresters." Thus, in the opinion of Sir John, are thieves to be called. Does a rogue need this kind of terminology? Indeed, the aim of thieves is to conceal their trade and pass themselves off as honest men.

Children play cowboys and Indians. The greatest pleasure of the games consists in the names: "How, great chief of Sioux nation! I am white brother!" Sonorous words and luxuriant nicknames must replace ordinary expressions. "Paleface speaks with forked tongue!" Or do we seriously think that the child is getting ready to scalp his playmate?

A merry game is going on at the Boar's Head. From player to player sail verbal balls to be caught in flight; sentences somersault in midair and turn over to become puns. What is the point of this sort of pastime?

In the beginning of the first book of *Gargantua,* Rabelais said that there is neither evil nor contagion in it, but only grounds for laughter. Humor is a quality inherent in man. Rabelais concluded his apostrophe to the readers thus:

> It being all my view
> To inspire with mirth the hearts of those that moan,
> And change to laughter the afflictive groan.

Falstaff and the Prince appear before the audience after a court scene—national strife has come to a boil, and revolt is at hand. Disaster visits England. ". . . the poor abuses of the time want countenance," says Falstaff. And yet, "the true Prince may, for recreation sake, prove a false thief."

Falstaff himself is a false thief, one who robs for general amusement. Nevertheless, it is immediately learned that all the participants in the proposed robbery betray one another. Poins makes an arrangement with the Prince by which they will steal the booty from Falstaff and make the fat man lie about his adventures. The Prince betrayed them all: he pretended to be a simplehearted "wag."

The first skirmish takes place on the highway, near Gadshill. They give Falstaff a drubbing and make him run himself into a mortal sweat. The joke finds its conclusion in the tavern. Jack falls into the trap and is exposed as a coward and a liar. Yet, this is mere semblance; it is not a legal proceeding, but a tournament of jesters. The merriest wins—he gets the last pun. No matter what traps they lay for Falstaff, he gets out of them with ease. The Prince of Wales is beaten by the prince of comic poetry.

The tournaments continue through both parts of the chronicle. It is a duel of metaphors. The combatants' appearance provides the topic for their competition. The Prince plays up the corpulence of his opponent, but here Falstaff is not delinquent in his debt.

" 'Sblood, you starveling, you elf skin, you dried neat's tongue, you bull's pizzle, you stockfish! Oh, for breath to utter what is like thee! You tailor's yard, you sheath, you bow case, you vile standing tuck——"

The last word goes to the fat man.

Training of the wit precedes the contest. Everything that catches the eye becomes a target. In an offhand manner, Falstaff composes poems on Bardolph's nose—and what doesn't this nose resemble! . . . There is born an image of a bonfire on the poop of an admiral's ship; the title of Knight of the Burning Lamp is conferred upon the possessor of such a nose. Stunned by the attack of these nicknames, Bardolph tries to defend himself.

Bardolph: Why, Sir John, my face does you no harm.

Falstaff: No I'll be sworn, I make as good use of it as many a man doth of a death's-head or a memento mori. I never see thy face but I think upon Hell-fire and Dives that lived in purple, for there he is in his robes, burning, burning. If thou wert anyway given to virtue, I would swear by thy face; my oath should be "By this fire, that's God's angel." But thou art altogether given over, and wert indeed, but for the light in thy face, the son of utter darkness. When thou rannest up Gadshill in the night to catch my horse, if I did not think thou hadst been an ignis fatuus or a ball of wildfire, there's no purchase in money. Oh, thou art a perpetual triumph, an everlasting bonfire light! Thou hast saved me a thousand marks in links and torches, walking with thee in the night betwixt tavern and tavern. But the sack that thou hast drunk me would have bought me lights as good cheap at the dearest chandler's in Europe. I have maintained that salamander of yours with fire any time this two and thirty years, God reward me for it!

In vain Bardolph tries to parry the witticisms and to insert a joke of his own:

Bardolph: 'Sblood, I would my face were in your belly!

Falstaff: God-a-mercy! So should I be sure to be heartburned.

In his short story "The Skylight Room," O. Henry wrote, "Tried out, Falstaff might have rendered more romance to the ton than would have Romeo's rickety ribs to the ounce."

There were any number of facets to the distinctive romance of

Falstaff's humor: buffoonery, parody, philosophic grotesquerie. There is one theme that merits particularly serious contemplation.

They lie side by side on the muddy earth after the historic battle—the dead knight Hotspur and the coward Falstaff, feigning death. Once he has looked about and ascertained that the battle is over and that there is no more danger, Falstaff raises himself carefully and begins to philosophize. He says that he has done well to pretend to be dead, otherwise "that hot termagant Scot has paid me scot and lot too."

"Counterfeit?" Sir John asks himself. "I lie, I am not counterfeit. To die is to be a counterfeit, for he is but the counterfeit of a man who hath not the life of a man. But to counterfeit dying when a man thereby liveth is to be no counterfeit, but the true and perfect image of life indeed."

The mirthmaking force is directed at the fearful enemy. A favorite image of the Middle Ages: dead men beat drums and play flutes; scantily dressed in his rags of rotted skin, a corpse-skeleton drags ploughmen, kings, clergymen, knights, and merchants by the hand.

"You are all counterfeits!" howls Death. "Wait for the trumpets of the Last Judgment, prepare for your resurrection. And always remember: the scythe is raised, the wheel of fate is squeaking, death dances, join the dance!"

To the round dance of death, Shakespeare opposes the round dance of life.

Only the daring of Shakespeare would venture to compose this conclusion to the scene: Falstaff, alarmed at the thought that Hotspur has only lost consciousness, decides to plunge his sword into the knight's body a few more times, anyway—as insurance. This prime coward stabs and slashes the body of the man of courage with a cry of "Therefore, sirrah, . . ." and later hoists the body onto his shoulders like a sack of potatoes and carries it off to get a reward.

What is the meaning of this unnatural cruelty and, it would seem, immoral violence to the body of a dead man, this mockery of the dead? . . . Did the author finally decide to evoke abhorrence of Falstaff? Yet, even, after a scene like this, neither the audience nor the reader really conceives any hatred for Jack. The very witty and, in its own way, convincing monologue about honor, and this conversation, is not concerned with the dignity of humanism, but with a militant vanity, which is inhuman by its very nature. It was not a simple matter to spit in the ugly bloodstained face of such vanity.

"Diseases desperate grown/By desperate appliance are relieved, /Or not at all." This is said in *Hamlet*.

The English historian Christopher Hill reminds us that Cromwell ordered the horses stabled in cathedrals so as to put an end to the order under which people were lashed and branded for unorthodox views on the mystery of the sacrament.

"There is Percy," announced Falstaff, dumping the corpse of "the king of honor" at the feet of the Prince. "If your father will do me any honor, so; if not, let him kill the next Percy himself."

Shakespeare often evinces a different attitude toward the concept of "honor" than towards that of "conscience." Honor is a limited category; the feudal honor of Laertes leads to the dishonorable substitution of foils at the contest and to the use of poison. Hamlet delays in carrying out his debt of honor; but there is not a moment's hesitation either in the Danish Prince or in the Venetian Moor when it is a matter of conscience—of the unshakable sense of inner truth.

There is much external beauty in the appearance of feudal honor, and the poet expresses the ideal of Hotspur in the full magnificence of its knightly imagery. But the gilt peels off quickly when fat Jack becomes involved in the matter. Like a great adipose beast, he goes into the temple of the loftiest class ideals and, chuckling with satisfaction, tramples and pollutes the notions of warriors regarding knightly glory.

Once humanity had dared—according to the famous words of Marx—it broke off with the past. It was a dark and fearful past, and jokes about it were anything but good-natured.

The future was not imagined as gay, either.

True, sometimes the tavern rocked with laughter, but suddenly underground tremors were heard and the Boar's Head turned out to have been built on a volcano.

In the second part of *Henry IV*, there is a stronger thematic and stylistic difference between historical and Falstaffian scenes: the action breaks down into a parallel development of lines. These lines have more inner connection in the movement of contrast and parody than in any development of conflict. The two lines are brought together only in the end with Henry V's accession to the throne.

Until his meeting with his dying father, Prince Hal did not have his own dramatic movement, nor did he appear to be more than an ordinary participant in the Falstaff scenes. If, in Part I of the chronicle, Hal is the central hero and Falstaff is his satellite, now Sir John confidently takes over the center of the state.

The King is ill. His heir fears that his grief will seem false to those about him, so he prefers to make merry again in the company of Falstaff. The author points out once more that Hal does nothing without reflection. There are various ways of treating the scenes with the dying father, but the theme of aspiration toward power seems to be expressed with greater cogency than the motif of filial sorrow.

At the beginning of Part II of the chronicle it is clear that the battle of Shrewsbury has not brought peace to the country. The contradictions are not resolved. The death of Hotspur is no more than an episode in an interminable civil war. The first part is structurally repeated in the second. Rebellion is prepared, and its participants betray one another. This time there is no feudal figure equal to Hotspur.

The Earl of Northumberland and his friends thirst for revenge. The images that portray the time are close both to tragic poetry and to pictures of a sick era.

> The times are wild. Contention, like a horse
> Full of high feeding, madly hath broke loose
> And bears down all before him.

As it is in *King Lear,* human anger is blended with a violent uproar of nature.

> Let Heaven kiss earth! Now let not Nature's hand
> Keep the wild flood confined! Let order die!

The landscapes of *Macbeth, Hamlet,* and *Julius Caesar* already appear in Shakespeare's poetry. People of the iron age leave the stage; they hurry off to sharpen their swords and saddle their chargers.

Silence. No calls to bloody vengeance are heard, no thunder of curses, no threats. And then the sound of a normal human voice: ". . . what says the doctor to my water?"

Accompanied by a small page, who was picked up by way of contrast to his unbounded figure, Falstaff appears again. It is possible to live, breathe, and laugh. The sinful world is still spinning on its axis. Sir John still continues his dissolute existence, and doesn't give a hoot for calls to blood and revenge. Threatening portents do not distress him in the least.

The two lines collide stylistically. The language of the chronicle of national events becomes all the more pathetic, and the tale of Falstaff's pranks becomes all the more ordinary.

National heroes never come down from their tragic heights: their declamations are resounding, and the metaphor and hyperbole pile up. Next to these rhetorical beauties, in the next scene, is the chatter of different people concerned with petty daily matters and everyday cares. Here, everything is palpable, three-dimensional, precisely spelled, and with a definite address. Bardolph betakes himself to Smithfield to buy a horse; Falstaff acquires a saddle in Pie Corner and is about to dine at the Lubber's Head in Lumbert Street at Master Smooth's, the silkman. Sir John cannot stand applejohns; Doll likes wine from the Canaries; and Poins has two pairs of stockings, one of them peach-colored.

Reproaching Falstaff for his thoughtlessness, Mistress Quickly reminds him of the circumstances of their past love. The widow is plunged in lyric reminiscence:

Thou didst swear to me upon a parcel-gilt goblet, sitting in my Dolphin Chamber, at the round table, by a sea-coal fire, upon Wednesday in Wheeson week, when the Prince broke thy head for liking his father to a singing man of Windsor—thou didst swear to me then, as I was washing thy wound, to marry me and make me my lady thy wife. Canst thou deny it? Did not goodwife Keech, the butcher's wife, come in then and call me Gossip Quickly? Coming in to borrow a mess of vinegar, telling us she had a good dish of prawns, whereby thou didst desire to eat some, whereby I told thee they were ill for a green wound? And didst thou not, when she was gone downstairs, desire me to be no more so familiarity with such poor people, saying that ere long they should call me madam? And didst thou not kiss me and bid me fetch thee thirty shillings? I put thee now to thy book oath. Deny it, if thou canst.

The short tale is almost a finished pattern of style. Both the choice of the hero, and the manner of describing his life, the daily round, the objects which surround him (and at which the narrator stares fixedly) are profoundly important. The importance lies not only in the fact that every detail of the life of a tavern hostess becomes significant to literature, but also in the wedging of the hostess' tale into one of the fate of kings and generals.

Figures commonplace in a performance of popular comedians happen onto a stage where the history of the nation is being acted out.

These figures are far from being masks. In one brief monologue, there is a whole symphony of human feelings. Here is the vanity of the man in the street (goodwife Keech "ere long . . . should call me madam") and a simplehearted faith in the promises of Falstaff. Here is the painted lyricism of memories of broken heads and of thirty shillings lost without a trace. And here is a hope that the threat of an oath on the Bible could frighten Falstaff. Feminine reproaches and touching solicitude and important homely matters (her neighbor had prepared a dish of prawns and didn't have enough vinegar) and hopes for a happy ending (he loves me all the same!)—they are all here.

The abundance of this kind of detail, and the love of these details, anticipates much that is to come in the development of literature.

Later generations cherish the memory of men of genius. They erect monuments, and marble slabs notify the passer-by that a great man once lived here. A special kind of memorial is sometimes built. A bond between artists stretches across the centuries.

In the nineteenth century, a noted English writer set out for the suburbs of London to find the place where, according to legend, the Boar's Head Tavern had been located. Here the boon companion of the Prince and the faithless lover of Gossip Quickly was said to have given his feasts. Here shone the blazing nose of Bardolph, and here the beauteous Doll Tearsheet was wont to mince. It was right here that Charles Dickens wanted to settle and write his books.

Balzac built the gigantic structure of his *La Comédie Humaine* according to a system of different cycles: "Scenes of private, provincial, Parisian, military, political, and country life.

"Such is the foundation, full of actors, full of comedies and tragedies, on which are raised the Philosophical Studies—the second part of my work, in which the social instrument of all these effects is displayed, and the ravages of the mind are painted, feeling after feeling." Thus wrote Balzac.

Within the bounds of the two chronicles, Shakespeare tried to develop these kinds of cycles simultaneously, in depth and in length.

In *Henry IV,* there coexist scenes of political, military, London, and provincial life, philosophical études, and the portrayal of the destructive storms of thought, "feeling after feeling."

Shakespeare's works include in themselves drama, the epic, and the lyric. Despite their clearly stated theatrical form, they also qualify as novels—as we now understand the term. They contain landscape, life environment, and the frank voice of the author.

Like the torments of the heroes of the tragedies, the destructive storm of thought sets in during the hours when Henry IV cannot sleep.

> Then you perceive the body of our kingdom
> How foul it is, what rank diseases grow,
> And with what danger, near the heart of it.

The King remembers the prophecy of Richard II.

> "The time will come that foul sin, gathering head,
> Shall break into corruption."

It has been fulfilled.

Similar feelings torment the leader of the revolt. These thoughts prey on the mind of the Archbishop of York:

> . . . We are all diseased,
> And with our surfeiting and wanton hours
> Have brought ourselves into a burning fever,
> And we must bleed for it. . . .

The disease of the world consists in both feudal uprisings and royal power. The debate is not between sickness and health but between the greater and the lesser ailment. The treatment given is bloodletting. Both sides are prepared to make lavish use of it.

And, for the time being, the earth keeps on spinning.

In a quiet little garden in Gloucestershire, in front of the house of a Justice of the Peace, two foolish old men sit on a bench and sluggishly converse about life.

Shallow: . . . And to see how many of my old acquaintances are dead!
Silence: We shall all follow, Cousin.
Shallow: Certain, 'tis certain, very sure, very sure. Death, as the Psalmist saith, is certain to all, all shall die. How a good yoke of bullocks at Stamford fair?
Silence: By my troth, I was not there.
Shallow: Death is certain. Is old Double of your town living yet?
Silence: Dead, sir.
Shallow: Jesu, Jesu, dead! A' drew a good bow, and dead! A' shot a fine shoot. . . . How a score of ewes now?
Silence: Thereafter as they be. A score of good ewes may be worth ten pounds.
Shallow: And is old Double dead?

They are born, they die, they love, they hate, they fight in the name of their beliefs and interests; they kill one another—people live. Life seethes, full of contradictions, varying convictions, divergent roads, irreconcilable interests, and somewhere, to one side of everything, lives the man in the street. No matter what happens in the world, he senses the passing of time only by the changes in the price of livestock.

This is the way of human existence: "To be or not to be" interests some; others only care how much bulls bring now at Stamford fair.

Falstaff continues his peregrinations. Hoping to recruit soldiers, he arrives at the Gloucestershire home of his old schoolfellow, the Justice of the Peace, Shallow. The great Corpulence visits the great Leanness. Shallow is not only an insignificant man, he is the Great Insignificance. This figure embodies all the inanity of the existence of a man who lacks the gifts of thought, desire, action, pleasure, and pain.

Every one of Shakespeare's characters has his own rhythm. Blood rushes through the veins of Hotspur, and impatience urges on his thoughts and passions. The breathing of Henry IV is heavy and labored. Shallow's existence is so peaceful, slow, and monotonous that it seems as though a minute stretches into a decade for him. Thought has a very difficult birth. The sentence congeals on the spot and becomes like a crack in a phonograph record: the needle sticks and the same noise is interminably protracted. This is the mode of speech of this man "like a forked radish, with a head fantastically carved upon it with a knife."

Give me your good hand, give me your Worship's good hand.
It is well said, in faith, sir, and it is well said indeed. . . . Good phrases are surely, and ever were, very commendable. . . . Very good, a good phrase.
Where's the roll? Where's the roll? Where's the roll? Let me see, let me see, let me see. So, so, so, so, so, so, so. Yea, marry sir, Ralph Mouldy! Let them appear as I call, let them do so, let them do so. Let me see, where is Mouldy?

The record has three cracks, all told: school reminiscences about trifling escapades, instructions concerning the farm, and the price of cattle. This is all there is to life. The school memories involve some strumpet and a childish scuffle; things still happened in the life of the estimable squire in those days. Later, time ground to a halt. Everything died and was covered with dust. There remained only a growing list of the dead and the going price of livestock. Shallow's world was focussed on the bucket for which a new link must be bought and the sack that William the cook lost at Hinckley Fair—he had to recover the value of the sack.

Shakespeare takes delight in this image of infinite tedium.

As two poles of human existence, Falstaff and Shallow meet. Corpulence mocks cachexy.

Everything that comes into Falstaff's view is transformed by means of his wonderful talent into an inexhaustible source for humor. His field of vision is wide in scope. Life serves him as a warehouse filled with phenomena suitable for a number of whimsical comparisons, luxuriant metaphors, and unbelievable contrasts. Shallow's globe is limited to the diminutive space where his oxen graze, and on this little speck he drags out his existence.

However, Shallow is not only stupidity, banality, and cachexy incarnate, but also a protagonist of the provincial theme. Shallow is a landed gentleman and a justice and is full of comic vanity and a sense of the greatness of his own person. On his little plot, the landowner is power and law. He is a part of the social system, and

Falstaff's meeting with him concerns government business: the recruiter from the capital comes to the Justice of the Peace. Falstaff's characteristics are already known. Now the nature of the government activity of Shallow is ascertained.

Davy: I beseech you, sir, to countenance William Viser of Woncot against Clement Perkes o' the hill.

Shallow: There is many complaints, Davy, against that Visor. That Visor is an arrant knave, on my knowledge.

Davy: I grant your Worship that he is a knave, sir. But yet, God forbid, sir, but a knave should have some countenance at his friend's request. An honest man, sir, is able to speak for himself when a knave is not. I have served your Worship truly, sir, this eight years, and if I cannot once or twice in a quarter bear out a knave against an honest man, I have but a very little credit with your Worship. The knave is mine honest friend, sir, therefore I beseech your Worship let him be countenanced.

Shallow: Go to, I say he shall have no wrong.

Feature for detailed feature, and despite apparent digressions, Shakespeare draws his age. The tale of sick times is told sometimes with hatred, sometimes with irony, sometimes poetically, and sometimes in emphatic prose. The ulcers of the disease are visible in a provincial farmstead, as well as in the royal palace and the castles of feudal barons.

Rabelais devised the term "Pantagruelism." Perhaps the last here who lived in the spirit of Pantagruelism was Falstaff. Three centuries later, a new definition appeared: "the Pickwick spirit." Narrow outlooks become material for distinctive poetry as well as for humor.

Shakespeare's view of this little world is devoid of sentimentality. Boredom and stupidity rule in a swamp where time has stopped and where a man without a drop of Falstaffian blood holds sway.

Prince John of Lancaster agrees to conclude a peace. As soon as the rebel leaders disband their armies, the Prince sends the betrayed conspirators to the block. This is the sum total of the talk about honor. After knightly oaths, the command: "Pursue the scattered stray."

The revolt is over; Henry IV dies.

Before the last breath of the father has time to leave his lips, his heir takes over. At this crucial moment in the history of the state, the Falstaff theme crops up again.

The dying king is afraid that his son will pluck off "the muzzle of restraint" and that plunderers will stream into the English court as "the wild dog/ Shall flesh his tooth on every innocent."

It is difficult to compare Falstaff with "the wild dog" and to picture the bodies of "the innocent" surrounding him. It is also of some significance that the image of power is not given by majestic representations but is compared with a muzzle. In order to explain the metaphor, Henry IV tells his son ". . . to busy giddy minds/ With foreign quarrels, that action, hence borne out,/ May waste the memory" of the subjects concerning "the former days."

The King's heart stops beating. The time has come for Hal to fulfill his former intention:

> I'll so offend, to make offense a skill,
> Redeeming time when men least think I will.

The youth of the Prince of Wales comes to an end, and the age of Falstaff is over. The two stories—that of the English King and that of Jack the merrymaker—are caught in a firmly knotted bundle.

The heavy hand of the law falls on the shoulder of the jovial old fellow. The luminary ends its era, and the constellation disappears. Soon the flaming nose of Bardolph will be extinguished; the widow Quickly will die in the hospital of the malady of France; Doll Tearsheet will be dragged into Fleet Prison. The period of gay adventure on the state's cruel earth is not long. The clank of iron and the roll of drums are heard here far more often than laughter and gay songs.

Nevertheless, the author intended to make merry again at the end of Part II of the chronicle. The Dancer, who speaks the epilogue, invites the audience to come to the next première. In a new chronicle—a history of the renowned King Henry V, the hero of Agincourt—the audience would, the epilogue promised, see Falstaff again "if you be not too much cloyed with fat meat. . . ."

But times settled down, and this rarely promises a Shrovetide.

The promise was not kept. In *Henry V*, one could only hear the tale of Sir John's death.

Why did the author part with his favorite? . . . One phrase in the epilogue, obscure for the modern reader, states that Falstaff is not Oldcastle—"for Oldcastle died a martyr, and this is not the man"—and thus makes it possible for scholars to create a hypothesis concerning the intrigues of the descendants of Oldcastle.[2] Other Shakespearologists are convinced that the playwright cut the part because the comic actor Will Kempe was on tour. It was probably not a question either of influential heirs or of acting personnel but one of the essence of the figure itself.

Falstaff says of himself, "I am not only witty in myself, but the cause of wit in other men."

The point is not only that Jack is a butt for jokes; it's more complicated than that: not only does he laugh and is humorous of himself, but everyone who comes into contact with him is funny and loses his dramatic power.

It is common knowledge that it is but a step from the sublime to the ridiculous. The step is even shorter when you stand next to Falstaff. The Lord Chief Justice and other highly placed persons recognized this. Haloes lost their luster in his neighborhood, and bombast grew more tame.

Falstaff could be a companion to young Hal, but what would he be to the king? . . . And what would have remained there then from the greatness of the victory at Agincourt, and from the hymn to the model king? . . .

He had to die soon after the coronation. It is said in *Henry V* that he died with a childlike smile, "and a' babbled of green fields."

They can be seen along the road to Stratford—quiet fields of a tender green, the soft lines of low-lying hills, the peace of nature, like a park. . . .

But Sir John returns again in every century. Again people watch his sad story and laugh. They beat him with cudgels on a road near Gadshill; mocking his stoutness, they put him in the infantry; they

[2] John Oldcastle, Lord Cobham, one of the leaders of the Lollards, and a friend in arms and boon companion of the Prince of Wales, was burned as a heretic when the Prince became King Henry V. The author's slip of the tongue in the epilogue makes it possible to suggest the consanguinity of Falstaff and the historical Oldcastle. Cobham was subsequently recognized as a martyr, and jokes about him came to be dangerous.

drive him, gasping with short-windedness, out into the night; they send him to prison. And he dies.

And the audience laughs itself to tears. His very torments are a prologue to fun.

This is an old theme in folk poetry; it is thus that a merry and intoxicating drink is made. That which gladdens people's hearts gets its buoyant strength from suffering.

Robert Burns spoke of how the merrymaking force rages in liquor after having passed through many torments. John Barleycorn is the undying victim.

John angered kings, and the kings ploughed him down. "But cheerful spring came kindly on," and merry John got up again from the earth. The kings, however, were not content; "the sober autumn entered mild" and a ringing scythe cut John down. They cudgeled him with chains, "hung him up before the storm," heaved him into a "darksome pit," and flung him into "scorching flames." The miller crushed his heart between two stones. But John did not perish.

> And they ha'e ta'en his very heart's blood,
> And drank it round and round;
> And still the more and more they drank.
> Their joy did more abound.

The foaming glasses are raised, and men give praise to him who has brought them gaiety.

> Then let us toast John Barleycorn,
> Each man a glass in hand;
> And may his great prosperity
> Ne'er fail in old Scotland!

Appendix

Ten Years with *Hamlet*

FROM THE DIRECTOR'S DIARY

Many times I have had to answer the question: How many years did you work on your production of Hamlet?" *I am afraid that my answers have varied as to length of time. This is not due to a poor memory, but to the difficulty of determining the point of inception, the beginning of it all. Of course, there is nothing complicated about specifying the dates of a film production; the studio has a record of the day when the script was approved and of the day when the initial shooting began. But does the work of a director begin there? Life itself is often the "period of preparation," and the first sequences arise in the mind long before they manage to be filmed.*

My relations with the Danish Prince were especially prolonged. I produced Hamlet *in the theatre and wrote a study of the tragedy. Yet the beginning of our acquaintance was formed much earlier still.*

The director Sergei Gerasimov recently recalled the distant past: it seems that I suggested to him (then a student at our workshop) that he rework the famous tragedy, using a modern tempo, and perform it in pantomime. This all happened in FEKS (Fabrika Ekstesentricheskogo Aktëra, or the Factory of the Eccentric Actor)[1] about forty years ago. Luckily for me, no materials concerning this experiment have been preserved. And also luckily for me, I was able to make such experiments at the age of eighteen.

[1] In Petrograd, one of several Russian theatrical workshops where the most varied and fantastic theories were tested during the early 1920's [trans.].

I can define my closer acquaintance with the Prince in a round figure—ten years. It was at roughly that time that I began to jot the first entries into my diary. By that same time, I had already thought of a film production.

When you conceive of this work as everything that you see and hear and read, it becomes a nutritive imagic medium, even though at first glance it has no direct bearing on the material of the work. This explains the pages that are not connected with Hamlet. Sometimes I cite quotes and excerpts from letters, all of which are important for me. Since many of my entries dating from certain performances became the rough material for my book, they will not be used here.

If readers who have seen our film wish to compare these thoughts to the sequences in the picture, they will probably find quite a few contradictions. It could not be otherwise. For a director, the production plan is not a regional map for a prospective trip but, rather, the baggage needed for the journey.

I

1953–1954

(*Performance of the Pushkin Academic Theatre of Drama in Leningrad*)

Modern English and, especially, American Shakespearologists have revealed the psychological characteristics of Elizabethan audiences which do not resemble ours. Englishmen of the sixteenth century were accustomed to sermons from childhood; legal eloquence was part of everyday life; metaphor and hyperbole were accepted as ordinary speech. These people imbibed a feeling for allegory with their mothers' milk.

In the opinion of several scholars, this permitted them to understand the images of Shakespeare perfectly.

Our audiences have not studied Cicero and Seneca in school, and rarely think in the allegories or figures of rhetoric. Nothing along this line was absorbed with their mothers' milk. Yet they understand Shakespeare perfectly, and they do not like it when his sense of justice is considered rhetorical.

A very great misunderstanding—the solitude of Hamlet. How can he be alone if all of us in the house are with him?

He speaks for many people, and defends their dignity and their idea of good and evil. This is central in the hero. But he is alone in the court of Claudius. Each one of us would have been alone in Elsinore.

■

Francis Bacon wrote of the idols that hindered the development of human knowledge. There are idols that interfere with productions of Shakespeare. There are broad concepts—"Shakespeare's every word is sacred," "Shakespeare needs no ornamentation," "The main thing is naturalness and simplicity"—and they are, of course, true. However, the truth of general statements helps but little.

When he heard of Stanislavski's interpretation of *The Seagull,* the director of the Imperial Aleksandrinski Theatre, who had made a mess of the play in his day, would probably have shrugged, "Chekhov doesn't need ornamentation. Vera Komissarzhevskaya (the finest Russian actress of the period) managed without frogs croaking backstage."

Ornamentation was not needed by Aeschylus, Maxim Gorky, Molière, and Ibsen. But if the director is good for anything, he must produce each author's work distinctively.

In the old days, the actor and director Lenski bemoaned the style of a noted actor: "Unfortunately, his acting evinced a depressing naturalism and the kind of simplicity which is worse than thieving."

The definition had more merchandise than could be sold; the time had come to take inventory and scale down the price.

■

At the outset, Hamlet is attractive because of his tender and youthful beauty. He is ingenuous, cannot yet hide his feelings.

After the meeting with the ghost, which was a shock of tremendous impact, a bitter taste pervaded everything. Slowly and heavily, loathing rises and swells; anger boils.

Revolt and revenge.

And, later, a sage peace is achieved through suffering. He has returned from a long trip, which had taken him throughout life.

Without haste, he quietly disembarks from the boat and steps onto the shore. He knows that death awaits him here.

If we talk of his inner life, then, figuratively speaking, ten years pass between the first and second acts. Another decade passes after the fourth act. How old is Hamlet? . . . At the beginning, twenty —and forty at the end.

■

Attention to the vital, human passages in the tragedy.
The main enemies: pathos and bombast.

■

Yuri Tolubeev is my favorite actor. It is a pleasure to work with him. But it is necessary, unfortunately, to lessen the force of his charm.

Polonius is one of the pillars of Elsinore. A frightening figure— the might of stagnation, the pathos of "knowing the job," "the golden mean." The living environment is important, the atmosphere of his home. The sleepy, sullen old man trains a hired scoundrel to spy on his son. Let this be more coarsely naturalistic than conventionally theatrical.

He scratches himself sleepily, yawns, puckers up his face from heartburn, chews some pills or other. A foul courtier, a slovenly house.

With the King he is adroit and elegant.

The purple pig's snout of Elsinore. A Danish edition of Skvoznik-Dmukhanovski.[2]

It's time for him to retire, but the old devil still goes to bend his spine and gaze sweetly into the Queen's eyes.

He knows everything, pries into everything; it is all clear to him.

■

(*from a letter from B. L. Pasternak*)

27 October, 1953

Dear Grigori Mikhailovich,

I was in a hurry, and in the letter accompanying the corrected text of *Hamlet* in the old and more circulated edition, I forgot to say the thing that had prompted me to write the letter.

[2] A character from Gogol's play *The Inspector General.*

Cut, abbreviate, and slice again, as much as you want. The more you discard from the text, the better. I always regard half of the text of any play, of even the most immortal and classic work of genius, as a diffused remark that the author wrote in order to acquaint actors as thoroughly as possible with the heart of the action to be played. As soon as a theatre has penetrated his artistic intention, and mastered it, one can and should sacrifice the most vivid and profound lines (not to mention the pale and indifferent ones), provided that the actors have achieved an equally talented performance of an acted, mimed, silent, or laconic equivalent to these lines of the drama and in this part of its development.

In general, dispose of the text with complete freedom; it is your right.

■

(from a letter to B. L. Pasternak)

Dear Boris Leonidovich,

. . . We are working with precisely that version of the translation which you sent. With every day's rehearsals, we are more convinced of its merit. It is hard to find a script that pleases the actors, especially when it is a translation; sentences strike them as incomprehensible and difficult to pronounce. This time everyone is content: the lines have a fluidity; the meanings are clear.

Thank you for your permission to "cut and slice," but I will try not to take you up on it. *Hamlet* is more than a play—you, of course, know this better than I. Its expressive energy lies in the integrity of the poetic movement. One can understand little outside of the poetry in the tragedy. "Prosy word-for-word translations" should not be made; the philosophic-psychological structure is inseparable from the poetic.

I am in complete agreement with your thoughts on the advantages of "acted, mimed, silent, or laconic" equivalents, but this requires a screen. In the cinema, with its power of visual imagery, it would be possible to risk achieving equal forcefulness. On the stage, the spoken word is king. . . .

■

Nina Mamaeva is an excellent actress. She must only be convinced that madness is happiness for Ophelia. Drama cannot be created by dramatic acting. To the contrary, the happier the madwoman feels in her madness, the more tragic the situation.

The role has a dramatic beginning: pestering and tormenting her, they give her no peace. They do not permit her to realize her own feelings. She has not yet said a word, but everyone already knows what life is for her. Her father and brother instruct her, compel her to renounce love and, later, to take part in some sort of shady business. She is confused and understands nothing. Elsinore chains her to lifeless ceremonial. She is "the minister's daughter," the "first young lady" of Denmark. And she is not suited by her spiritual constitution for all this.

She lost her reason and found happiness.

■

"The mystery, the baffling vital obscurity of the play, and in particular of the character of its chief person, make it evident that Shakspere had left far behind him that early stage of development when an artist obtrudes his intentions. . . ." Thus writes Dowden, the nineteenth-century critic. "It is a remarkable circumstance that while the length of the play in the second quarto considerably exceeds its length in the earlier form of 1603, and thus materials for the interpretation of Shakspere's purpose in the play are offered in greater abundance, the obscurity does not diminish, but, on the contrary, deepens, and if some questions appear to be solved, other questions in greater number spring into existence."

The vagueness of the artist's intentions is relative. Can it be suggested that Shakespeare loved Claudius, hated Hamlet, thought Polonius a sage and Horatio dishonorable?

The "mystery" mainly inheres in the monologues of the chief person. The Prince now curses himself for his inertia, now reaches for his dagger, and now envies suicides. The "obscurity" emerges when the principal motif of the play is deemed to be revenge, and Hamlet's so-called vacillation is attributed to a delaying of revenge—in other words, when the play is returned to its pre-Shakespearean version.

Shakespeare did not superimpose onto the old drama of revenge a variation of that genre, but life itself. Claudius then proved more than a villain; he was a clever ruler after his own fashion, and his passion for Gertrude was sincere. Polonius displayed worldly experience and paternal love. The contours of stage business vanished; people appeared, and took on flesh.

Hamlet is foreign to the world of these people. The tragedy does not lie in that he is not suited to vengeance; it is more profound: he is not suited to this kind of life.

Even if Claudius had not killed Hamlet's father (let us imagine such a blasphemous hypothesis), nothing would have been changed. The Prince could not swim with this current. The conflict of his spirit, trained by Wittenberg, with the realities of Elsinore is inevitable.

For a lifelike situation, it is important that Claudius is a murderer. This is a natural road to power.

■

Hamlet is not only a play but also a novel. The very scope of the hero's thought is indivisible from the picture of "overwhelming onrushing life" (*Gogol*) which is portrayed in the tragedy. The breadth of its outlook on an epoch and its depth of psychological research are fused into a combination that defines the novel. The same thing is implicit in the nature of the film.

The monologues are also related to the novel. They seem confused because they sometimes seem to be lyrical digressions on the author's part, rather than speeches of the character.

■

The noted "firing arms" went off with much more dash in pre-Shakespearean melodrama. Shakespeare uses the firearms in his own way. Romeo's first beloved does not appear on the stage in order to rouse Juliet's jealousy; in fact, her image does not even revive in Romeo's memory. This "fires" too: the contrast of superficial attraction to love.

No play of Shakespeare's has so many frank speeches as *Hamlet*. Here, there is uninterrupted teaching, preaching, and instruction. Elsinore is represented in the fullness of its ideology. In answer to it, there is the passionate propaganda of the monologue about the "pipe." This is what has "to fire"!

■

The problem is not that this tragedy is a reflection of life and that it is up to the director to translate reflection into reality. The Elizabethan period is well enough known. *Hamlet* is not a mirror but a mine detector: old shells not yet deactivated are concealed in the flesh of every century, and, in thoughts concerning this tragedy, they reveal their presence.

■

One need only distinguish the contemporary from the topical. Composing a broadcast that combines the tragedy with newspapers is a worthless affair. The tragedy discusses skirmishes of humanity with inhumanity, and although they change form, they are not likely to die out quickly.

■

There should be no superficial romanticism in Hamlet. That would be the same "show" and "suits of woe" which are repugnant to him.

■

At every step, hiding behind every exclamation mark and every series of dots, the "neurasthenic" with his surface exictability, his alternation of shrieks and whispers, lies in wait for the director.

■

Ophelia's madness is a social event. People listen to her gibberish and look for a secret meaning in its nonsense.

The government reels. This madwoman is a sign of disaster. The consciences of Gertrude and Claudius come to life.

■

A pupil of the best dancing teachers, Ophelia walks with a fluid, courtly gait. She is in heavy mourning velvets. A servant bears the train of her dress; his face is twisted with fear.

Before the emptiness, she drops a low curtsy. She finds it uncomfortable, close; she tears off the collar, which strangles her, and unfastens a corset. She gets out of the huge unyielding dress as though crawling out of a black shell; she steps out of her high heels—a small, slender girl who was born under a cold northern star. Now it is well, and easy for her. She frisks and plays about in the dark, empty halls.

■

The revolt of Laertes is a feudal rebellion. A mode of the insanity of family vengeance. Laertes in a torn shirt, boots gummed up with mud. A heavy medieval sword in his hands.

Madmen converge on one corner of the eye. A raucous deranged voice. A bloody bandage on matted hair.

■

The closet scene.

The Queen at her toilette. She has removed her dark wig; under it the hair is touched with gray. A tired woman, no longer young.

■

Hamlet is tanned, with an unruly shock of blond hair.

■

Rosencrantz and Guildenstern—once people who shared Hamlet's faith. Now there is no time for daydreaming of the loftiness of man's destiny. The cards didn't fall, and they are bored on provincial estates. And now: a break!

In unfashionable, dusty costumes (fresh from the road), they pass the courtiers. Strangled by nerves, they stand before the King. They are ready for anything.

Then they said, "Fortune has come! . . ."

Hamlet calls Fortune a prostitute (it is far stronger in the original).

The childhood friends set out on a career.

■

Polonius, Rosencrantz, and Guildenstern are by no means villains. They are not even evil people. The horror is that they are ordinary people, moderately reasonable, moderately honest, moderately kind.

It is exactly this moderation which does not suit Hamlet.

■

The gravedigger wanted to spit on the grandeur of death. He digs a grave and sings merry ditties. It's the usual thing.

In Denmark, they are used to everything.

Hamlet had arrived from Wittenberg; he had no habits.

■

Hamlet studies the nature of toadying.

He makes experiments. Talking with Polonius about the form of a cloud and with Osric about the weather, he purposely affirms contradictory things. Each time, his companion readily agrees with him. They are ready to agree to anything. This readiness increases with the years.

"Yesterday, it seems, you were not quite so tall?" Khlestakov asked Zemlyanika.

"Very possibly," agreed the Trustee of Social Welfare Institutions.[3]

■

Polonius is extremely energetic. He follows the spiritual development of his daughter, extracts her secret, sends a spy to observe his son. He personally spies from behind the arras in the Queen's closet.

He wears the kind of naval coat sported by plainclothesmen, only it is lined with ermine.

He noses around, peeps furtively, eavesdrops.

On the basis of this sort of activity, Hamlet really is a hero of inactivity.

■

Gordon Craig maintained that Claudius's throne speech is completely absurd. "If you will read the words in the play," he wrote, "you will see that they are pure caricature."

The speech is formal oratory. Claudius is eloquent. But the content of the scene should have something else: a new ruler usually shows old courtiers the "lash" and the "cake." The actor must play not the content of the speech but the taming of the ministers.

His meaning is clear: it's time to stop wearing mourning.

The form is evasive, diplomatic. Two sentences sit in the pans of the scale: "Though yet . . . it us befitted to bear our hearts in grief" and "yet . . . hath discretion fought with nature."

The silk whip, with a mahogany handle. The cake is not a large confection, but very tasty. All this takes place among people of intelligence and grace, who catch other's meaning at once.

■

Act three.

The murky twilight of an unpleasant day. The comedians guide a van into the courtyard. They fold back one of its walls, and a sideshow platform is formed. They hang a threadbare curtain—the show's backdrop; they arrange beggarly props. Their costumes are sewn from cheap material; the crowns are made from foil, and

[3] From Nikolai Gogol's *The Inspector General.*

coarse beards are made from tow and tied on. The musicians take their seats and tune their instruments.

Against this sober and lifelike background, the conversation between Hamlet and Horatio takes place.

Servants light torches. Immediately there is a change in mood: the feverish, shadowy light changes forms and colors. The rhythm becomes different—fast and troubled. The shadows grow, the cheaply bright colors of theatre costumes catch fire.

There is a "white ball" in the palace. The courtiers are in white. Hamlet is black. Bloody spots on the mantle of the player-king.

■

(from a letter to B. L. Pasternak)

Dear Boris Leonidovich,

. . . I cannot work out a finale at all. I don't understand the image of Fortinbras very well, and, in the theatre, his entrance usually winds up being operatic: a feather on his helmet, banners, fanfares, a crowd of extras. . . .

■

(from a letter from B. L. Pasternak)

Dear Grigori Mikhailovich,

. . . The end seems natural to me. It is the roar of life's general continuation after the silence of isolated death. Such contrasts are not rare for a Shakespeare curtain. They are premediated with him, and clear as to intention. . . .

■

"To be or not to be." A dull northern day. A church in the distance, the leisurely tolling of a bell. The poor are buried. Hamlet envies the lowliest of the dead.

■

If it would be possible to make the army of Fortinbras pass through according to the military etchings of Callot and Goya . . . Burned villages, the carrion of cattle on the muddy ground; an oak tree: the wind swings the bodies of the dead. The officer is a drunken mercenary. A merry murderer.

In the theatre all these would be props.

■

Why do the actors who play Claudius never pay attention to the words about the King's smile? It is not the bared fangs of the murderer which persecute Hamlet, but his smile. Shakespeare emphasizes Claudius's gift of seduction.

His figure strikes me as a perverted unity of something heavy, coarsely powerful, bullish, and at other moments affectedly refined.

There used to be winged bulls, and here another kind of nonsense: a bull with peacock feathers. . . .

■

His struggle with Hamlet is only a surface line of Claudius's action. Far more important is the interior motif, deeply concealed: the struggle with conscience.

On this plane, both Claudius and Gertrude, and—to a lesser extent—Laertes, suffer from "hamletism."

■

(*from a letter to K. V. Skorobogatov, who played the King*)

Dear Konstantin Vasilievich,

I felt like jotting down a few thoughts after the whole play was rushed through.

The relations between the royal couple do not work yet with us. Unfortunately, there is no text for it, but maybe in the first scene, we can find a place for the meeting of glances: the people lost control of themselves for a moment. They seem as though they were to themselves in a locked room. Hamlet—and we look at life through his eyes—sees in Claudius not only the usurper of the throne but the lover of his mother.

It is glad news that you have gotten a grip on the prayer. We will try to extract its complex meaning. In essence, the scene is not religious but philosophic: Is there a court to judge the deeds of man, and does it have full punitive power? The court of man over man. No one can refuse to place himself under its jurisdiction. Claudius understands that there is no salvation for him, but he argues with his conscience and tries to outwit it.

This is both tragic and grotesque. The King is an orator able to wield the most subtle sophistry. He tries to convince us of his righteousness by casuistry, oratorical fire, threats, and flattery.

The judge is silent. He is not there; he is inside of man. There is a horror to this.

Claudius is brave when Laertes advances on him with sword in hand. He is seized with fear when he pays heed to Ophelia's ravings; his conscience comes to life.

Despite Mamaeva's excellent acting, the mad scene still does not work. The fault is mine. The blocking must be changed: everyone must be drawn into the action, but at the moment, we have a solo mad Ophelia.

No waste of energy on taming Laertes. Jobs like this are most elementary for Claudius.

■

Torn from the whole complicated thought process, a sentence inevitably dies, its meaning effaced. In prerevolutionary Odessa, some vaudeville actor sang couplets about "sad Hamlet with his 'to be or not to be.' "

The old cloak was so worn that its frayed edges began to appear on the vaudeville stage, even in Odessa.

There are more important words in the famous monologue. So much attention has been paid to the inertia that its cause has been forgotten. The Prince says at the end of the monologue, "Thus conscience does make cowards of us all."

The man of iron and blood can easily tame it.

> Conscience is but a word that cowards use,
> Devised at first to keep the strong in awe.
> Our strong arms be our conscience, swords our law.

These are the words of Richard III, a man of action.

At the end of a Shakespearean tragedy, heroes like this are ruthlessly killed, slaughtered like animals. Their corpses are dragged like carrion.

Shakespeare orders Hamlet buried like a soldier, with all the ceremony of a military funeral.

It is not always necessary to believe what people say about themselves.

■

(from a letter to B. A. Freindlikh, who played the Prince)

Dear Bruno Arturovich,

Of course, it is idle to pick apart details, to discuss what was played better one evening and worse on another. The main thing is the direction of the role.

Better the failure of an individual performance, than to turn from the path we have chosen. Better that it not "get across" than to "get across" by methods that we had rejected. Indeed, it is not the Shakespearean profundity which "gets across" in this case, but melodramatic passion with its big mug.

They reproach you (it is my fault) with inadequacy of "tragic style." And I do not quite understand what this is. Yet, the benevolent Chekhov wrote, in the last century, of the Hamlet of the celebrated Ivanov-Kozelski that "he hisses like a foolish country gander" and was exasperated with his weeping: "tears are rare with men, and all the more so with Hamlet."

Too often, they take for tragedy cheap consumer goods, like arms raised to the skies, bombast, and the phony pathos generated by screams as the curtain descends.

During rehearsals, I was attracted to a certain characteristic of your talent—I would call it "diffidence." You never permit yourself to imitate passion, to intensify a form without genuine feeling. I understand; everything changes when the house is full. You have to "give out."

Do you? . . .

I am completely sure that the audience will grasp and love your Hamlet, and will begin to draw near to it spiritually (this is central!) even if the forms of expression are most modest. People of great spiritual complexity are restrained. The noise is made by those whose souls can be bought for a dime a dozen. . . .

The scene with Ophelia and the closet scene are going well. Rashevskaya's acting is so precise and human. Your success with the monologue about the pipe invariably delights me—it seems to me to be the most important passage in the tragedy.

My notes from the time of the theatre production end here. During these months, I would come home from rehearsal hoping that the evening and night might pass, and the next day come more quickly and bring another session with the actors of the Pushkin Theatre, all of whom had become genuine friends.

However, I am a movie director, and often, in the middle of the beautiful theatre which Rossi had designed, I missed the northern winds and the broad spaces of the sea. . . . The opportunity of looking into the very depth of Hamlet's soul was not enough for me. I desperately needed a movie camera.

I began once more to prepare myself for a new production of the tragedy.

The first copies of my book, published in 1962, were presented to my co-workers on the movie version of Hamlet.

II

1962–1964

(*Work on the Movie*)

There are certain books which you cannot claim to "have read"; you "are reading" Shakespeare every time.

Having produced it in the theatre and written a study on it, I am still reading *Hamlet*.

■

There is nothing more fruitless than writing down one's conceptions of this play. The most valuable thing is that which remains outside the limits of each of them.

"In order to know a subject well, one must embrace it, study all its facets, all its connections and capacities. We never fully achieve this, but the demand for thoroughness cautions us against mistakes and mental numbness" (*Lenin*).

"Thoroughness" or "numbness."

A conception or life.

■

"Prejudice is the bane of thought," Pushkin wrote to Katenin.

"On one theme," Lev Tolstoy wrote in his diary, in reference to George Eliot, "I can't write that way."

Shakespeare couldn't either.

■

The architecture of Elsinore does not consist in walls, but in the ears which the walls have. There are doors, the better to eavesdrop behind, windows, the better to spy from. The walls are made up of guards. Every sound gives birth to echoes, repercussions, whispers, rustling.

■

The imagery of a bull fight. Claudius as a huge corpulent hulk. Hamlet is thin, well-proportioned.

■

One of the most important qualities of the spiritual constitution of the hero is vulnerability: a man with a thin skin.

■

His faith: resistance to evil.

■

Claudius and his nobles are to be found in a certain vacuum. There is a guard in the space from which the air has been pumped out, and watchdogs.

■

Success and failure must be analyzed. At the Pushkin Academic Theatre of Drama, I was delighted by the applause after the monologue about the pipe, and was not at all pleased when the house flinched at the sight of Hamlet bringing the goblet to his lips. The dramatic mechanism went so smoothly that no one paid any attention to the cup itself—a prop from the days of the old Aleksandrinski[4] (a terrible piece of hack work; in no way could I get a requisition for another one).

■

(from a letter from Innokenti Smakhtunovski)

Dear Grigori Mikhailovich,

I am proud, happy, embarrassed, and grateful, but frightened more than anything else. I do not know to what extent I will be able to justify your hopes—I have never had anything like this to do either in the theatre or in the movies. For this reason, you will understand my perplexity. Terrible, but no less terribly wanted.

I am not at all sure of myself as Hamlet, and if you can inspire this faith in me, I will be very, very grateful.

In general, to be or not to be. . . .

■

The music of the whole thing. The interrelation of parts, developing in impetuous motion. From the beginning, the propulsion of a number of little wheels and casters. Interdependence of each of the movements.

Hamlet not only moves, but is moved, propelled, by a number of circumstances.

[4] An imperial theatre in St. Petersburg, designed by Carlo Rossi, and opened in 1832. It was renamed the Pushkin Academic Theatre of Drama in the Soviet era [trans.].

Two interconnected beachheads for the struggle are revealed in the impetuous, alternating movement: the narrow field of one man's soul, and the space of history and of events on a universal and historical scale.

■

"Conscience? What is conscience? I make it myself. Then why do I torment myself? Force of habit. The universal human force of habit which has existed for seven thousand years. Then, get out of the habit, and we shall be gods" (the words of Ivan Karamazov in Dostoevski).

Hamlet defends the universal human habit. He does not permit Claudius and Gertrude to become gods. This is his activity, goal, and revenge.

The King and Queen understood that it is not they themselves who make conscience. Conscience is seven thousand years old.

■

In the dramaturgic mechanism of so much melodrama, theatrical situations are so spectacular that their effectiveness should be measured with a micrometer.

Shakespeare often abandons action for thought, poetic imagery, his own personal digressions. To travel this route means to express these digressions above all else and not "the main thing," the plot.

The acting, the melodrama, becomes banality. Chekhov's idea —that when a man suffers, he does not grimace, but is silent, or jokes and whistles—is true here.

Hamlet "jokes and whistles."

And "Hamlet's jokes make your hair stand on end." This is already found in Pushkin.

"The most terrifying part is when he laughs," wrote Herzen.

Mayakovsky knew how to laugh this way. And Hamlet's mourning is a version of the woman's yellow jacket. He waves it in front of Elsinore.

■

Again, a word on what might be the main thing: the intonation of the story. Two guides come to mind. One of them gave a whole performance at Holyrood castle in Scotland, complete with tragic cries and ominous whispers. He "served up" the rooms of Mary

Stuart to the tourists, and "played up" the hall where David Rizzio was killed.

The other guide was calm, spoke softly, and put no part of his tale into italics. He led us through the premises quietly and unhurriedly, and patiently showed us everything and spoke about it all.

This was at the Auschwitz museum.

The Holyrood guide sweated and climbed out of his skin to make the affairs of distant history seem effective and dramatic. He tried, in hope of tips.

A number was burnt into the arm of the man at Auschwitz. By chance, he survived. To tell how it all really was became the meaning of his life. That the story be remembered in its full scale and with accuracy of detail. That it might seem to every man that a number had been burnt into his own arm.

Those who see our movie must feel that it is they who had befriended Rosencrantz and Guildenstern, that Claudius owned them body and soul, that Polonius taught them morals. And that now, with Hamlet, they smash the very foundation of Elsinore.

■

Et tout le reste est littérature, as Verlaine wrote. "And all the rest is mere scribbling."

■

The motif of "this canker of our nature," which eats away at the essence of man, is the key to the fates of the protagonists. The spark of desire blazed into the fire of lust and incinerated Gertrude's conscience. The cancer of ambitions corroded the spiritual world of Claudius. From a microbe of careerism, the soul became leprous—Rosencrantz and Guildenstern obliged the block.

Pushkin wrote of the diversity and multiplicity of the qualities of the Shakespearean character. The diversity and multiplicity are indisputable. But the tragedy is formed, and ripens, because one of the qualities not immediately obvious (Macbeth does not display ambition from the start) begins to grow and to supplant other qualities.

Research has still not defined the nature of cancerous tumors, the cause of their origin, or the dynamics of their growth. It is easier to define in Shakespeare's characters.

Time, the historical process, society. In the very air of the times lives all that nourishes and hastens the growth of these cells with appalling force.

■

This kind of cell in Ophelia is eavesdropping. It leads her to spy on her beloved. In Laertes, it is the tribal reflex of revenge which had been forming for generations.

■

Well, and in the hero himself?

Here the situation is at the most complicated. Shakespeare tries to contrive a line of love for the "pale cast of thought," by which "the native hue of resolution is sicklied o'er."

Was it not this sin which revealed the world to the human being and formed the human in man? . . . In the words of Pascal, it made the reed "un roseau pensant."[5]

In Gertrude's soul, "the native hue of resolution" became "such black and grainèd spots as will not leave their tinct."

■

The friendship of Rosencrantz and Guildenstern with Hamlet was not severed because they had changed of themselves or had become evil people. Most of all, the time had changed. It no longer lent itself to childish friendship.

Hamlet did not start wasting his time over trifles either. In a hurry to chop off heads, he forged a royal order and applied the seal.

■

In a film that is peaceful, and sometimes even prolonged, digressions from the external action are needed; the shadow of reverie seems to muffle the colors and to soften the abruptness of movement.

■

Some woman or other asked the director I. Shapiro what sort of film *Hamlet* would be, "A performance, or from life?" . . . This is the main task: "from life" with no traces of "performance."

■

[5] "A thinking reed."

Our cinematographers have learned in the past few years to show life through the eyes of a child. We have seen the very fine *Serëzha*[6] and others, and the imitators have already mastered this particular point of view; it is that of a reed, but not yet of a thinking one.

It would be good to master yet another point of view: that of a grown man. How he looks on life, and what he sees in it.

Thence—*Hamlet*.

Art created by adults for adults.

If, as Marx put it, ancient art is healthy childhood, then Shakespeare is the age of both the loss of childish illusion and the acquisition of courage of thought.

■

Monologues must be separated from the general course of the film. They are not speeches but currents of thought. The inner world of the man becomes audible. From the chaos of sensation, ideas are formed. They are still in movement; no sediment has formed.

It would be desirable to achieve a sound montage along the lines of Anna Akhmatova's verses:

> It happens thus: some kind of languor;
> In th' ears unceasing strikes a clock;
> And distant rolls subsiding thunder.
> From voices captive and unknown
> I seem to hear complaints and groans,
> Some kind of secret circle narrows,
> But in th' abyss of chimes and whispers
> Arises one all-conquering sound. . . .

The rhythm of his father's burial arises in Hamlet's memory. Later, the words of the ghost. In an instant, the laughter of courtiers and the music of a ball. And ousting all this, again the command of the father.

But nothing can be read from his face. He knows they follow him; even a shift in his glance will be noticed.

Hamlet unhurriedly walks past the courtiers, apparently quite

6 Released in this country as *A Summer to Remember* [trans.].

calm. The sequences must be much more violent in the dynamics of inner life than all the noise and scurrying of Laertes' revolt.

■

Sometimes in Shakespeare, you will find a completely un-Shakespearean phrase. It is surprising in its contemporaneity of intonation. After the scene with Osric (it is linguistically antique, a parody on euphemistic affectation), the Prince speaks of "many more of the same breed."

■

In the same scene, he speaks of "a kind of yesty collection which carries them through and through the most fond and winnowed opinions."

In Elsinore there is an extraordinary diversity of tone in the tenors of life: a plurality of standards and contradiction in manners.

Callousness and inner disintegration lend unity to everything.

The growing tumor is an oft-repeated metaphor in the tragedy.

Fathers, sons, and even grandsons (Osric) are incurably sick, and are doomed to destruction along with the government-prison.

■

Evgeni Enei made an excellent sketch of Polonius's house. Huge cupboards, coffers; hangers-on cower in dark corners.

The artist defined it as "the Ostrovski of the sixteenth century, so to speak."

■

In the great hall, we decided to paint a fresco over the fireplace anyway. An expensive, fashionable thing. By order of the minister.

■

The boundaries that separate scenes must be destroyed. The boiling of life. A maelstrom. No film transitions: no black-outs, fade-ins, or double exposures. The life of government, individual, and military flow together, merging.

Hamlet's thought penetrates this motley, speeding world, and exposes the cancer cells and the decomposition of the organism.

■

One of the great dangers of directing is the endeavor for emotionality—for the easily attained, superficial variety, of course.

I have in mind the kind of influence on an audience which springs directly from that which happens in a given sequence. It is here, first and foremost, that melodrama necessarily emerges.

There is another sort of infectiousness, more complex, which is needed to stir up a whole swarm of living associations.

The screen must convey the enormity of history, and the fate of a man determined to talk with his epoch on equal terms, and not to be an extra, with no speaking part, in one of its spectacular crowd scenes.

Then there will be no necessity for emotional little scenes.

Theatrical fervor, the sense of nervous rhythms, and expression by distance perspective must all be excluded as modes of influence. Everything Shakespeare said is too important for us. It's no time to fool with the movie camera, and the fire and lightning of "movie idols."

■

The movie must be clear, and within everyone's reach. This is a human story; it deals with life.

It is no good, however, if the story is so stated that it becomes overly obvious. It is precisely the possibilities for implication which permitted each century to fill in the details in its own way. And each man has the opportunity to think the tragedy out in his own way, to look for his own meaning in it.

The means of expression must be measured in microscopic dosages, because Hamlet and Claudius are self-possessed, restrained, intelligent people.

The spectator is to believe that he grasps everything.

■

There is an instructive old anecdote: a man sits at home stark naked ("No one will come.") but has a collar on ("What if some should suddenly show up anyway?").

Either a movie, or the scrapping of theatre aesthetics. A prose translation. Retain the thoughts and feelings of the characters, but cut the declamatory passages. Transfer most of the scenes to nature. Monologues are processes of thought, not speeches.

The powerful film management of action is on the planes of life in real surroundings.

As far as possible from the naked man with the collar around his neck.

■

An academic production of *Hamlet* is probably a contradiction of terms; the very combination of subject and epithet would make it impossible.

Edmund Kean and Pavel Mochalov did not resemble academicians. Each generation communicated the main idea of the tragedy, its vital meaning, in its own way.

And has there ever been an "uncontroversial" production of *Hamlet?* That kind of academic performance would probably have retained every word and utterly lost the life-origin and the fermentative energy.

Before Auditions

Today's rehearsal serves as a model: What is the work of a director with his actors? First came the actors, trained somewhere "in the system." They sat around and talked. They left, and were replaced by a ballet dancer. A beautiful face, but he began to sweat as soon as he opened his mouth.

Our brother is to be helped—the excessively eloquent performer must be helped to stop talking, the silent ones to speak up.

■

For some reason, all stage Claudiuses have a workaday look. But he is a satyr, a sensual beast with moist lips and languid, protruding eyes. A seducer of women and ministers of state. There is a special kind of Renaissance obscenity to the man: all those earrings, laces, chains, and signet rings.

■

The word "queen" hypnotizes actresses playing Gertrude. However, other, ordinary words are essential: "mistress," "mother," "woman." She has an only son and the last lover of her life.

■

The flesh of this tragedy is verse. A rich tightly woven fabric, its threads are so intertwined that it is hard to pull any out separately without destroying the cloth itself.

Cuts, even theatrical ones, begin to tear it at once.

If integrity of film rhythm does not replace the verse harmony with a new fabric as rich in its way as the verbal one was, the movie could become a dock-tailed Trishka's caftan.[7]

The main danger: snatches of action with the harmony of spectacle.

Laurence Olivier followed his own method in his film: he cut lines belonging to Rosencrantz and Guildenstern, Fortinbras, and both the monologue on the greatness of man and the revolt of Laertes. To make up for it, there are almost no cuts in the remaining lines.

Having seen his movie (excellent in its way), I wanted to film *Hamlet* even more. Olivier cut the theme of government, which I find extremely interesting.

I will not yield a single point from this line.

Where shall I find an instructive example?

In Galina Ulanova. Her Juliet is the finest ever done, a truly Shakespearean heroine, although she utters not a word. Her art *is* poetry, and therefore you don't try to remember the verses. Her triumph is due to her having danced the role through. A new fabric was formed of her own harmony.

And so, we will *film Hamlet.*

■

The significance of "milieu" should not be overrated! . . .

Stanislavski gave a perfect description of how Salvini saw such devices in a production of *Othello* (the abduction of Desdemona in the gondola, and the like). The Italian actor noticed everything, but simply did not pay special attention or lend meaning to it all.

These devices were cinematographic.

The cinematographic quality, used only externally, is not so powerful on the screen.

It is useless to enrich *Hamlet* with sets and crowd scenes at the cost of cutting the text.

The reincarnation of one art in another is another matter. This

---

[7] From a fable of Ivan Krylov (1769–1844). Trishka mended worn elbows by taking cloth from his sleeves, which he then repaired with fabric from his coattails. Trishka was content, but the garment no longer resembled a caftan [trans.].

is not a "movie version," but cinematographic poetry. It's easy to say! . . .

∎

Working with the designer Virsaladze, we found an important device: the costumes were to be historical only in contour. We rejected quaintly refined period detailing. In other words, a silhouette, but no ornament and no imitation of ancient fabrics. I consider it my great good fortune that this man is working with me. He has a precise feeling for style, and an aversion for historical naturalism.

This is important for the plastics of Shakespeare: the generalized features of a given time, without geographical and historical detail.

Neither archeology nor aesthetic lispings about antiquarianism have anything to do with Shakespearean plastic arts. Attention to everything authentic: the texture of leather, iron, coarse fabrics. The cloaks people wear on the road to keep warm and sheltered from the rain. Boots for riding. Silk is absolutely never to be used.

Court costumes are black with white, a kind of evening dress for receptions.

∎

Ophelia does not love Hamlet with any sort of exalted abstract emotion, but probably as Juliet loved Romeo. I speak of passion. In the beginning, Polonius's daughter must have all the nuances of these first feelings toward a man: the sinking of the heart, the expectation, passion, and breathlessness.

∎

In the beginning, it is important to show Hamlet's friendliness toward various people: Laertes, Horatio, Rosencrantz and Guildenstern, the players. Only later, after much as happened, the suspicion and the cruelty begin.

People—"this quintessence of dust"—have made him lonely, and have turned "this majestical roof fretted with golden fire" into the stone ceiling of a prison.

∎

The people who are driving Ophelia to madness and death love her very much. Both Laertes and Polonius, and Hamlet. In every scene of violence of her feelings and will, it must be perceptible that they demand her rejection of happiness only because they love her. A tender brother, an affectionate father, and an ardent lover drive her to the grave in the name of the finest emotions.

■

Self-restraint is of necessity difficult enough for the director. Whatever he can deny himself, he must discard. To guide the film to clusters of the important and basic things. To remove ornament. To compose one's variations, apropos of the tragedy, with exceptional simplicity.

It is hard to find filmic imagery. It is even harder to cleanse a director's work of the bravura of gadgets, of the device annexed to Shakespeare. One must be natural and irrefutable in one's ability to persuade in regard to the current of life.

■

The visual character and the manner of executing a portrayal may not be limited by one quality. In this case, the concept of style is flexible. As in Shakespeare: an arc from generalizations, even utter abstractions (the third act of *King Lear*), to naturalism and a physiological sensation of the stuff of life.

For *Hamlet*, there must be sequences that show the sinister power of the state, where the plastics tend to hyperbole, and also sequences that show the ordinary quality of the graveyard. In this kind of moment, everything becomes clear: the hole in the ground, damask and refreshments by the edge of the grave, the skull, the rotted fool's cap.

The funeral of Ophelia and the morning after the meeting with the ghost must be filmed in unpleasant weather, without "mood."

■

In a few sequences, one wants to achieve a confluence of picture and music. This sort of plastic poetry is important for the image of Ophelia.

■

Probably the search for a means of poetic expression of time—the struggle against the "historical" "costume" picture—goes on in my work from *The Overcoat* (1926) to *Don Quixote* (1957).

However, the best sequences were not those of the torches in the storm of *S.V.D.* (1927),[8] but those of the outskirts of St. Petersburg in *The Youth of Maxim* (1935) and of la Mancha in *Don Quixote.* Anything but external poeticism.

■

A way of overcoming the props of historical movies was revealed in *S.V.D.* It consisted in the poetry of plastic sensation: windstorms, snow, fire—later, in *The New Babylon* (1929), of rain and fog. In *The Youth of Maxim* and *Don Quixote,* something more complex and significant was revealed: how the material can propel itself. The reality of the particular epoch lays bare its own special expressiveness. The red wastes of la Mancha, burned by the sun, or the dead primness of a ducal court, are not devices but are included in the material itself. They had only to be exposed within the material the images brought into focus, and the extraneous elements excised (much as the greenery was removed for the shooting of *Don Quixote*).

There are bases for visual imagery in *Hamlet:* the north; the state, its life fenced off from life in general and secluded by the walls of its fortifications.

■

Gordon Craig saw the visual imagery of *Hamlet* primarily as the interrelation of scale: the scale of huge walls, and that of the small figure of a man. It was a revelation of no small importance.

■

Hamlet interests me mainly by its proportion and conformity with contemporary life. It is terrible if a glib radio exchange with the evil of the day is joined to this complex inner connection: a cabbage worm with dramatic inflection.

They often stage *Hamlet* in modern dress, but tell a tale of ancient life. The tragedy must be played in sixteenth-century costume but must be dealt with as a modern story.

■

I have been attracted to caricature and to poetry since childhood. It was much later that I understood the strength of realistic prose. But realism only pleases me when caricature and poetry are admixed to it. Only then does a liking for the material come to life,

8 Usually translated as *The Club of the Great Deed,* this film concerns Russia's Decembrist revolution of 1825 [trans.].

and a previous conception of the image arises. Again: learn from Shakespeare!

∎

Directing is defined by quite a few tasks, among them to create an honest representation of the author's figures, and to unite people in their various work by a single conception. And the director is really occupied by all this; it all has its place. . . .

But there is still another aspect of this profession; it's like the work of test pilots. The same expressions can be used in directing: "throttle wide-open," "go for broke."

Stanislavski went for broke in *The Seagull,* threw the throttle of Chekhov's dramaturgy wide open. The commercial flights came later. They "truly showed" and "united"—and the altitude of the play was reduced, and reduced again. Why did it happen this way?

The academician Ivan Pavlov wrote, "However perfect the wing of a bird, it could not fly if it did not rest on air. The air of the scholar is facts."

The air of a director is contemporary life as experienced and thought by himself. It is the history of his century.

This is the job: to increase the altitude of *Hamlet,* to throw the throttle wide open in contemporary terms. And to do this, to rest the tragedy on contemporary reality, the air of our time.

Neither Goethe nor Belinski interpreted Shakespeare "correctly." They increased the tragedy's altitude and rested it on the air of their times.

∎

It's only worth attempting a production when you have already sensed the hidden capacity of the play, of the material, and of the actor—capacity that has not been exposed in past productions.

∎

Meyerhold's significance for the history of theatre is immense, and consists in that he opened the throttle of precisely those elements which had previously been ignored. And he almost totally ignored all the standard "commercial runs."

From the point of view of the well-known and pre-eminently reasonable conceptions, any old provincial production of *The*

Inspector General was—by and large, according to Belinski—far more "correct" than the Meyerhold version. This, however, was not directly grasped. As everyone knows, *The Inspector General* was not retained in the repertoire.

In art, that which is indisputable often proves to be inert. No co-authorship arises from the audience.

Meyerhold opened the throttle of the poetic, fantastic, and grotesque in Gogol's art. In his production, which was "questionable, by and large," were revealed the strata of the play's content, imagery, its picture of an unnatural system of government and of a society made soulless, its empire of façades and of spectral "non-existent reality" (*Belinski*).

Not only the genius of the director was needed to see Gogol this way, but also a review of history as affected by the revolution.

Perhaps the reason why Gogol himself ran away from a Petersburg production in despair (although Sosnitski was in it, and Diur, too, who was probably not a bad actor) was that "the terrible blizzard of inspiration" had enveloped him, . . . and what he saw was only a comic play fit for children's matinees.

■

It so happens that, by itself, the activity of a people—its selffless devotion to duty, its bravery—can be evaluated only when the goal of that activity is known. Sometimes the artist need not be explicit about the goals; the audience will perceive the action on the screen as though it were tuned in on a definite wave length of spiritual activity by an associative force, tuned in on a conditional reflex of attitudes toward good and evil.

During the Second World War, William Wyler directed his *Memphis Belle*. The film contains shots of a bomb run by flying fortresses, the life of the pilots, their military work, the return to base under fire.

The chronicle is filmed as entertainment: it shows the characters of the pilots, their mutual relations, tastes, customs. Their tastes are not demanding. A picture is painted on the side of an airplane: a bathing beauty sticks out her rear end. Returning from a run (the mortal danger and the bravery of the crew is indicated; there are quite a few seriously wounded), the pilots slap the Memphis Belle on her behind: it's a custom.

In this case, neither the drawing itself nor the conduct of the men is in any way attractive of itself. Wyler does not show the enemy: bombings are filmed from the plane (little squares for objectives, the smoke of explosions, shell craters). But the audience sees the movie as though tuned in on a certain wave length: hatred for fascism is already a conditioned reflex.

The American fly-boys, their bravery, and even their joke about the girl in the bathing suit, all seem attractive, profoundly human.

Now let us imagine this film in its entirety as taking place in Korea. Just as any turn, however insignificant, of the radio dial will tune in another station, so here everything becomes different and the interpretation makes an about-face. The men are murderers; their life is coarse. And the bawd in the bathing suit becomes a symbol: here are the ideals and the culture in the name of which these thugs have flown across an ocean in order to annihilate a people fighting for their freedom and human dignity.

■

Nothing caused such damage to Shakespeare and the kings about whom he wrote as did the notions of actors about Shakespeare and these kings. Usually, stage fright immediately seized people here; some particularly high-flown Shakespearean speech or magnificence of royal manners will be missing.

Queen Elizabeth was in the habit of using the most startling abuse, and often spat in the face of her courtiers. When an ambassador asked after the health of the Earl of Essex, she ordered a small chest brought in: in it lay the skull of her beheaded lover.

As regards high-flown speeches, Shakespeare once pleaded: ". . . o'erstep not the modesty of nature."

The revolt of Laertes is a court squabble with a little throat-cutting. A mixture of feudal fanaticism and a "rub-out." They knelt, bowed, and later, having lost their heads, they tore through the halls, took care of the guards, and busted open the locks. And that's all.

Lines like "the rabble call him lord" and "Laertes shall be King!" could not reasonably be seen as indicating the scale or the popular character of the revolt. Shakespeare did not bother to mention the suppression of it.

The mutiny itself came to nothing when Laertes ran to the royal chambers. A few dead bodies, a broken door. And no more.

■

The actress must play Gertrude in her struggle to hide her sensuality from strange eyes. Externally, she is reserved and modest. But when she raises her eyes, or touches Claudius's hand with her fingers, she gives herself away.

It is then that the hateful fire that burns her very being can be seen.

She is a most modestly dressed woman next to the overdressed Claudius and his court.

■

Actresses playing Ophelia substitute academism for the frailty of her emotional world. One should probably pay attention to the tone of the north in her poetry. This is a girl from a pale world. In the strong lines of her face, hair, and dress, one must seek a plastic art more medieval than Renaissance. This helps to avoid the sweetness of a "Gretchen," of loose flowing hair with little flowers and so on.

Juliet and Desdemona are girls of the south. Ophelia is of the north.

How good it would be to do the mad scene in the winter!

They force her to be a court lady. She is crammed into finery and smothered with a corset. She is utter naturalness, but they cripple her with conventional etiquette, mutilate her simple language with artificiality.

It is not true that she was "too noble for the world" from her very birth; she is "too noble for the time."

As it often is in Shakespeare, the conflict is between nature and time.

■

The ghost is a poetic image, not a mystical one. Side-show movie miracles would be particularly vile: the transparent contours, double exposures to introduce an element of fear, and so on. There should be no deviltry. From what can the poetry take shape? . . . Hamlet thinks he hears his father's voice everywhere; it is alloyed in natural sounds and arises in them. Hamlet alone begins to live in a world filled with vibrating memory: the wind makes a noise, the sea roars, thunder sounds in the distance—and in it all, "Adieu, adieu! Remember me."

Only the son sees the father distinctly. The audience must be able to sense the presence of the dead king, the atmosphere of his apparition, but must not be able to see his features. Perhaps, from under a raised visor, only the eyes will become visible for an instant; they are full of sorrow. Hamlet sees this gaze in a dusty mirror, in the sea, in flames. A cloud recalls the contours of a figure in a blowing cloak; the shadow of a tree lengthens—perhaps it is the shadow of a cloak. Words are heard in the rustling of leaves. The father does not forsake his son again. They are together: Hamlet and the memory of duty.

Chekhov's Vanka Zhukov wrote "to grandfather in the country"; after the flight of the cosmonauts appeared an address "to all humanity." Art is magnificent when it writes to both these addresses at once—putting it simply, to each and to all.

"To all, to all, to all . . ." the absurd handmade radio rapped out in the first days of the revolution; a ravaged, ragged, and hungry country addressed all humanity.

The sense of authenticity does not depend on a complete representational likeness to nature at all. It depends, rather, on similarity to the outward appearance of nature. You are hardly apt to meet a Chaplin complete with Chaplinesque trousers and gait on the street, but when you see his best films, they seem completely true to life. The reason for this lies in his artistic inspiration.

Only inspiration gives vital movement to everything in a sequence. The power of an artist's spiritual essence is passed on to the material and overcomes the resistance of that material.

This affects everyone who works on a film.

I believe that Virsaladze spent several months on the costume of Hamlet. He puttered over each detail for hours at a time. And the material became spiritualized: something of the soul of the designer himself began to live in the fabric.

Only part of oneself, given from oneself, will give life to the figures. And we often think that inspiration can be realized to order.

If, instead of with fuel, the tank is filled with water, even distilled water, how can a spark light it? . . .

■

The labor of a designer is a kind of donation. It is not cutting and fitting (using the material of the client) like a tailor, but a blood transfusion.

■

In the plastic art of *Hamlet*, the picturesque and the movie reproduction of ancient paintings want to be avoided. Sequences that involve state councils, crowds of guests in a reception hall, gatherings of embassy officials must be taken as "news of the day," as the newscasters call it.

■

From the very first scenes, the film must be populated with vital figures, people with no resemblance to made-up actors. Immediately a number of real faces of different types and characters, men, women, children—not, of course, similar to people, not movie extras.

Not a touch of greasepaint.

■

Like every civilized tongue, the language of the film has now become national. There is little in common among the compositions, rhythms, and tonalities of the art of Akira Kurosawa, Federico Fellini, Ingmar Bergman, and Luis Buñuel. In our most contemporary art, the ancient world views of the Japanese, Italians, Scandinavians, and Spaniards come to life.

However much we might try to reproduce the English or the Danish world, the film—if it turns out—will be Russian. We still have our Hamlet from the times of Belinski and Herzen.

■

If it could be said that *Othello* is a tragedy of jealousy, and *Macbeth* of ambition, then *Hamlet* is the tragedy of conscience.

Shakespeare establishes a colloquy on this subject among many characters on the huge material of life and history.

9/1/62

The first test footage, without sets, and with the sea as background. These sequences provide good material for analysis.

First of all, neither the characters, nor the costumes, nor the situations of this tragedy will resemble life (in the Shakespearean sense, not with any idea of "verisimilitude") without the particular poetic atmosphere that gives everything *its* truth, *its* strength, *its* meaning.

Ophelia is not only the character of a young girl, delicate and weak-willed, but also the whole atmosphere of her image. It is interesting that thoughts of Ophelia recall flowers, above all, and a willow growing "aslant a brook."

Learn from poetry. Is it really possible to create an image of Aleksandr Blok's Unknown Lady with acting, even the best acting? Both her appearance and her charm are inseparable from the cloudy mirrors of the restaurant, the conversation and laughter behind the local barrière, the golden doughnut on the twilight sky of Pargolovo, and later the rustle of silk, black ostrich feathers on a hat, the ring on a slender finger, the smell of perfume. . . . The image condenses and loses the real outlines of its parts. An epithet forms and gives character to everything.

And then the appearance of heroines in Dostoevski!

■

The poetry of Ophelia must be formed in the unity of fixed qualities both of the human essence and of objects. The charm of pure fragility in everything that surrounds her. As in Gogol's *Dead Souls*: a chest of drawers equals Sobakevich, a house equals Sobakevich.

There is, among the rocks of Elsinore, a strange aerie, the rooms of a little girl; it is painted with fabulous unicorns and birds, as though it were a copy of the spiritual world of Polonius's daughter.

Enei wants to use more gold in the set. Through this little porcelain world passes the iron of the age.

■

In rereading Bunin, I found a poem falling right into the course of this reasoning:

THE ARTIST

He crunched along gray pebbles, passing
A sloping garden, glanced at reservoirs,
And sat on a bench. . . . Behind a new white house
The ridge of Yaila rises close and heavy.

All weary from the heat, a slate gray crane
Is standing in the bushes. Lowered crest,
And legs like canes. . . . He says, "Well, bird?
Not bad to go to Yaroslavl, to the Volga!"

And, smiling then, he thinks of death,
How they will take him out—how gray like doves
The mourning rizae[9] in the sun
The yellow fire is, the white on blue a house.

"The bulky priest, with censer, leaves the porch
And leads the choir out. . . . The frightened crane
Begins to jug, appealing from the fence—
And, well, to dance, to rap his beak against the bier!"

A tickle in the chest. The dust from off the road
Is hot, particularly dry.
Removing his pince-nez, he coughs and thinks,
"Ye-es, vaudeville. . . . All the rest is tripe."

The force of this Bunin portrait of Chekhov lies in its rethinking of completely real objects in relation to death, *his* death (the crane on the coffin, the artist's power of observation, the love for detail, even when it concerns his own funeral). And what is particularly forceful is the combination of the situation (the funeral) with the confusion of vaudeville. The attitude toward life and the Chekhovian intonation are especially powerful here. It is a combination of vignettes in the spirit of Chekhonte[10] musing about imminent death.

In a few verses, Bunin was able to draw a portrait, a life milieu, the symptoms of a disease, and the character of the artist's thought.

∎

[9] Metal mounting on an icon [trans.].
[10] An early pseudonym of Chekhov [trans.].

There is genuine poetry in that this introduction of objects and situations is neither for fun nor "for mood": the objects are organic, even necessary (you couldn't manage without them), and natural in this passage. Not only are they poetic in themselves, but also trivial. This goes both for Blok's Pargolovo and for Bunin's Yalta.

To tell the truth, there is no poetry either in a dusty street or in the local pub.

■

What is knowledge of life and of "material"?

The answer would appear to be natural: the actor is especially good at playing people he knows and among whom he has spent his life.

Let us remember Stroheim: precision of expression (to the last detail) in both the outer and the inner world of a German officer, and in the very spirit of the caste—from the monocle to the gait. The uniform is actually the man's skin.

The origin of these figures is revealed by the actor's biography. This kind of people surrounded Stroheim from childhood, and once he was such a man himself. His full name was Erich Maria von Stroheim; his father was a regimental commander, and his mother a lady-in-waiting to the Queen. He studied in military school, as a boy, later served in an aristocratic regiment, and was subsequently a military attaché in various European embassies. A mysterious story (cards? love?) and the Prussian officer left the military, and he went to Hollywood. He played the characters best known to him, and acted what he himself had lived.

Everything is clear; it is an obvious example of outstanding knowledge of one's material.

I read an article about Stroheim in *Sight and Sound*. His biographer went to Austria to gather materials. He ran down some evidence about Stroheim's birth: Erich was the son of a Jewish tradesman. The "background" was fiction, and the sonorous collection of names all invention. He had never lived in the milieu that he had portrayed; the characters he played had no relation to his family and friends, nor to the actor himself. As to the "sabers and saddles"—that came from the publicity department of Metro-Goldwyn-Mayer.

There is a perfect knowledge of material which neither experience (in exactly that milieu) nor diligent study and observation can give.

This is the force of love and hate. These feelings involve a kind of clairvoyance. The clairvoyance of hatred revealed the soul of a Prussian officer to the son of the Jewish merchant.

■

One must look for the points in which Elizabethan costume resembles modern feminine fashion. Perhaps in hair styles? A certain sense of unnaturalness in the backdrops will do no harm: life at court and at fashionable receptions does not seem natural today. In close-ups, this sense would be murderous. Here, there must be simply life, simply people.

Neither Hamlet's costume nor his wig should force the mind into the past. A modern haircut, jacket.

■

The quest for the human—its "own image" in all the characters (in other words, "good in evil")—can rob the tragedy of meaning. You gain minor points, and lose the main one. Of course, Claudius is not a stage villain, but a man; Laertes is not simply a murderer; Polonius is not only an intriguer; and Guildenstern aspires to more than just spying. This is all true. However, in this tragedy, man—in the noble sense—is Hamlet. Only he.

As to the rest: "human-people" and "animal-chickens," as it's put in Gorky. And those who seem incapable of murder are murderers nonetheless. Intriguers direct the ministry; noble youths become poisoners. What, then? Do we cry over their sad fate? Or is it perhaps more reasonable to suffer because Hamlet was thrown into these circles and into the course of these lives. And to be with him in spirit when he angrily and painfully refuses to swim with the current.

■

It is disastrous for the director to lose perspective of the plan of the play. This would be reflected first in the rhythm. Life and action develop like a loosened spring, a spinning top. Everything speeds up its action; people hurry, rush toward their goals—from Laertes (to get to Paris sooner; later, even more quickly—to kill!)

to Rosencrantz and Guildenstern (who so adjust Fortune that the spokes of her wheels flash into view for only a moment).

Hamlet alone does not hurry. He sticks in the perfected tuned pace of the wheels of government mechanism. They grind him up. Yet he all but broke the machine.

■

You cannot be attracted by a single line of itself. A difference in the rhythm (slower) and the means of expression (more detailed) must only exist between the scenes of Hamlet and those of all the other characters.

■

The theatre critic Vlas Doroshevich wrote intelligently about so-called tragic acting: the curtain goes up; on the stage there is an actress boiling jam; her expression would seem to indicate that she was boiling it out of her own liver.

■

Hamlet's mind is so finely tuned that he doesn't have to look closely or listen intently to understand the state of mind of another. He sits with his back to the door. Ophelia enters. He senses her entrance without turning. Nothing is changed in Guildenstern's intonation, but it is clear to the Prince that there has been a double cross.

It is impossible to read anything on Hamlet's face.

In such scenes, his thought processes are hidden from the audience. God forbid that the situations be sculpted—graphic articulations of the action into "bits of business," the arrangement of periods and commas, fragmentation of the central idea by using italics.

The mask of madness lets all the punctuation marks get muddled.

His answers to the questions that the King puts to him seem senseless. And at the same time a sinister meaning is felt in every sentence but is not easily comprehended.

■

In trying to define the plastic motion that can express *Hamlet,* you arrive at a strange word: "seriousness." "Smart" does not fit (the velvet oiliness of black), nor does "expressive" (the loss of

the proportion of real relations effected by a wide-angle lens),
nor—of course—"commercial" (the glitter of brocade and rhine-
stones, close-ups of pretty girls).

The words of the tragedy are suitably serious; we will strive for
suitably serious sequences.

■

Beware the directorial technique of Tom Sawyer! Tom thought
that a secret should be disclosed (it had already been disclosed)
only in a properly mysterious set.

Chekhov parodied the set made sinister "for mood."

We must play tragic scenes in out-of-the-way places where there
is rubbish scattered around, where hens are cackling and grooms
are unharnessing horses. Into this sort of place, which is natural in
action, the van of the players arrives. The first player turns the
dirty yard into a forum by the sheer force of his passion.

■

S. A. Tolstoy recalls that Lev Nikolaevich said, "It is not hard
to write something, but it is hard not to write." That is to say, it is
hard to restrain yourself from extraneous twaddle. "Idle vision,"
"idle sight" in the plastic arts: roaming sequences, extreme close-
ups, reckless foreshortening.

■

The complexity of the figure of Claudius (especially in a
movie), hypocrisy and play acting, are native to him as a man. By
nature, he is a poseur and a windbag.

In the documentary *The Life of Benito Mussolini*, all the
mugging that Il Duce does in front of the camera, all his caricature
hamming (which even the worst of provincial actors would not
risk) are frightening because the audience knows that it's for
real.

How can the movie persuade the audience that the play acting is
a personality trait and not the style of an actor's performance?

■

In theatre productions, they pay special attention to contrast
between the festive court and the Prince in mourning. The fundamental contrast is a different one: of festivity and military preparation (in Shakespeare: strengthening of the watch, alarm, border

disturbances, "sweating labor" to make ready for war). With a subtext like this, the first scene acquires the character of a feast in time of plague.

Out of everything written about *Hamlet,* perhaps the wisest thing said is contained in the lines of Pasternak:

> O! All Shakespeare, maybe, is the way
> That Hamlet chats just casually with the ghost.
> So very casually! . . .

Sometimes the hero needs a collocutor. Hamlet turns then to a man who is much closer to him in spirit—far more—than Horatio. He can say everything to this man, and he will grasp the measure of Hamlet's sorrow and anger, and the horror of life in Elsinore.

What I have in mind is Herzen's groan: "Future generations—will they grasp it, will they value it?"

Once in the film (in a monologue), the hero can look directly into the hall. This scene must be especially quiet. So-called demagoguery, the fire of oratory, has no place here (nor has it any in the whole film, as a matter of fact).

One of the monologues originated "on the move"; thoughts alternate in the rhythm of his walk.

The interior monologue will be particularly interesting if it is successful in giving the impression of an explosive force of thought which betokens danger for the government of Claudius. Spies have instructions to shadow this dangerous man, and not to let him out of their sight. And Hamlet unhurriedly and calmly strolls about the room. The camera goes closer; we hear the words of his thoughts, but the sleuth who clings to the door hears nothing. He has nothing to write down in his report: steps, quiet.

Hamlet . . . thinks. There is nothing more dangerous.

Test footage of the entrance of the royal couple. Probably, in Elizabethan reality such an entrance would be even more theatrical. In these shots, the King must be surrounded by flatterers and frightened dignitaries, and by the ugly faces of the secret police. There is less masquerade in such figures.

■

(from a letter to I. M. Smakhtunovski)

Dear Innokenti Mikhailovich,

I felt like writing to you. The results of the first months of rehearsals seem so important to me that they must be profoundly contemplated. This letter will help me to define my thoughts more accurately, and you can read it over again whenever you feel so inclined.

I have already said several times that you are successful in many things: humanity, nobility, and—most important, perhaps even decisive—the certain inner light that burns in the soul of our hero.

This is of no small importance. But it's still not everything.

There has shown up a danger both of making Hamlet goody-goody instead of good, and of grinding off the sharp corners of the figure and telling little of his strength, bravery, and implacable hatred.

"I must be cruel only to be kind" is an immensely powerful formula. If he is not cruel when he talks about the renunciation of the loathsome brutality in life, he will become sentimental. . . .

My dear Innokenti Mikhailovich, we have a magnificent role in front of us, but clichés are stuck all over it and it is not easy to find your way to its heart. Nor is it easy to give up the clichés; they lie in wait for you at every step. And you yourself don't notice how you follow the old trails. They lead not to a revelation of the vital content of the figure but to easy success and communication of the usual, superficially charming, pretty, and likable.

Yesterday, I reread what I had written several years ago about the character, about the folksy truth of a person who speaks with inveterate liars—even with the ones to whom he is close—with "words like daggers," about the power of opposing baseness.

We are about to make him a luxurious court costume. And why the hell does Hamlet need it? . . . Not only does he not adapt himself to Elsinore etiquette, but at every step he insults it. Better that he come on—one among many—in a rumpled shirt, with tousled hair and an evil gleam in his eye. For Shakespeare, in every play, madness always denotes the privilege of speaking the cruel and ugly truth about those who have come into power and about the vileness of careerists and flatterers. Let our hero sit in the place prescribed by etiquette, and behave like a young Maya-kovsky in fashionable drawing rooms.

It pleases me very much that you seek action everywhere. This is the only way one can work. But, you see, action to what purpose? . . . Do we care about the Prince's doubts concerning the truth of the ghost's words? Is there a man in the modern audience who cares whether the ghost was lying or not? . . . There is, really, such a motif in the play, but it's antiquated, already a dead level of the tragedy.

Action? Of course, action. But in the name of exposing the very foundations of Elsinore, to wash off the gilt from façades and to show people, modern people, the collapse of this kind of society, and the abomination of human relations that disgrace man—who can and should be "the beauty of the world," "the paragon of animals," and not "this quintessence of dust."

Yes, Hamlet is kind and spiritually beautiful. But he is also cruel and rough when they screen infamy with pretty words. He answers force with his attack: he feigns madness, and the fearless-ness of the thoughts he expresses before the forces of terrible power takes your breath away. He is not a tender young man at all, but a heretic who attacks, burning with the intoxicating joy of struggle. It is an unequal struggle: power is against him and his only weapon is thought.

But thought won, echoing through the centuries, and we repeat with enthusiasm: Man is not a pipe! These, yes and others—there are a number of them in the play—are great words. Fill them with energy (of course, I would advise nothing like "verbal fire" and thundering outbursts) and with the inner strength of struggle, of opposition to evil. Fill them with hate. And with pain.

I loved you during the rehearsals, and it is a great pleasure for me to work with you. I am sure that you can take care of these qualities in the role.

Don't rush. Think.

∎

The first monologue—without stopping, in the midst of the stream of events and people. Hamlet is hidden by other figures; he has his back to the camera. So far, no attention has been given to anything in his appearance or personality. Nothing has yet come into the foreground, nor shown any special significance. The scene develops in the bustle of a crowded court. Many people participate in it. Hamlet is among them; the camera should not reach him or be able to focus on him.

But now, unnoticed, he approaches the audience; the courtiers have passed from the foreground and have exposed Hamlet—he is even closer to the lens. The words of his thought become audible. Simultaneously, in distant rooms, the gay music of a ball begins to play, and you can hear laughter, chatter.

■

The audience must ascertain Hamlet's relation with life, history, a gallery of people, moral giants.

■

The very atmosphere of the scene and its movement can determine the rhythms of the thoughts. Let us imagine "to be or not to be" in the stateroom of a ship during a storm. The floor heaves, furniture and objects keep falling about. Huge black swells crash down on the ship.

■

The basic tendency of the film is that of life; the tone is realistic. But somehow another scale is wanted—a mixture of time and space. The meaning of "to be or not to be" will be revealed differently if the time is from dawn to sunset and the space is from a smallish room to the vastness of the ocean. If the weather, then the character of the light and the range of space also change. The beginnings and ends of the changes are barely noticeable: the unity of action in the foreground hides the transitions from sequence to sequence.

How long has he thought—an hour, a day, a week?

And perhaps he, too, changes imperceptibly, as though he were passing through years. . . .

■

Reason out the sea motif throughout the film. In Shakespeare, everything is in a process of movement, of change. The sea, the sky, and the earth should develop their themes in the background. Movement—the course of huge massifs. Here, there should be both a door into the room and an entrance into the world.

People live in rooms and in the universe.

∎

Hamlet is the standard of what centuries of the development of human nature have achieved. The impossibility of agreement to brutish ethics and animal habit is almost a reflex sort of thing.

∎

In his *Towards a New Theatre,* Gordon Craig quoted the first monologue of Claudius in full, and wrote: "If you will read the words in the play, you will see that they are pure caricature, and should be treated as such."

Craig is doubtless right; this is a caricature. But life itself is made up of just such caricatures, although contemporaries take the caricature either as an ode or as a reasonable reality.

∎

For the lines of the image of Ophelia—not only Botticelli, but also El Greco (hands!) and Picasso of the blue period.

∎

The Three Musketeers is a Franco-Italian production. The movie does not present any special interest, but it is instructive as an example of a historical costume picture. Commercial realism: the insignificant details and the sets are lifelike, but the characters are decidedly not. Even within the limits of the aesthetics of Dumas.

But the furniture is real, and the set designer skillful—he has taste.

Only the internal force and contemporary depth of thoughts and emotions can overcome the "historical epic," the "costume movie" —the most infamous of the various kinds of movie.

∎

Hamlet must not be produced; it must be suffered. As soon as "production" begins, everything turns to dust.

∎

A unique piece of dehumanization happens with Ophelia and Laertes.

◼

Ever since Gordon Craig, a plastic image of *Hamlet* is futile. The solitude of the hero amid the immensity of walls and columns. But in Shakespeare, it's extremely different: solitude amidst the boiling of court life. It is not at all the architecture of the castle that stifles Hamlet, but the organization of life and the spiritual atmosphere of the century.

◼

On the screen, there has only to appear an epoch meticulously depicted, and any sense of Shakespearean imagery is lost. You have the "historical epic," which I have so passionately hated since childhood; it is characterized by the aesthetic that I have fought from the time of my *Overcoat*.

But how much easier it is to write of the poetic than to subdue the screen to it!

◼

Which painters make you think of *Hamlet,* at least in some aspect of their work? Not one of the illustrators of the tragedy (Delacroix is, perhaps, better than the others). The closest to Shakespeare of all of them are Goya and the Picasso of "Guernica"—by their sense of the tragic.

◼

(from a letter to D. D. Shostakovich)

Dear Dmitri Dmitrievich,

May I beg you to compose a short number?—"The Dance of Ophelia," the beginning of the scene in Polonius's house. An old woman is teaching various dances to Ophelia. The instructress is playing simple music on an ancient little fiddle or clavecin, and Ophelia learns the steps by heart under her directions. Thus the scene begins, and it ends in the same way.

We want to show how they denaturalize the girl. (The term is stupid, of course, but nothing else comes to mind.) And here is how the figure is conceived: a sweet girl, half a child, whom they turn into a doll—a mechanical plaything with artificial movements, a memorized smile, and the like. They force her to renounce love and to look for a dirty trick in everything. This, essentially, is the cause of her madness. . . .

In later mad scenes, it will be possible to repeat and develop the theme.

The time allotted to the number is as brief as possible, so that a repetition of the same thing can be more significant. . . .

I don't think I have to tell you what a pleasure it is for me to work with you again.

I forgot to mention that in the first scene (the dance lesson), the music would be in the spirit of the time, as though it were authentic. In the later devlopment (if it seems appropriate to you), it will already be a musical image, outside the framework of the Shakespearean epoch. . . .

■

(from a letter from D. D. Shostakovich)

Dear Grigori Mikhailovich,

Here is the "dance lesson." It would be preferable to perform it on a violin, with a piano or guitar accompaniment. In my opinion, it is not necessary to make a point of splitting hairs. . . .

■

Having heard a recording of this dance, Dmitri Dmitrievich thought a bit and said, "Let's try it without the piano."

We recorded the number again, as a solo violin performance.

The composer was still not satisfied. "Get a celesta," he said.

When I first heard the recording of the delicate sounds of the antique instrument, I heard Ophelia.

The work of the composer was similar to getting the focus in photography. He had now found a completely accurate sound image. This is also true in the plastic arts; there is a certain rhythm of line which is proper to Ophelia.

■

V. Admoni writes of the poetry of Rainer Maria Rilke and of the characteristics pertaining to the best lyrics of the turn of the century: "These traits consist in a thirst for the renewal of human life, a tense, if vague, expectation of decisive social change and of unique shocks which must affect every aspect of man's existence. ". . . a sense of exhaustion and of the intolerability of the existing forms of life. . . ."

∎

Rushes of the first takes (a "Gobelin hall"—Claudius's entrance). There is not enough richness of tone or enough power of events. A farce on the ferment of tragedy is wanted in the King's manner of behavior.

The feeling of dissatisfaction will probably pass only after the first nature shots, if they turn out. The sweep of landscape, the threatening force of the expanse of the sea, a glowering sky should all be seen on the screen a bit sooner. The point is not in the landscapes of themselves, but in the intonation of the narrative. The scale of the original material makes it easier to find the true tone of the film and to bring the characters into focus.

Strangely enough, they have always sought to film *Hamlet* in studios, but it seems to me that the key to reincarnating Shakespeare's words in visual imagery can only be found in nature.

∎

The tragic does not at all consist in gloom, pathos, or tearing a passion "to tatters," and so on, but in the density of ferment and the tenseness of tone.

∎

We have many fine character actors: evil ones, pompous ones, "types," but still no bland ones (on the screen), no sleek, artificial, permanently intimidated ones. And Elsinore consists in just this.

∎

The situations usually stressed in productions of *Hamlet* seem superficial to me, too graphic:

(1) *"Denmark is a prison."* So they make Elsinore look like a jail. But the whole point is that the government of Claudius is like a stone sack in which Hamlet's thoughts and soul are incarcerated. The prison constrains the feelings and aspirations of man but is hardly a damp and nasty bit of floor space. To the contrary. The palace is well-built and luxurious after its fashion. And the more luxurious it is, the more hideous becomes an existence in it.

(2) *Hamlet is alone*. Here they show his solitude by the emptiness of rooms and the immensity of apparently uninhabited halls, where the Prince wanders alone.

The genuine tragedy lies elsewhere: in solitude in a crowd. Read carefully into the picture of life which is described in detail in the "to be or not to be" passage. This is why I try to shoot the first monologue in a crush of courtiers, amid the noise of a court reception.

∎

The inceptive, developing element of production plan is the artistic idea: it must not be specified to the point of becoming a symbol, which was something that occupied us all in previous times (in *The Overcoat*, we filmed the Significant Person from below, and Bashmachkin from above). For the time being, the following don't seem bad to me—precisely because the thought did not become a symbol: the meeting of Hamlet and Ophelia across a balustrade—a meeting of prisoners (a grille would have been bad, though); Hamlet's conversation with Horatio about the ghost against a background of the flames in the fireplace; Hamlet lying against the gilded lion next to which Claudius had given his first court speech; Hamlet opposite two empty armchairs at the table in the secret Council.

∎

The protagonists have their chorus, a kind of echo: Claudius's is in the ministers, the dignitaries, and the guard. Osric is a plurality.

∎

Preparation, reasoning everything out to the last detail, a precise working scenario, and so forth, are all necessary for freedom of improvisation in the filming. And if something worthwhile turns out, then it is but the result of a detail that has been discovered in the subject for the first time, or of a sudden confrontation with an actor's individuality.

∎

Ophelia's madness. The greatest difficulty lies in the standard of poetic expression. Just that—poetic. Pathology and clinical symptoms of insanity, etc., have nothing to do with it.

You want to find the "persecuted tenderness," as the novelist-journalist Ehrenberg put it.

■

Spirituality—a conception about which you contemplate more and more often. You want to convey the mad Ophelia in an almost religious key. Not in the modern concept of the word, of course, but the folk, the medieval—as in the wooden madonnas of the countryside.

■

We seem to have found the elements of the scene: the iron of weapons, the coarse faces of soldiers. The slender silhouette of Ophelia. A tragic philosophy: the only happy man in a mad world is the real madman. But this is not a situation reminiscent of Samuel Beckett—the quiet cretinism of life made senseless; here we have the Shakespearean hostility and mutiny against this kind of life.

■

The madness of Laertes: a furious dash toward a meaningless goal. To annihilate the prettiness of his suit, to dirty his face. A mask of vengeance—blood-stained, soiled, twisted into a grimace. The eyes of a madman. The insanity of the rebels (crown whom instead of Claudius? . . . Laertes?). The madness of the mercenaries, the tough faces of war. The twisted arms of captives. There is not "a single level place, but only footprints filled with blood" (*Leonardo da Vinci*).

And only one happy person, already gathering dirty, broken branches instead of little flowers—Ophelia.

■

Attention to the authentic: faces, iron, stone, wood.

Only no attempt at bluff by using the clichés of movie revolutions! . . .

■

Everyone is in a rush; everyone has a clear objective. Everyone but Hamlet.

■

Scholars have not paid any attention to the style of what seems to be the most melodramatic of the scenes dealing with the conspiracy of Claudius and Laertes. According to the canons of the drama of revenge, a sinister condensation of metaphor and hyperbole is due here. But Shakespeare does not have Claudius declaiming like a villain, but speaking prose—that is, slowly, thoroughly, with stops at the everyday details of life: life at court, details of sport, and reminiscences about some newly arrived courtier (even the surname is given) although he has no relation to the plot.

In this smallish scene (giving us the motivation for the substitution of the rapier and for the poisoning) are contained both the traits of Hamlet's psychology and the details of the characters of Claudius and Laertes.

Realism and the novel exert pressure on convention and the theatre. And this struggle between genres takes place in a passage hardly advantageous for realism: the plot group of criminal agreement.

■

There is something lifeless and mechanistic in the spirit of the term "film version." It's as though you put a literary work into a slot in some computerlike machine and push the button: a snap of the fingers, the noise of levers and wheels, and from another aperture the reels of film come rolling out. A prefab product.

■

We need a period of earnest search, origination, verification, and rejection of working hypotheses. "That's going too far"; at top speed, you dash into a blind alley and break your head open—the despair of your own lack of talent, stupidity, inability. . . . And after thousands of unsuccessful experiments, a little thread of artistic thought suddenly begins to weave itself into something. You can become firmly convinced of something only from rejections verified by your own experience, and not from the words of others.

■

This is the way Smakhtunovski works. Somehow he got to rehearsal, "But don't be alarmed! It's utter gibberish!"

And he showed me the monologue on man; literally every phrase was accompanied with a gesture of his hands. The nervous, trembling fingers could not calm down.

Of course, there could be no question of filming such action. The bizarrerie, affectation, and gestural conglomeration were all too evident. And it was also evident that the actor was testing out his "working hypothesis." The actor had to forget about his habits and his usual manner.

What he showed me was, above all, talented.

Time passed, and this monologue was played completely differently. But Hamlet's hands did, however, appear in other scenes.

■

Like every minister serving under a tyrant, Polonius is in mortal fear of Claudius. Fear—like a general mutual guarantee—is in the very air of Elsinore.

■

The boiling cauldron of history: wars, rebellions, the changes of power, and the flight of hopes; the iron of violence. . . . Will all this be in the film?

■

The King, Mikhail Nazvanov, was not fully dressed when he came into the studio. A white body could be seen under his unbuttoned shirt. In Claudius, this could not be. I asked make-up to try to glue hair onto the chest. The look of a "costume part" immediately disappeared, and was replaced by something bestial. We will perfect this "shagginess."

■

There have been hundreds, if not thousands, of interpretations of Hamlet—stage and literary—and today every one of them (indeed, even all of them put together) evokes the impression of insufficiency: Shakespeare's hero is deeper, spiritually richer, has other qualities. What is the secret of the inexhaustibility of this figure?

People of various eras and talents have tried to establish one single theme for explaining Hamlet. But Shakespeare wrote life, which contained an infinite swarm of germs for ever-new ideas.

■

Shakespeare has roles that are contours. Only the most general sketching, and a total absence of detail. This is Fortinbras.

Is it accidental?

You have but to compare Osric and the Norwegian Prince, and it becomes clear that Fortinbras is vastly more important. Nevertheless, his outline is not filled in at all. Doesn't the answer to this lie in that the story itself fills in outlines like this? There isn't much of the human in that.

∎

What sort of sound is it that one can distinguish in Pasternak's roar of continuing life at the finale?
The thunder of drums, the tramp of soldiers' boots.

∎

A picture described by journalists many times: a quiet studio, the inspired director creates: the actor gives his lines over and over, but the director is still not satisfied. A demanding artist, he is looking for something else, something better. The words are repeated again and again. Everyone is already in a sweat, worn to the limit of his endurance, when finally, a decisive voice: "Lights! . . . Camera!"
"The director has achieved what he wants; a miracle of art was performed before our very eyes."
And I say: Tripe! Nothing usually happens except that the few phrases become stultified.

∎

Art means to film quickly, almost without rehearsals, keeping the spontaneity and catching the improvisation of the actor.
Living, inspired human movement, inimitable and first born before your eyes, is difficult to catch on the wing. So is getting the very quiver of spiritual life onto film.
And you have to get it before the first takes. This is how we prepared *Don Quixote,* with Cherkassov and Tolubeev (six months of rehearsal), and *Hamlet,* with Smakhtunovski (three months of daily meetings at my home).
We even took test footage of the role of Hamlet almost in toto before we began to film it. Every time there was test footage of the other characters, I had to call out Smakhtunovski. We selected the test sequences in such a way that some one trait of Hamlet, in relation to the others, would be revealed.
Months of rehearsals, innumerable fittings, getting comfortable

with the costumes and make-up (this was also rehearsing in its way), still tests, and screen tests. . . .

And later, when we began shooting, to repeat everything that we had already discovered? Just the opposite; we began everything anew. It is easy to open a door and walk into a world where everything is familiar; here you can risk going on to meet unforeseen circumstances.

The wave on which an image must be built has been determined.

A good actor is easy to hinder and hard to help.

He often hinders himself. In many ways. Sometimes, instead of playing the one role written by the author, he plays two at once. The second is his own creation; the line of business here is varied: "the intellectual actor," "the simple, charming guy," "the nervous artist."

The "intellectual" not only works, but tells us how he works. Sometimes he talks about it so long and in such detail that he can no longer work.

The "simple, charming" sort fascinates everyone who drops into the studio by his simplicity and charm.

The "nervous" type points out how hard it is to work in front of the cameras; nothing is creative any more.

The actor actually has to keep wearing these images for quite a while, or else the third one—his own natural one—will get worn out.

At rehearsals, Konstantin Skorobogatov would complain that "it's hard to jump." He didn't accustom himself to a character, but "jumped" into it.

I read Blok's poetry from morning till night. In order to "jump" into a scene.

Before the takes, Smakhtunovski requests, "Let's warm up!" . . . And he fences with passionate attacks, rehearses without a break.

"Warm up" is also a good term.

Helping a good actor means removing everything that hinders complete freedom and peace in his spiritual life. To clarify, to make the vital qualities of the figure visible for him, to tune him into a harmony of the associations connected with his own life.

■

To act very well means not to act. This, however, is inhumanly difficult. A type, a man from the street begins to act in front of a camera: tense, constrained, unnatural.

■

It is necessary to see a number of things simultaneously while shooting: the eyes of the actor—are they empty? . . . The crowd scene in the background—did it come into someone's head to gesticulate wildly? . . . The interworkings of light on the characters and on the set—one pair of the "wrong" boots (the wardrobe mistress gave them out by mistake) among the feet in the crowd. . . .

■

The lens is an insidious and evil thing: even a good lens might not pan out and, since the least slip caused by it cannot be detected until the film is on the screen, it can spoil the whole sequence.

■

Can realism, even poetic realism, have any relation to the ghost?

The ghost, as a being deprived of flesh, does not let me get hold of it in any way. I cannot think of anything that could be apprehended by the senses. Despairing of contriving anything, I went to the armory at the Hermitage before the filming, in search of perhaps an external appearance for the role. Nothing inspired me along this line. I went through hall after hall without result: helmets, breastplates, cuirasses—all for the Stone Guest of an opera performance. Suddenly, an object appeared before me—I could never have dreamed up anything like it. . . . A helmet lay in a showcase: the visor was a face forged from steel. Its features betrayed some sort of proud suffering and ominous power. The fact that it was made of steel, impossible for a human face, communicated horror. I immediately imagined a combination of two faces: the steel one, thrown back as though convulsed with pain, and behind it, appearing for an instant through the slits of the helmet when insulted love is mentioned, two eyes full of sorrow.

The helmet had been fashioned in the middle of the sixteenth century by an armorer in Nuremberg. Even the period was right for our film.

■

The time strata must seem to be laid bare in the visual development of Elsinore. The layers of the centuries become evident, like the rings on a huge cross section of a tree.

The scene with the ghost is an ancient medieval layer, a stratum of romance: the stone faces on bas-reliefs, coats-of-arms, ancient masonry, the battlements of fortresses. Later, another formation: the frescoes and Gobelin tapestries of the Renaissance—the world of the youth of the Wittenberg student (the rooms of the Prince). And, finally, the last ring: the affectation of gala halls, remodelled by order of the King.

Expedition. Tallin. Kejla-Ioa.

No matter how strange it might seem, when Hamlet opened doors to go from room to room, I came upon a fairly significant discovery in the style of the studio shots. Let them be ancient oaken doors, but they must be doors through which everyone enters and leaves. I never saw this in the theatre. It became essential that there be doors in Elsinore—doors that opened and closed.

And now against a background of nature, it is necessary that Hamlet be able to enter the world, and to rise above it. To leave it.

■

It is not an easy matter to work with the fantastic in our day. Yesterday some frontier guards dropped into our castle. Seeing the ghost—prepared for filming in cuirass, helmet, and an immense cape—a lad in a green service cap exclaimed joyously, and without a moment's hesitation: "A cosmonaut!"

■

"Elsinore" is a speculative concept in Shakespeare. It is impossible to translate it directly and completely into plastic form. The screen must show separate parts: the general plan can only be imagined. Otherwise, everything seems small, reduced. The walls must have a continuation in height and length beyond the frame of the sequence: the towers—only a few of the towers.

The boundaries should not be distinct, nor forms complete.

The state, and not only a palace or a fortress; life itself, and not only the way of life at some given time.

The state with its armies, police, and holidays, and not a feudal castle or the throne of absolutism.

■

It seems that the basic elements of the plastic arts are formed against a background of nature. In decisive places, they should oust period stylization (of the Tudor era, and of English affectation) and express the essentials.

I have in mind stone, iron, fire, earth, and sea.

■

Stone: the walls of Elsinore, the firmly built government prison, on which armorial bearings and sinister bas-reliefs had been carved centuries ago.

Iron: weapons, the inhuman forces of oppression, the ugly steel faces of war.

Fire: anxiety, revolt, movement, the trembling flame of the candles at Claudius's celebrations; raging fiery tongues (Horatio's narrative about the ghostly apparition); the wind-blown lamps on the stage erected for "The Mousetrap."

Sea: waves, crashing against the bastions, ceaseless movement, the change of the tides, the boiling of chaos, and again the silent, endless surface of glass.

Earth: the world beyond Elsinore, amid stones—a bit of field tilled by a ploughman, the sand pouring out of Yorick's skull, and the handful of dust in the palm of the wanderer-heir to the throne of Denmark.

■

The death of Hamlet. Remember Prince Andrei in *War and Peace:* "an expression of the highest spiritual life." Some sort of transparent intelligibility of the central idea appears on the man's face. For the first time, true peace and clarity and wisdom.

Three modes of death: Claudius's kicking the bucket like an

animal, the convulsions of Laertes, and Gertrude's grimace of pain. And the peace of Hamlet.

In the faces—deathmasks—with full cinematographic naturalness, the sum total of the life of the "slaves of passion" and the victory of Hamlet.

To use Russian poetic associations, Hamlet is Lermontovian in the "Mousetrap" scene, and Pushkinian at the end.

Methods of directing the action. Montage: the joining of pieces, their length, and the correlation of their salient points are finally determined only in rehearsals, as though they had formed themselves in the spiritual activity of the actors.

One must not be afraid that the lines won't go over. Shakespeare wrote them. It is not the text which has to be gotten across. But it must not be dropped; if particular care is used to carry it, it will be dropped all the more easily.

In one of the most tragic passages, Othello speaks of catarrh. Before his meeting with the ghost, Hamlet asks what time it is.

Hamlet's meditation on the skull is thought to concern the futility of human effort and the meaninglessness of life itself. But the Prince says nothing about the work of the ploughman or of the carpenter; it's hard to imagine a Shakespearean hero asking the skull of a farmer, "Well, what good was farming? What was so necessary about the bread you gave people?"

It is the aspirations of tyrants, courtiers, and officials that are meaningless.

I will state it again: The general view of the castle must not be filmed. The image will appear only in the unity of sensations of Elsinore's various aspects. And its external appearance, in the montage of the sequences filmed in a variety of places.

One of our sequences has a lowly origin. In Gurzuf, some merchant built a preposterous building on the side of a mountain; it is not large, but it is composed of "all styles" and is called "Swallow's Nest." It's one of the sights of Crimea; picture postcards of it are sold on every corner. One of our sequences of Elsinore shows a shadow on the sea, cast by this merchant's *dacha*. During the filming of it I trembled with fear: will people suddenly know that?

■

The flow of verse must become a swarm of visual images of the same poetic quality. Here, in the visual aspect, the subtext is even more complicated than it is in the audible one. Behind the crowds of Elsinore, men are thrown about by the whirlwind of history. Included in its very ominous movement are the march of the army of Fortinbras, the flight of the rebels, and the bustle of the courtiers. And the basis of everything is the force of thought, mournful and angry.

The storm of history and the chaos of the iron century could not bend the "thinking reed."

■

Sometimes, when you feel, above all, the rhythm and movement of a scene, it will turn out. The first royal entrance would have come out rather well—Gertrude and Claudius at a rapid pace, almost a run, go past candles, torches, applauding courtiers, and a round dance performed in animal masks. This galloping space, saturated with people and flame, seems to me to be charged with Shakespearean energy.

The scene was to have been shot to its end, but so far—nothing. The pace, which was the basis of the image, had stopped short.

■

In the theatre, they usually pronounce the words "Denmark is a prison" against a background conducive to thoughts about imprisonment.

I am beating my brains out to find a set that is delightful to look at. I have already filmed the passage through the fashionable main hall; charming women in court dress conduct pleasant conversation, exercises are being played on the clavecin. With a respectful bow, a disciplined lackey takes the Prince's cloak.

Another variation: a park—a fountain glistens in the sun, children play on the path, a girl passes on her pony.

It is in these surroundings that one must talk about Denmark the prison.

■

I have never felt such a necessity to revise the methods of expression which I had used in my past work. Does this result from the fact that the art of the cinema has developed newer and more modern devices? . . . No. It is because I found in a six-teenth-century play a modern and novel story about life, history, and man.

Well, and the form?

> Not very young is the mode of the ballad,
> But if the words ache,
> And they tell how they ache,
> Younger again is the mode of the ballad.
> —Mayakovsky

■

The "newly hatched" motif in Osric is that of the new genera-tion at Elsinore. What is necessary is the scale of the phenomenon, and the novelty of the type. Here comes this frivolous figure against a background of fortress towers. A book in his hand (he too has his hamletism), a skeptical smile on his face, and flabby, enervated movements. And approaching are others like Osric: little bows, little smirks. Here comes the future Elsinore. They stare at the Prince impudently (he is in disgrace—they even say he has lost his reason), they wink at one another.

■

There is an infinity between listening and hearing. Many times, I have listened to a whole Shakespearean text in the theatre, and often did not hear what was basic.

The picture of life, the relation of man and state, the impossi-bility of existence in a world without souls—all this, I am sure, can be expressed on the screen more completely than is possible on the stage. Yes, more completely, and with fewer words.

It is also possible to keep the poetry, but to speak in prose. The meeting of Hamlet and Ophelia after the scene with the ghost is played without a word, but follows Shakespeare to the letter. I hope that the figure of Ophelia and the poetic atmosphere of her scenes keep their Shakespearean qualities, although neither a dance lesson nor madness amidst iron is in the original play.

It seems that Claudius is, primarily, a smiling villain. This smile is described a number of times by Shakespeare. It drives Hamlet mad. I have never seen it in the theatre; it is probably difficult to smile and speak verses at the same time.

The particularly difficult Fortinbras scenes begin. With a heavy tread, covered with dust, long unshaven, wearing dirt-stained boots and heavy armor, the men of fire and iron march. They go to act. The man of heart and thought is dead.

The death of Hamlet. A moment of complete silence. The camera moves slowly over the stiffened figure of the Prince, the stock-still Horatio, a rocky cliff. Stone fills the wide screen; it is chipped and overgrown with moss. Silence. And after this long and absolute quiet, from a distance, there is a scarcely audible sound: a hum, a noise, a whisper. Barely closer, but already louder: the tramp of feet, a clanking, a rumble.

The sound becomes louder; everything is drowned in the heavy tread of soldiers' boots.

The last scene. A combination of an ordinary war theme (winded horses, tired and heavily armed men, an army at the end of a march) and stern honors given to the unarmed man. They give Hamlet a soldier's burial, not with the grand ritual of parade, but with austere ceremony as performed by an active army. They lower their lances and dress them with pieces of a banner shredded in battle. Four captains with huge, overgrown beards come up to the dead Prince, who rests peacefully against the rocks as though asleep. An officer raises his sword; ordnance is shot off. They raise a litter with the body over the battlements of Elsinore. A volley. The state flag is lowered.

Not a handsome "army," but "soldiery" in the everyday sense of the word. This is what is important for these scenes.

■

The death of Ophelia, of which the Queen speaks in detail (the witness is important enough), is, for some reason, subsequently considered suicide. The motif is not necessary for the plot. What is the meaning of the gravediggers' conversation, and, especially, of the words of the priest? . . . It is one more detail in the picture of society. The poor girl is not only denied happiness and the right to love but is not permitted a normal grave in the cemetery. Only "strewments" of "pebbles" are allowed this most poetic being—a dog's funeral.

■

"To be or not to be": walls, into which Hamlet bumps—as he wanders interminably about Elsinore, passing through its life from the play of children to the training of soldiers, and is again set into a blind alley of walls. The famous monologue is only the beginning of thought; its completion is in the peace and clarity, and in the smile on Yorick's skull.

■

Hamlet . . . Denmark . . . the sixteenth century . . . how complex it all is. But look how simple it is to a poet from Dagestan, Rasul Gamzatov:

> During life the Djigit[11]
> Had fought with wrong,
> Injustice is with us till now,
> But he is not.

■

In the sequence, we want to achieve what Gogol called the "abyss of space," taking this not to be a distance embraced in a field of vision, of course, but a multiplicity of associative possibilities, a connection effected by the most varied of regularities. It is to have many strata, but this is not to be noticed externally: the action is natural, the movement lifelike.

■

[11] *Djigit:* A skillful horseman (especially in trick riding) from Circassia [trans.].

Every time we take nature shots, there are tourists from the castle and transient movie makers. I hear their enraptured conversation: "How beautiful!" "Simply wonderful!"

And we are dripping with sweat, working to prevent these beauties from being evident on the screen.

What a pleasure it is to film Smakhtunovski sitting on the ground and wearing a long, loose garment, dirty and torn. The sky (without any picturesque clouds), the earth, the lapping of waves, stones; a man who is acquiring a beard is joking with a peasant who is digging a hole.

■

In Russian there is a word that means "my sufferings are over"; when, at the end, Hamlet finds the happiness of peace, this word describes it.

■

Here, a principle of directing: the quality of an isolated thing is always more important than general quantity. Five original pieces of armor from the Hermitage, or a few carefully made costumes, are more important than crowd scenes with thousands of extras. Our largest court scene has forty or fifty people, so each person was selected as though he were to act a large part.

■

The notorious "weightiness, crudity, and visibility" usually are translated on the screen into the lightweight, the really coarse, the naïvely graphic. Bad actors "embellish" the text and underscore the "main" words, so that everything will get across. But the job is to give a push to the audience, propelling it toward creativeness in order that it become a co-author.

■

Smakhtunovski tells the story of how he, lousy and sick with dysentery, lay under a bridge, after having made off from a party of prisoners. After the German escort convoy had left, a peasant woman dragged him into a tent. Spotting some bread, he pounced on it and immediately began to tear greedily into it. The housewife ripped the piece of bread from his hands and slapped his face. "Fool," she yelled, "you'll kill yourself!"

This is the kind of person who must play the Prince.

■

The sense of form is probably an anxiety that must not be quieted. But not a style chosen with calculation. It makes its own mold, if you work seriously.

■

Works of genius are immortal precisely because they are mortal. They have only one life, and, at the same time, an incalculable number of deaths. What are we to understand by this? The embryos of infinite lives lie in the combination of the particles contained in the work with the life of a new century, the cells of new social contradictions. The atrophy of some particles is the demise of the contradictions of a past epoch. Thus, *Don Quixote* loses its level of parody, and *Hamlet* its theme of feudal revenge.

Not only does the individual motif die out, but so does the manner of writing: the prose of *Hamlet* runs with the juice of life, but some of the metaphoric verse has fallen into decay.

Immortality is defined by the possibility provided for these animations and atrophies. It has nothing to do with the notorious pedantry of "every word of Shakespeare's is sacred."

■

Philosophy, according to Hegel, is an epoch that has been seized in thoughts. In ages of material upheaval, at the crossroads of the old and the new, iron audits the understanding of man's nature and his relation to persons, humanity, and the universe. Breezes from every era fanned the Shakespearean bonfire, and once more its flames illuminated a black sky.

■

We are accustomed to see the apocalyptic scenes in Shakespeare as usual imagery: on the catastrophic day, some sort of wild monsters appear and beasts crawl out of their lairs. There are specialized studies of these metaphors and hyperboles. All of this is interesting, of course.

However, it was not long ago that I read a description of a catastrophe—without metaphor and hyperbole: After the explosion of the atomic bomb, fishes threw themselves onto the shore and propelled themselves among the bushes by their fins; birds dug their shelter deep in the earth.

Professor Yasuo Suehiro of Tokyo University has spent many years collecting facts about the appearance of strange marine life on the eve of great earthquakes (according to *Pravda*). In 1963, the people who lived on the island of Nii-jima caught a "sea monster," an unknown deepwater fish six meters in length. Two days later, there was an earthquake.

Our day is reviewing the concept of the "fantastic." Sometimes it proves very down to earth, and certainly pertains to life.

This is when I understood the Tolstoyan "sharpening, in order to penetrate." As in the theatrical performance, the monologue about the pipe is important.

The now academic English method of reading the full text in a rapid rhythm leads to a blunting of perception. In this flow of verse, the thoughts and images are not grasped, do not "penetrate."

It is quite possible to speak all the words and to say little.

I have strived all this time to transfer the tragic scale of events and conflicts onto the stage—however, to express them not by the generic methods of tragic acting and producing, i.e., by an especial loftiness of imagic structure and by a mannered exposition, but, to the contrary, by completely realistic and natural movement.

That everything might be "the way people live."

We tried to dub in the Queen, because of Elsa Radzin's Lithuanian accent. Her lines were read by a good dramatic actress. We achieved a perfect synchronization: the sound agreed exactly with the movement of the lips. But we lost something important from the figure.

What had gone? . . . Scale. Gertrude became small and ordinary. But lofty tragic bombast was foreign to Radzin's whole performance.

The force of suffering was lost. The depth of spiritual wounds. And it was in this that the "Shakespearean" quality consisted.

We speak of "truthful portrayal." But the end of art is something else: "to seek out truth." This is the reason for the tragedy of Hamlet.

Is there anything that art has not proceeded from, if we are to heed the experts: the sexual instinct, the processes of labor, religious ceremony. . . .

Art is diverse and, so, is of diverse parentage. The art toward which I am striving probably developed from a sense of justice— people do have this sort of instinct. It is a strong reflex, one that makes people wince and experience physical pain from contact with injustice.

This sense, hypertrophied, was possessed by artists of whom I am especially fond. It was possessed particularly by the men of letters in nineteenth-century Russia. It's not for nothing that the titles torn from them were shouts and groans: *I cannot be silent!*, *What is to be done?*, *Who is to blame?*

Sometimes, you hear that an artist must be objective, unbiased. What fuel propels him then? . . . Photographic developer? . . .

Of all the lessons Hamlet reads to the actors, the most important one is ". . . let your own discretion be your tutor." In that is the heart of the matter. An artist is impotent when his inner discretion is replaced by the horror of silence. His voice then has to be dubbed in.

Hamlet is for me a work that includes everything that I have loved throughout my life, everything to which I have aspired since childhood, albeit still unconsciously—the forms of expression and feelings and thoughts (those I understood much later): from the wandering players to the theme of man and time. I found myself surrounded by all of my old friends and teachers in this film: with me were my first favorite clowns, Fernandez and Friko, and my close friend Yuri Tynyanov.

There is room in the shadow of Shakespeare for everyone and everything.

The strength of the director does not lie in an obstinate execution of every detail in his plan, but in mercilessly throwing out everything personal, everything that does not organically belong. Life and ideas are the test and measure of everything. They compel the artist to strike out the superfluous, the lifeless, or the empty of thought.

What I want to remain on the screen is the "past and thoughts" of Shakespeare. The play was written in 1600 and performed in the forty-sixth year after the October Revolution.

Leningrad, 1965.